A Private in the Texas Army

A PRIVATE IN THE TEXAS ARMY

At War in Italy, France, and Germany with the 111th Engineers, 36th Division, in World War II

JOHN A. PEARCE

The Texas Center
Schreiner University • Kerrville, TX
325-660-1752 • www.mcwhiney.org

Cataloging-in-Publication Data

Names: Pearce, John A., author.
Title: A private in the Texas army: at war in Italy, France, and Germany with the 111th Engineers, 36th Division, in World War II / John A. Pearce.
Description: First edition. | Kerrville, TX: State House Press, 2021. | Includes bibliographical references, illustrations, maps, and index.
Identifiers: ISBN 9781649670052 (soft cover); ISBN 9781649670069 (e-book)
Subjects: LCSH: World War, 1939-1945 – Regimental histories – United States. | World War, 1939-1945 – Personal narratives, American. I United States. Army. Engineer Combat Battalion. 111th – History.
Classification: D769.335 111th (print) | DCC 940.54

First edition 2021

Cover and page design by Allen Griffith of Eye 4 Design

Distributed by Texas A&M University Press Consortium
800-826-8911
www.tamupress.com

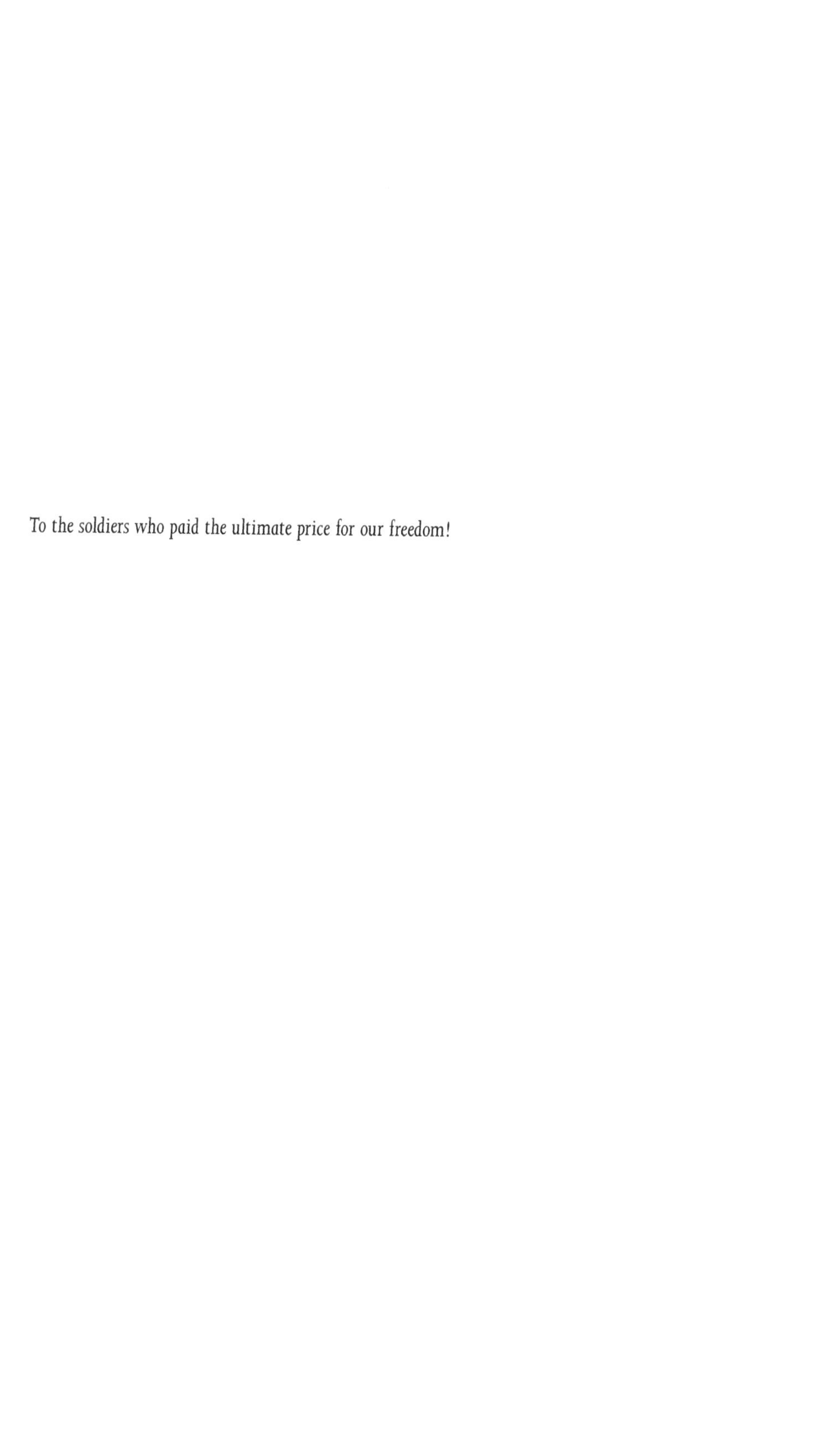

To the soldiers who paid the ultimate price for our freedom!

Contents

Understanding Division Breakdown

Military identification of the 36th Infantry Division is presented in a universally recognized fashion as found in the official *A Pictorial History of the 36th "Texas" Infantry Division* published shortly after the war.

Maps & Pictures

Maps and pictures are both from the official *A Pictorial History of the 36th "Texas" Infantry Division*. The map illustrations were drawn by R. A. Huff and make for a clearer understanding of the areas the 36th fought. Pictures used are from contributors and private collections of veterans. In September of 2014, the 36th Division Association Board of Directors, in a rare move since World War II, approved the use of their maps and pictures for this book.

Acknowledgments

Frank Webster Pearce, my dad, kept this diary during the worst of times, and then entrusting me with it's future. Surviving the war, his love for his family, and his devotion to God and to his country his entire life highlighted my family's lives and values as we grew up in the tranquil 1950s and turbulent 1960s. This is a debt I could never repay.

State House Press rescued this project form obscurity and helped shepherd it along. Thank you, Susan Frazier, for your patience, and Don Frazier for helping to move this project along. To Allen Griffin, the designer, I owe much. His patience helped get this book close to perfect.

To all the World War II generation who battled to keep our country free despite the price. We owe them a debt that, as time passes, can never be forgotten. Thanks, too, for everyone who volunteered pictures and stories of their family members who fought with the 111th Engineer Combat Battalion. Without them, this story would have been incomplete. To the 36th Division Association Board of Directors for granting me the privilege of using pictures and maps from "The Fighting 36th" book published shortly after the end of the war.

To the two petty thieves who robbed our home in 1984 and stole a bag containing Dad's diary among other valuable things. On the way out of the house they found something more important to put in the bag and dumped my Dad's war pictures and diary leaving them scattered on the floor of our home. In doing so they left the most valuable thing I treasured of my father's possessions. Otherwise, this book would have been lost in time.

I reserve my greatest thanks for my wife Jaime of fifty plus years whose patience, advice, editing, encouragement and love made this book come to life. Without her this would never have happened.

A Private in the Texas Army

Introduction

Frank Webster Pearce's informative diary and letters home create the backbone of this in-depth look at Texas' own 36th Infantry Division and the 111th Engineer Combat Battalion. The Division's story has been told before, but never from start to finish by a combat engineer whose legacy is measured in the footprints left from stirring the sands of three invasion beaches, wallowing through the mud, and trudging in the snow of every battle. From training in the United States to the war's end in Austria, Pearce chronicled it.

With this combination of diary, numerous letters home describing the wants and needs of a private, and official Division reports, you have the most complete look ever produced on the engineers and their war with Hitler's Germany.

This is a primary account written daily, in a sometimes not politically correct way by current standards, as the events unfolded. It was the war years. Here you find out how to properly bury a man in the water-soaked Italian soil, a foolproof way to smuggle liquor from the US to the soldiers overseas, the foul stench of death reeking across the battlefield, and the beauty of exploding artillery shells in the night sky.

This is his collection of thoughts and letters as he wrote them. Pearce used the limited space in a small diary to scribble down each day five or six lines of what was important to him at that moment in time, despite the horror of war crashing around him. If he fought, it was written down; when he drank too much, it was scribbled line by line; and if he had strong feelings about someone—good or bad—he jotted it there also.

The external events exploding around him, when his diary was written, are also here in a sequential format and keep his story flowing through the war years. These were critical years for the United States, and many of its finest young men.

The story starts in the United States, travels across the Atlantic to North Africa, sails the Mediterranean to Italy, forges forward through the rain and mud of the Italian boot to the Rapido River and Cassino, takes a short boat trip to assist in the breakout at Anzio, races northward to enter Rome, and then concludes—after another beach landing, fighting over blood-stained ground—to victory in France, Austria, and Germany. This book will lead you with those fighting men—day by day, step by step—through it all.

1 ROAD TO WAR

"Take a cue from me and stay on the straight and narrow as the folks probably depend on you more than they do me. But it's just like it's always been, I just made another mistake. As you say I was always a little impulsive but there is no use in crying over spilled milk."

Born in 1915, Frank Pearce grew up in Sulphur Springs in Hopkins County Northeast Texas. The square jawed, five foot eleven Texan, sported a wiry muscular one hundred fifty pound frame, boyish, steel blue eyes, Clark Gable ears, and wavy black hair. He was twenty-four years old when he entered military service in 1940. Prior to enlistment, his life was typical of many small-town Texans facing a changing world in the 1930s.

Pearce managed to graduate from high school despite missing long periods of time working to help his family struggle through the early years of the Great Depression. There was never time for high school activities, much less the potential of college for Pearce, his sister Iona, or brothers R. A. and Marvin. His high school years were highlighted by pumping gas at a local station, battling mosquitoes while picking cotton in the nearby fields, and doing odd jobs anytime, anywhere.

By the time Pearce received his high school diploma in May of 1933, Adolf Hitler was in complete power in Germany, and America's thirty-second President, democrat Franklin D. Roosevelt, had begun what would be the longest tenure of any president in American history.

Following the end of his formal education, Pearce went to work for his father, Robert Andrew Pearce, selling wholesale automotive parts to the oil field maintenance sheds and filling stations dotting Northeast Texas. Life on the road was hard. Constant mechanical breakdowns and flat tires plagued travel from spot to spot, plus automotive parts to vend

Frank Webster Pearce.

were scarce. With this being the only life he knew, Pearce continued peddling auto parts from town to town until beginning his military obligation.

With American emotions of anger and outrage inflamed by local economic woes and worldwide sorrows, 1940 became a time for action. Highlighted by a new popular national theme, "Americanism: Let's Re-Sell It to the World," and serious concerns of global affairs, both pride and fear filtered down to the 5,417 residents of Sulphur Springs entering a new decade.

On Tuesday, October 22, 1940, after considering the pros and cons of conforming to military discipline and training, Pearce and several friends navigated their cars westward from Sulphur Springs down Texas State Highway 67 through the tiny dairy communities of Brashear and Cumby to Greenville, the county seat of Hunt County. They brought their vehicles to a stop in front of the military armory recruiting station and, with little fanfare and after several bold strokes of a pen, each enlisted in the 36th Division, Texas National Guard. On this red-letter day, the National Guard membership grew as James "Arnold" Glenn of Yantis, J.P. "Popeye" Johnston, Daniel "Muley" Junell, Pearce and several others from Sulphur Springs became soldiers.

As members of a National Guard unit with only a one-year commitment and new uniforms displaying publicly their passion for country, they became ineligible for any upcoming military draft, received a small but much needed amount of pay, and only reported to duty once a week in Greenville for training. Regretfully,

Top left: J.P. "Popeye" Johnston. *Top right*: Arnold Glenn.
Bottom left: Frank Pearce. *Bottom right*: Daniel "Muley" Junell.

Pearce and friends soon found they wouldn't be around Sulphur Springs long enough to enjoy the magnitude of respect their new uniforms brought or the freedom from long-term military service.

To each enlistee's surprise, the Guard activated on November 25, slightly more than a month after Pearce's enlistment and over a year before the United States would enter World War II. On that date, due to the escalating action in Europe and the threat of Japan in the Pacific, the 36th Division, Texas National Guard, under Presidential Executive Order number 8594, mobilized into the Army of the United States. The mobilization of the 36th necessitated, for combat conditioning, a move out of Hunt and other Texas counties to Camp Bowie near Brownwood, Texas.[1] The once-a-week training sessions abruptly came to a halt, and life for Pearce as a member of Company C, 111th Engineer Combat Battalion began.

Over the next two years, the 36th traveled throughout the United States training for war first at Camp Bowie, joining in on the Louisiana Maneuvers (September '41), and then back to Camp Bowie (October '41), before moving on to Camp Blanding, Florida (February '42).[2] Requiring additional improvement, they journeyed north to participate in the Carolina Maneuvers (July '42), and finally to Camp Edwards, Massachusetts (August '42-April '43).

In the early months of 1942, the 36th became what was known in military terms as a triangular division. A triangular division, consisting of 14,000 plus men, was an innovation designed to create a more efficient chain of command, flexibility in deployment, and superior movement without weakening its total firepower. The newly named 36th Infantry Division, its size reduced by several thousand soldiers, now consisted of three infantry regiments instead of four, one engineer and one medical battalion instead of engineer and medical regiments, four artillery battalions instead of six, and reduced special service units.

Pearce and John Benedict of Ocala, Florida, training at Camp Blanding, Florida, in June of 1942.

Pearce and Luther Bruce of Telephone, Texas, at Camp Bowie.
They are wearing the updated M1917A1 World War I style helmets.
These were replaced with the M-1 "steel pot" helmet in June of 1941.

On General Fred L. Walker's orders, military regulations were strictly enforced, the mood of those in command serious, and shenanigans of any type not tolerated.[3] Traveling to Boston in a military convoy to unload supplies for the trip overseas, the lure of Bean Town beckoned. To see it in more detail, Pearce and several others took a truck and hit the city on their own. The consequences of being Absent Without Leave was never a consideration when an entire city lay at their feet. Upon their return, it was discovered they had taken the truck illegally.

Pearce, as the ranking soldier of the adventurous GI's, faced the primary disciplinary action. His continued ability to dance into trouble would dog him constantly, this time costing him a future opportunity to attend Officer Candidate School. The paperwork had already been completed when the misguided Boston adventure began. Instead of a potential officer, Pearce was busted from staff sergeant to buck private. The rest of the AWOL soldiers with him were never reprimanded.

Notwithstanding, the Division, nearing the date to go overseas, was victimized by soldiers permanently going AWOL. Not every American boy felt it was a patriotic duty to fight for his country. Some had mothers write letters begging to leave their son behind; families with money solicited lawyers to work on the disgruntled GI's behalf; other soldiers faked illness, and the most desperate disappeared into the countryside. Three days before embarking for Africa, over seventy-five men had deserted. Thirty-five of the deserters scurried like roaches on one single day, March 29.

Five different times before February 1, the 36th was instructed to begin preparation to leave Camp Edwards for a new area of operation. Each time, the last on January 17, the order was immediately revoked. The soldiers, grumbling over the series of phantom commands from the War Department, continued into February training at Camp Edwards. Then out of the clear blue, new orders were issued on February 17. The Division was scheduled to leave Camp Edwards and move south to Camp A. P. Hill in Virginia. The move south eliminated the possibility of the 36th shipping overseas any time soon, and more drilling for the agitated men seemed imminent.

Just ten days after the command to move to Virginia, this order was also rescinded. The majority of the Division was to stay put at Camp Edwards. Additional troop ships were now available for transportation, so the 36th would get their chance to face the enemy. Where was not clear, but combat was definitely in the cards.

Saturday 16 January '43

I believe it was around this date that I had my last furlough.[4] It has turned out to be my last for a long time.

Monday 1 February '43

Returned to Camp Edwards and found things in a mess at the motor pool. My Sergeant was having trouble with the Lieutenant. So, it was there on my back from them all until I got tired of it and told them off which resulted in my being marked for a bust.

Saturday 13 March '43

Was reduced from rank of Staff Sergeant to private. Reason is not clear. Couple of days ago I accompanied convoy to Boston and went off in truck while there and was three hours late getting back. Main reason was because a few officers didn't like me because I wouldn't kiss their feet.

Pearce (left) awaiting a landing craft during training exercises in Massachusetts.

(March 13 letter to Marvin concerning demotion)

Seems as if we are both back where we started from or I should say on an equal footing.[5] You don't understand what I mean but from now on my rank is Private. Yes, I got busted today for something that is no business of yours, but the folks will probably tell you as I wrote them and told them about it. It seems the cards were stacked and this time not in my favor but I'm not kicking as I probably got what I deserve, and it could have been worse. Take a cue from me and stay on the straight and narrow as the folks probably depend on you more than they do me. But it's just like it's always been, I just made another mistake. As you say I was always a little impulsive but there is no use in crying over spilled milk.

2 A DOSE OF REALITY—AFRICA

"The hardest jolt to a soldier's morale is to receive word in a round about way that LuLu or Gertie married a defense worker who celebrated the occasion by throwing a beer party and nearly choked on his false teeth."

The 36th Infantry Division, anxious for action, sailed out of New York Port of Embarkation on April 2, 1943. The Division, housed on five separate transports named Brazil, Argentina, Gibbons, Barry, and Hawaiian Shipper, arrived without incident in Oran, Algeria, eleven days later and bivouacked initially near Ossie Bin Oka. Originally scheduled to participate in the November 1942 North African invasion, the lack of ships, landing crafts, and other means of transportation stranded the troops in the United States. When the Division finally arrived in North Africa, the fighting was reaching its end.

After leaving Ossie Bin Oka, the 36th moved a hundred miles into Algeria to Magenta. The Division was held in combat reserve until the German Africa Corps was defeated by Allied forces. Despite the excitement of possibly seeing action, they did not enter combat while in Africa.

★★★

Left Camp Edwards Massachusetts by train and went to Staten Island, New York, where we boarded ship that night. "Henry T. Gibbons"[1] Left dock at 4:30 AM. Am quartered on E deck. Proceeded south as near as I can guess. Quite a few boys seasick.

As I have not kept a diary until beginning in July, I will attempt to fill in space. We had an uneventful trip. I could see about 25 ships in our convoy. Rumors have it several ships were lost. Our ship was a new one and this was its maiden voyage. We fell behind several times with minor troubles. Always lots of destroyers close by. Out of Gibraltar our destroyers dropped depth charges, so we guessed a sub or two were nearby. Went thru Gibraltar at night and proceeded up the Mediterranean Sea (April 12). On the evening of April 13, we docked at Oran (French Algeria). We disembarked at ten o'clock with all our equipment and bags. I had hurt my back so I really had a hard time.

Our first contact with the natives was amusing. Kids and grownups running along beside us begging for cigarettes. They knew a few words of English (all bad words). No cigarettes being given we were called bad names. Trucks carried us out to bivouac area close to Ossie Bin Oka where we stayed a couple of weeks.

We then boarded a train in Oran. Rode in box cars, very short and smelly. Went to Sidi Bel Addes and then on to Magenta back in the mountains. Stayed

Traveling North Africa in smelly box cars.

there about a month. There I witnessed a shooting between two soldiers and three M.P.'s in which one M. P. was killed, one soldier killed and one M.P. wounded (May 10).[2] Wine (vino) causes all these troubles.

About the last of May, we started South by truck. Left Algeria and spent first night in Oujda. French Morocco was entered.[3] Second night was spent at Guercif, a filthy Arab town. Trades day so there were lots of Arabs. Kill goats on spot and even sell the guts. Flies so thick you couldn't see the meat. I watched a French kid take a goat head and without removing a hair place it over a charcoal pot and roast it. What a smell. Old men laying around on the streets, covered with sores. Flies all over them and I was afraid one fly might land on me and transfer syphilis to me as I'm sure that is what they had.

Next night was spent at Meknes and I had my first decent meal in Africa. Had pork chops in a French restaurant. Towns have two sections, a French one and the old Arab one. Arab sections are all walled and crowded with narrow streets. These are "off limits" to us. Very filthy.

Passed thru Fes and other cities and ended up at Rabat (French Morocco). We bivouacked about nine miles out in a cork forest. Have been into Rabat quite a bit and down to Casablanca once. Are preparing to move back north to Arzew, east from Oran, for an invasion course.

(June 20 letter to the Perkins Store Force)[4]

To us boys who are now in Foreign Service a letter or a card means more than anything else we could get. After being away for a while the people and I might also say the girls seem to forget about the boys, whom I'm sure don't forget about them quite so soon. About all we have left is the memories of the things we enjoyed so much and all of us are looking forward to the time when we may return and take up where we left off.

But in the meantime, the only way we have of being in contact with the old life is the cards and letters we receive, which at the most are far from enough to satisfy us. A soldier never gets enough mail! I don't mean no one writes but it is just the fact that we live by mail.

The hardest jolt to a soldier's morale is to receive word in a round about way that LuLu or Gertie married a defense worker who celebrated the occasion by throwing a beer party and nearly choked on his false teeth. What's the matter with the girls? Do they think we aren't coming back and that they are all going to be old maids? Of course, we don't expect them to sit around and moon and twiddle their thumbs. But I dare say they have more opportunity to enjoy life than some guy over here that is mooning over them.

Thank the Lord I happen to be free of any such affliction at this date, so I sleep and eat as usual.

I've seen boys make extra trips to the mail clerk and insist that they have some mail and accuse him of holding out. I assure you that it does make a fellow feel pretty good to capture a few letters every day. Even an old sourpuss will put on a smile and may even laugh out loud about Tabby having a dozen kittens although he has always hated cats. That's what a letter can do! I know of nothing else that can do that unless it is the actual meeting of the people we all remember. When you feel like writing, even though you have nothing of interest to write, do it anyhow as it means quite a lot to us.

So now I will skip over to July 17 where this diary really begins. Lieutenant McTeer,[5] the officer who reported me back in the states as being AWOL and had me reduced from Staff Sergeant to Private, was killed at mine school at Guerceif in June. A Sergeant out of A company was killed by mine in late July.

LOCAL BOYS SAFE IN NORTH AFRICA

Mrs. Robert Irons of Sulphur Springs received a cablegram Tuesday from her son, J. P. Johnston, who is in North Africa with the U. S. Army, assuring her he is safe and well.

Frank Pearce and Muley Junell are two local boys who are with him in the armed service there.

Sulphur Spring Daily News Telegram July 1943.

Captain Ernest Petree.

Saturday 17 July '43

Cleaned ordinance. Put out washing. About fifty Moroccan soldiers are bivouacked near us for training purposes. One came over and I washed his tie and shirt. They have few clothes and plenty rough. One offered me two American pennies for pack of cigarettes. They don't know value of our money. Saw two fight and they fight to kill butting and kicking especially for the vital parts. One tried to use bayonet. Others interfered. French officers whip them in order to handle them.

Monday 19 July '43

Pulled out at 8:30 AM after policing up once more. Moroccans formed and presented arms as we pulled out. Passed thru Meknes, Fez, Taza, and ended up at Guerceif at 8:30 PM. Approximately 225 miles. Slow going as it was very mountainous and with our load we crawled up them. Sleeping on ground with my mosquito bar over me as that is enforced on account of malaria.

Tuesday 20 July '43

Passed thru Oujda and Tlemcen and bivouacked at Sidi Bel Addes. Went to town and found it to be the lousiest one yet. A Spaniard lives across the way. Swapped bar of soap for two quarts. Had a five gallon keg filled for three cartons of cigarettes. Lots of wine now.

Wednesday 21 July '43

Left out at 7:30 AM and got to Arzew at 11:30. Went to Arzew tonight to Red Cross to see show. Filthy town with sewage running down the street. Bad show "Should a Girl Marry." Very old. Couple of our boys had a fight after we came back. Penn Yankee and a Texas lad. Poor Yankee. He's been asking for it and he really got it. More vino troubles. Captain Petree hot. [Ernest Petree from Kilgore, Texas]

Sunday 25 July '43

Yesterday an Arab brought in an escaped German. Had a double barreled shot gun. Get $25 for prisoner. Italians seem happy to be out of war. Went to St. Barbe to unload train. Bringing in prisoners from Sicily (1500 Italians). Algerians guarding them. Use rifle butts to speed them up. Two turned on one and I thought he was going to use bayonet. More Germans brought in guarded by English.

John Benedict trading with a local.

Thursday 29 July '43

Moved out today. About eighteen miles in the hills. Took nearly all day to clear out brush and get tents up. Damn useless as there were plenty of cleaned space. Big bag of mail. Took nearly an hour to call out. I got one V mail[6] from Marvin.

Saturday 31 July '43

Pay day! I drew $31.20. Lost five playing rummy. Went over to a Frenchman's house late this evening to try to get keg filled. Arab in charge wanted fifty francs a bottle. Would take $20 to fill keg so I got none. (50 francs-$1) Rumors are we will be going somewhere in a few weeks. I hope so.

Monday 2 August '43

Talk on demolition this morning. Went to beach this evening for practice as tomorrow we demonstrate demolition to 143rd Infantry. Set off several Bangalore torpedoes[7] under wire entanglements. Fired my rifle quite a bit. Stick of dynamite for target. One boy had dynamite caps to go off in hand. Bunged up hand pretty bad. The Battalion has had several men killed over here at mine schools.

Friday 6 August '43

Show tonight "My Favorite Blond". It isn't safe to go out alone here as Arabs are pro Nazis. One of our boys was cut in the back last night and the other night three of our boys were rocked. They can throw straight. We're not allowed to carry protection. Oh these brass hats.

Saturday 7 August '43

Went back to beach 15 and instructed Infantry on demolition. Three causalities today. One pretty bad from shrapnel. Private Ellis [Gilmer Ellis of Port Arthur, Texas] and I went to Oreah and drank some wine. Jumped off truck at Clemenceau and had some more. Hitch hiked in. He went back tonight. Carried 4 sticks of dynamite with short fuses for protection. I expected him to blow up!

Tuesday 10 August '43

We went to Arzew and loaded on the USS *Samuel Chase* at 2:30 PM.[8] Did nothing else today. Have to sleep on deck as there are more men than bunks. Slept on hatch under a tank lighter (boat for landing tanks). I believe we will invade Italy before long.

Wednesday 11 August '43[9]

Only made one landing today which was easy. Boarded ship again by climbing net upside. Muley couldn't make it so we passed a rope over and tied it around him and hauled him up. Will not leave harbor but will stay here behind submarine nets. Had first coke and ice cream since leaving states.

Saturday 14 August '43

This is last day on ship. I hate to leave as we get good chow. Navy really feeds good.

Sunday 15 August '43

Completed the biggest mess of landing we've done. Got up at 2 AM and rushed to breakfast, hash and boiled eggs. At 4 AM we went over the side by the net into the L.C.T. boat.[10] Then we waited for a half-track and M7 tank destroyer[11] to be lowered. At 7:30 it was completed. Hit shore and took off over land. Hard going as it was hilly. Walked 5 miles.

Monday 16 August '43

Bed sure felt good after that steel deck. Went up close to Oran and practiced building Bailey bridge[12] adapted from English. A mess as usual but we did it. Received orders today what and how to pack for invasion. Rifle ammunition issued. I have 176 rounds. Have to carry my machine gun, rifle, tool kit, etc when I board ship. Some load. We will come off the ship on our half-track. Probably get knocked off by mine or artillery. It is a fact now that we are going. Seems we are beginning to realize that we are in a war. Kind of sobers up a fellow's thoughts as some of us won't come back.

Wednesday 18 August '43

Moved out at 10:30. Moved about twelve miles. Am bivouacked about two miles from Mediterranean Sea on a high hill about five miles from Arzew. Put up tents. These moves are worrisome especially when you move only a few miles. But that's the army way. Meat loaf on hash with synthetic lemon juice every day. Hope we board ship soon so I can get a good meal.

Monday 23 August '43

Practiced crawling and creeping this morning which is hard work. Night problem. Went about a mile over to a hill and defended it against 2nd and 3rd platoon. Had to carry a machine gun. Pretty tough going up those hills. Captured nearly all the boys. Got back to camp at 12:30. Believe we will go aboard ship soon.

Thursday 26 August '43

Benedict and I went down the hill to get wine. Had to go to Porte aux Poules. Fifteen francs a bottle. Went to show tonight "Gentleman Jim". Had a fight with a guy from Kansas who was cussing us Texas boys. I gave him a pretty good lickin. He didn't touch me. He went to bed all bloody.[13]

Tuesday 31 August '43

Captain said the General (Walker) said we had the hardest assignment ever assigned to a Division. Sounds bad but I am anxious to get started as we are getting stale. At 2 PM we put on wools and equipment, rifles etc. and marched down hill. Formed beside road so General could inspect. Terribly hot! Nearly passed out. Stood for one hour and then a one-star General breezed by in his Packard, then a two star and a few more. At 4 PM the big shots arrived. General Eisenhower[14] and Clark.[15]

Wednesday 1 September '43

On guard last night from 3 AM to 7 AM. Had last meal in kitchen. On C rations[16] tomorrow. Only have one blanket now. Ground sure gets hard. Officers studying maps. Keep all men away. They must know where and when.

Thursday 2 September '43

Lecture on aircraft we will come in contact with. Rest of day off. Went to Arzew with Private Ellis. Ate at Red Cross. Had a few drinks. Went to an Italian woman's abode and drank wine at twenty francs a bottle. Terrible place but interesting to see these places. One room with off set for kitchen and wine barrel. Had 4 kids. Lots of families live in each building the same way. Really got tite.

3 BAPTISM UNDER FIRE

"Can't tell who has who surrounded but looks like it is us on the little end. Germans breaking thru."

German ideas of conquest in North Africa were a dream of the past. Offensive operations, knocking Nazi and Italian forces back, were now the aspirations of American and British commanders. Surprisingly, their first surge forward produced amazing results in short fashion. With stunning ease, Allied forces booted the German and Italian armies off the island of Sicily in August.

Hungry for more, but unsure of the target, British and American leaders differed. Since January of 1943, Winston Churchill, prime minister of England, repeatedly called for a new front to be opened in Italy. While the American high command originally considered an Italian invasion rather pointless in winning the war, the powerful insistence of Churchill eventually wore them down. Churchill, referring to Italy as the soft underbelly of Adolf Hitler's entire Fortress Europe, would ramrod forward his plan for Italian invasion. On August 16, even before the last shot on Sicily was fired, Eisenhower finalized the decision by placing the bull's-eye on Italy.

The Allied 15th Army Group's attack on Italy, code named Avalanche, was under the command of General Sir Harold Alexander and comprised two armies. The British Eighth was led by General Bernard L. Montgomery and the Fifth, mixed with American VI Corps and British X Corps, was headed by Lieutenant General Mark Clark.

Eighth Army's first step on the continent was to be at Reggio di Calabria on September 3, to draw the Germans forces down the Italian boot to defend the toe. Then the Fifth would hit beaches several hundred miles farther up the peninsula near Salerno on September 9 and cut them off from the north. Regretfully, the Allied punch to this body's flabby midsection did just the opposite and aroused a washboard-hard antagonist. Veteran German troops, aided by their rugged environment, held strong.

The 111th Engineer Combat Battalion was divided and then attached to each Infantry Combat Team with Company A assisting the 141st, Company B with the 142nd, and Company C aiding the 143rd. When placed on the ships, they were separated even more. For example, Company C had its 1st platoon (with Pearce) on the USS *Chase*, its 2nd platoon on the USS *Stanton*, and its 3rd platoon on the USS *Funston*. Commanding each company for this first combat action were First Lieutenant Warren W. Ausland of Grants Pass, Oregon, with Company A, Captain Orvil W. Crisman of Wortham, Texas, over Company B, and Captain Petree leading Company C.

The British Eighth Army invasion of Italy met light resistance. By September 8, the British advance forces were already halfway up the toe of the Italian boot. On the evening of the same day, the Italian Government formally exited the war. Surrender occurred on September 3, but it wasn't announced until the 8th to coincide with the main Allied landing at Salerno. The delay was an attempt to keep the Germans from taking over Italian cities and various key defensive positions currently occupied by the Italian troops. Eisenhower broadcast the news to the troops aboard the ships bound for Salerno. To the cheers of men about to enter combat for the first time, he said "Hostilities between the United Nations and Italy have terminated effective at once."

Meanwhile, the Allies planned to unload three forces on Italian beaches in the wee hours of September 9. X Corps' landing spot was near Salerno with the directive to seize Salerno, the Montecorvino airfield and Battipaglia. A second force, consisting of U.S. Rangers and British Commandos, was assigned to take control of the rugged Sorrento Peninsula west of Salerno. Part of the VI Corps, a revved up 36th Division jumped off well south of Salerno near Paestum. Their objective, as the first American military force to invade the European mainland since 1917, was to secure a beachhead, capture the high ground overlooking the southern half of the Salerno plain and hook up with the British Eighth Army advancing to their right. Floating as reserves were two combat regiments of the

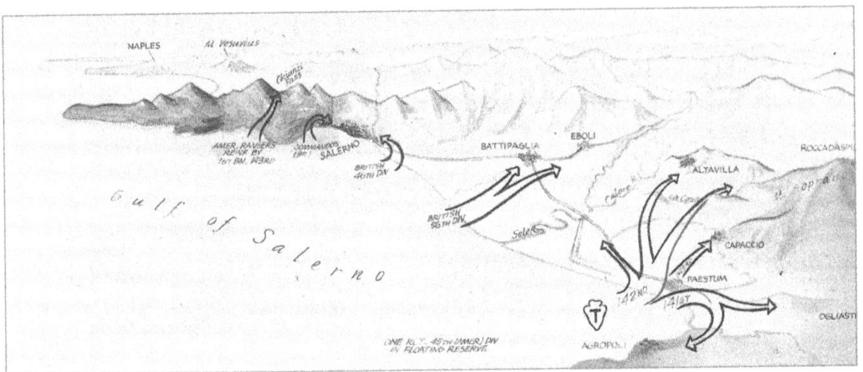

Invasion of Italy.

45th Division. The former National Guard unit, formed from the combined states of New Mexico, Arizona, Colorado, and Oklahoma, provided reinforcements as needed.

Fearing the power of German coastal batteries, the invasion fleet anchored twelve to fifteen miles off the mainland. With the moon setting minutes before 1:00 AM, the Allied force started to disperse to invasion craft for the 3:30 AM landing. Members of the 36th Division were ready to pierce the newly acquired German empire.

Aligned north to south, the beach landing zones were Red, Green, Yellow and Blue. Each colored landing zone averaged approximately seven hundred yards in width. As the invasion began, 141st plus Company A took to the beach on the right flank at the Yellow and Blue sectors.

Forty-eight engineers from Company A's 2nd and 3rd platoons under William Dold Jr. of Boston, Massachusetts, and James "Ace" Mueller of Macon, Georgia, landed with the first wave on Yellow Beach near Paestum. Their task, despite expected heavy machine gun, mortar, and tank fire, was clearing a path through any barbed wire or mines so the infantry could move freely ashore. As the engineers infiltrated the beach, they found the sands empty of Nazi mines or barbed wire. Only after daybreak did they receive small arms fire and later tank, mortar and artillery bombardments.

Company A's 1st platoon, led by Herbert Spearman of Columbus, Ohio, accomplished the same on Blue Beach. As the day progressed, Spearman, with aid

James "Ace" Mueller.

from Steve Boreczky of Cleveland, Ohio, managed to work his way past American lines into Paestum and destroy three German railway guns located there.

Brave soldiers appeared everywhere during the early stages of the landing. Two such men were Henry Gerdes of Victoria, Texas, and David Quisenberry of Campbellsville, Kentucky. For thirteen hours of uninterrupted death-defying work on a bulldozer, they avoided continuous German artillery and aircraft strikes to build six roads from the beach past the sand dunes.

142nd plus Company B hit beaches called Red and Green. 1st platoon of Company B, as they were loading for debarkation from the USS *Lyons*, suffered the 111th's first injury when George M. MacLaine of Houston, Texas, fell and suffered broken bones. Company B's 1st platoon, 1st and 2nd squads, under Robert M. Morton of Birmingham, Alabama, failed to land at their desired location on Red Beach. Avoiding multiple floating German mines, the engineers missed all four landing zones, unloading a mile and a half above Red Beach. The landing area was later named Red North. Instead of clearing a path for the 142nd, the engineers became infantry. Once their position was made known to American units, problems with friendly fire mistakenly aimed at them subsided.

Engineers at work as infantry storms the Italian beach. (U.S. Army Signal Corps)

Company B did manage to capture the initial German prisoners for the 111th. Starting with the first captured Nazi at an Italian farmhouse, the soldiers used a friendly Italian guide to lead them to German pill boxes overlooking the shore. In the infantry style encounter, George P. Pengressi of Pontiac, Michigan, killed an enemy soldier and helped capture eleven more.

Company B's 2nd platoon, 1st and 2nd squads, led by Omer E. Fortier of Lewiston, Maine, left the USS *Dickens* as part of 2nd Battalion of the 142nd and landed on Green Beach. Concentrated German machine gun and sniper fire slowed their advance but did not cause any casualties. With infantry aid the machine guns were silenced and 2nd squad under John A. Bettis of Goose Creek, Texas, cleared a path so more troops could land successfully.

Miles E. Hill of Ellisville, Mississippi, commanded Company B's 3rd platoon, 1st and 2nd squads' landing. Despite constant fire, the engineers crept forward until confronted with a far deadlier enemy—German tanks. Armed with only small-caliber weapons and trapped in a drainage ditch on two sides by thirteen German tanks, Hill gave orders for his sixty engineers to hold their fire. American aircraft and artillery fire, along with naval bombardment, knocked out five of the tanks around the trapped engineers. The remaining tanks retreated but were quickly replaced by five more tanks. American fire disabled two before the other three pulled back. Arthur Truman of Beckley, Virginia, separated from his friends, witnessed one tank being hit and disabled. As a German soldier attempted to escape the death trap, Truman eliminated him. No one else tried to escape from inside the tank.

Used in reserve, 2nd and 3rd Battalions of the 143rd plus Company C's 2nd and 3rd platoons unloaded between 6:40 and 8:00 AM on Red and Green Beaches. They received the same welcome as the other invaders. 2nd platoon of Company C, led by Thomas B. Gautier, Jr. of Charleston, South Carolina, arrived during a tank attack. Using their 37mm anti-tank gun and other fire to drive off the enemy, they suffered no wounded or killed. Loyd L. Patterson of Greenville, Texas, on the half-track he led, coordinated with infantry troops to eliminate a German machine gun nest.

Donald A. Curry of Madison, Wisconsin, and his 3rd platoon of Company C, landing north of Red Beach, had little difficulty getting on shore. A short tank battle with no damage to either side was the climax of their landing and inland movement. The orders for 143rd, after the engineers' demolition work on the beach destroying any barriers hindering movement, were to replace any faltering assault forces or take over an area between the 142nd and 141st. Once the latter course of action was decided, they advanced toward the tiny village of Capaccio.

After the *Samuel Chase's* landing craft disembarked its troops, smaller vessels made the fifteen-mile trip back to the beach. Time after time they unloaded the *Chase's* 88 vehicles, 13 two-ton trucks, 4 half-tracks, and 251 tons of ammunition, water, rations, engineers' supplies, etc. Pearce, lingering on the *Samuel Chase* most of the day, drove ashore from the LCT on the half-track he was assigned. Along with the rest of the 1st squad, his vehicle rolled onto Red Beach with 1st Battalion of 143rd in the early afternoon. Here they remained the rest of the day in support of the 1st Battalion, assigned to guard the Divisional Command Post being set up at Casa Vannulo.

The three infantry combat units of the 36th had varying successes and failures. By nightfall, the 143rd achieved a quick descent inland as the enemy disintegrated before them. They captured an abandoned Capaccio and the southeast slope of the area's major landmark—3000-foot-high Monte Soprano. A beleaguered 141st suffered the opposite. With limited exceptions, due to heavy German tank attacks, the 141st found itself pinned down only a few hundred yards from the beach. The 142nd, slowed but not staggered, continued forward on the left flank of the 36th attempting to acquire as much depth as possible from the beach.

The 111th, fighting side by side with these infantry outfits during day one, suffered two men killed in action and one wounded. Company A lost Jess W. Hudnall of Gauley Bridge, West Virginia. At 5 feet 10 inches tall and a thin 128 pounds, Hudnall, in the second wave ashore, worked with five other engineers utilizing mine detectors to clear a safe path for the infantry. Separated early from his landing party, he was later found nestled between two dead Germans. Their wounds and the blood on his bayonet said enough. Company B lost Truman A. Rice of Grand Rapids, Michigan. Rice, terribly wounded by shrapnel, was part of Hill's 3rd platoon cut off by thirteen German tanks. In order not to give their position away, he quietly suffered the excruciating pain until his death. Due to his heroic self- sacrifice, the platoon's vulnerable position was not revealed to the enemy. Hudnall and Rice each received the Silver Star Medal[1] for their bravery. Company B also had Joseph Abbott of Philadelphia, Pennsylvania, who was hit in the neck by enemy fire, successfully evacuated to an awaiting hospital ship.

Air strikes by the German Luftwaffe created some major problems, especially during the opening moments of the invasion. Allied fighter planes based on Sicily could only carry enough fuel to allow them to fight for fifteen minutes over the beach. Enemy air activity reached its height during the night of September 9 and the day of September 10. No injuries to the engineers were reported, but in one clamber to find cover, Company B suffered the loss of an overturned pot of hot coffee. The pissed off engineers, after a barrage of foul and profane language, returned to work.

Truman Rice.

Plans for D-Day Plus One were to occupy and secure the mountains inland from the beach. This would eliminate any German observation points there from directing their artillery positions' fire. These positions were currently raining accurate destruction down on the beachhead.

Facing only scattered enemy resistance on September tenth, the 142nd took the small town of Albanella. Monte Soprano, also under control of 142nd, was secured in case of enemy assaults. The 143rd remained predominately in the area around the town of Capaccio, a village on the slopes of the American occupied Monte Soprano.

After a night on the beach, the 141st carefully tread inland seeking to protect the right flank of the invasion force. Early in the morning they succeeded moving from the shore when the Germans, concerned about the fall of Monte Soprano, retreated.

There were numerous reported cases of British planes diving on and firing at Allied soldiers by mistake. Friendly fire remained a constant problem as the troops proceeded up the peninsula of Italy. This situation also worked in reverse. On September 11, two British Spitfires were shot down by American fire power as the nervous men manning the guns became trigger happy, shooting at whatever attempted to fly over the beach front.

The 1st Battalion of the 143rd, guarding the division headquarters, was moved from Paestum beach on September 11 to Maiori where they reinforced the US Rangers battling there.[2] None of the attached engineers accompanied the battalion as Company C's 1st and 2nd platoon took up the role of furnishing security for the 143rd command post. 3rd platoon of Company C exploited defensive slowdown measures when it placed over 760 mines beside a highway southeast of Capaccio. The 142nd, encountering only light enemy forces, succeeded in capturing the quaint village of Altavilla and Hill 424,[3] which had a clear view of the majority of the American beachhead plus any troop movements inland. The occupation of Hill 424 and Altavilla would be temporary. 1st platoon of Company B, while on reconnaissance near Altavilla, came under heavy German fire. Albert T. Phelps of Tyler, Texas, was injured when the resulting shrapnel penetrated his left arm.

As D Day Plus Two closed, the 36th Division beachhead extended six to seven miles inland except to its immediate left. Here the Texans bordered up against the American 45th Division. Elements of the 45th came on shore the night of the invasion and filled the precarious space between the British X and American VI Corps. To date they had enjoyed limited advancement into the Sele-Calore River corridor. This created a weakness between the two Divisions, providing many problems for the Americans in the days to come.

Sunday found the engineers on reconnaissance missions sizing up various situations like roadblocks, blown bridges, damaged roadways, and mine fields they would encounter. Company C advanced to the front line, about three miles southwest of Altavilla, to perform one of their highly trained specialties. That specialty was the dangerous task of clearing out mine fields, so troops could move forward. On this date, it was to allow for the future movement of the 143rd Infantry. These mined areas were reported as cleared by 4:30 PM.

The 1st Battalion of the 142nd, holding Hill 424 and Altavilla, regretfully became the initial unit of the 36th ravaged by the enemy. Determined German counterattacks came at daybreak on the twelfth against Hill 424 and then to Altavilla. They ripped apart the 1st Battalion and completely disrupted its combat efficiency, causing the loss of 260 officers and men. As stragglers of the battalion worked their way back to American lines, the Nazis resumed control of Hill 424 and Altavilla. On a day of horror and death for many 36th Division soldiers, the engineers, despite heavy German artillery hammering, only had a single man wounded. The infantry battalions, on D-Day Plus Four, would multiply that number by hundreds in dead alone.

1st and 2nd platoons of Company C, receiving radio distress calls from endangered troops, moved midway between the towns of Albanella and Altavilla and provided protection for two Field Artillery Battalions operating there: the 131st and 132nd. The artillery positions Pearce and his mates were protecting received heavy bombardment themselves. The overwhelming number of incoming shells and threat of ground attack eventually forced the Americans back.

Company A, in reserve, used the day securing supplies and preparing equipment for the expected upcoming engagements. 1st platoon of Company B, late in the day, was sent to remove an enemy roadblock northwest of Albanella. During the removal, Private Robert N. Jobes of Neptune, New Jersey, felt stabbing agony to his torso and legs as a hidden booby trap exploded.

German forces also struck hard with an armored attack against the 2nd Battalion of the 143rd, located northwest of Pearce's position. This battalion moved from a reserve position into combat status by filling the gap in the Allied lines in the low land between the Sele and Calore Rivers. The 2nd Battalion was hit by tank and infantry assaults that surrounded it and killed or captured most of its men. In a decaying state, it ceased to exist as a fighting force. This near annihilation of the battalion, with over 500 men lost, created a hole in the center of Allied lines that threatened the entire VI Corps landing.

With this win, Nazi troops gained full possession of the ground between Sele and Calore Rivers, and only heavy artillery fire from 45th Division artillery, with over 3650 shells fired, kept it from being a complete break to the beach. As the enemy exploited their advantage in the Sele-Calore area, German infantry crossed the Calore River north of Altavilla and pressed aggressively against the left flank of the 3rd Battalion of the 143rd.

The 3rd Battalion, assigned the mission of securing high ground around Altavilla, had moved into action, and succeeded in taking an unnumbered hill plus the few buildings still standing in Altavilla on the southwest slope of Hill 424. With the thrill of early success electrifying them, the perked-up battalion progressed on, trying to retake Hill 424. Heavy artillery and mortar fire plus a German counterattack against the 3rd Battalion short-circuited any effort to recapture Hill 424.

The German forces, which crossed the Calore River to the battalion's left, gained a threatening position behind 3rd Battalion and pressed firmly ahead with their recently won advantage. 3rd Battalion, their communications severed, gazed straight into the face of the same piecemeal destruction inflicted on the 2nd Battalion earlier. Retreat became the only option for survival.

A successful landing on the beaches of Italy by the VI Corps only days before was in the awkward and unexpected position of being pushed back into the sea. The Corps, in an unenviable position, was forced to shorten its front lines and regroup for the anticipated counterattack by the Germans.

Clark, concerned that the recoiling American section couldn't shoulder the brute weight of the Nazi surge, ordered contingency plans drawn up for the evacuation of the VI Corps and its redeployment in the British X Corps perimeter.

Fortunately, he did not underestimate the determination of the Texas Division and its will to survive. After further consideration, he accurately assessed that the defensive lines were in a favorable geographical position, and more troops were on the way.

The day ended on a positive note for the engineers, as several bold men of Headquarters and Service Company struck one more blow to slow down the enemy. Herschel Bridges of Cumby, Texas, Malcolm Cox of Annapolis, Maryland, James Foster of Saratoga, Texas, and Mack Murphy of Groves, Texas, worked past American lines at midnight, ignored incoming German fire, and blew up a Nazi tank near Altavilla.

Clyde Couch of Vernon, Texas, was the first combat death in Company C. Renowned as a tough but wise Sergeant, the college-educated native of the windy flatlands of North Texas was a giant loss to the soldiers relying on his leadership. He was reported lost around 9:00 PM when the company was replaced by parts of the 142nd and was withdrawing from the front lines. There were strong insinuations from fellow engineers on the scene he was a victim of friendly fire from the tank destroyers moving past Company C to bolster the front lines.

With the Division facing certain destruction, the situation demanded drastic action. After dark on September 13 came the much-anticipated order to withdraw. A last line of defense for the 36th was organized to defend the area between the Calore-Sele River junction and Monte Soprano, with the La Cosa Creek as a buffer in front. The creek provided a flimsy protective shield for the reeling GIs but was the most logical position to prepare for a last hurrah.

Located about six miles inland, it was fortified by elements of troops from every available unit, primarily because the 36th had suffered such a loss of manpower on the thirteenth. Since the retreat happened so fast, the German commanders believed the Americans were preparing to evacuate.

Pearce's 1st platoon, along with the 3rd, were stationed four miles inland at the extreme left sector of the Division's eight-mile-long defensive line. Mining all possible tank approaches, they defended them from the junction of the Calore-Sele Rivers (1st platoon) to the joining of the Calore River and La Cosa Creek (3rd platoon). The abiding positions were held by the 179th Infantry of the 45th Division to the left with an Anti-Tank Company of 143rd on the right.

These defensive spots were also dotted with any fighting men available. By early morning the Americans were dug in and waiting. 2nd platoon of Company C was in reserve and prepared to fight against any breakthrough or to cover the forced withdrawal of troops.

As midnight neared on the thirteenth, much needed reinforcements arrived. The 82nd Airborne, based out of Sicily, dotted the dark sky with 1300 white parachutes all arriving accurately in the landing zone near the Allied-held beaches.[4] Arriving ready to fight, the men of the 504 Parachute Infantry Regiment were hastily placed to defend the right flank.[5]

On the night of the thirteenth and the day of the fourteenth, hundreds of Allied planes, finally turned loose on the enemy, carried out one of the war's heaviest bombings. Naval fire power, especially when the British battleships Warspite and Valiant arrived from Malta, played a key role in the beachhead remaining stable.

Morning saw renewal of the enemy's hard-pounding charge. The Germans, trying to force openings in the defensive wall and drive the desperate defenders back into the sea, based the bulk of their offensive attack on their tank forces. One penetration of American lines was near Pearce's foxhole. Around 11:00 three or more tanks plus numerous self-propelled guns tried to ford the Calore River near a burned bridge and slightly northeast of it. Allied fire of all types beat the attempt back forcing a Nazi withdrawal. The 36th Division artillery alone fired over 4000 rounds on the fourteenth. Another major attack, consisting of twenty-five or more tanks, hit American lines on the level ground along La Cosa Creek just south of the Calore River. Some German tanks managed to penetrate the creek threatening defensive stability, but the American tank destroyers eliminated them in a few stunning, tension-packed minutes.

The remaining pockets of battle-weary Germans were ordered to retreat north while implementing an order delaying action on the Allies. Disengaging, the Germans ceased attacking along the La Cosa line. The only the sound of battle became enemy footsteps as they disappeared into the night. The crisis threatening the 36th was now over.

As the last rays of the sun fell on the debris-splattered battlefield, word reached Clark that the Texans had held. Clark, in his war memoir *Calculated Risk*, praised

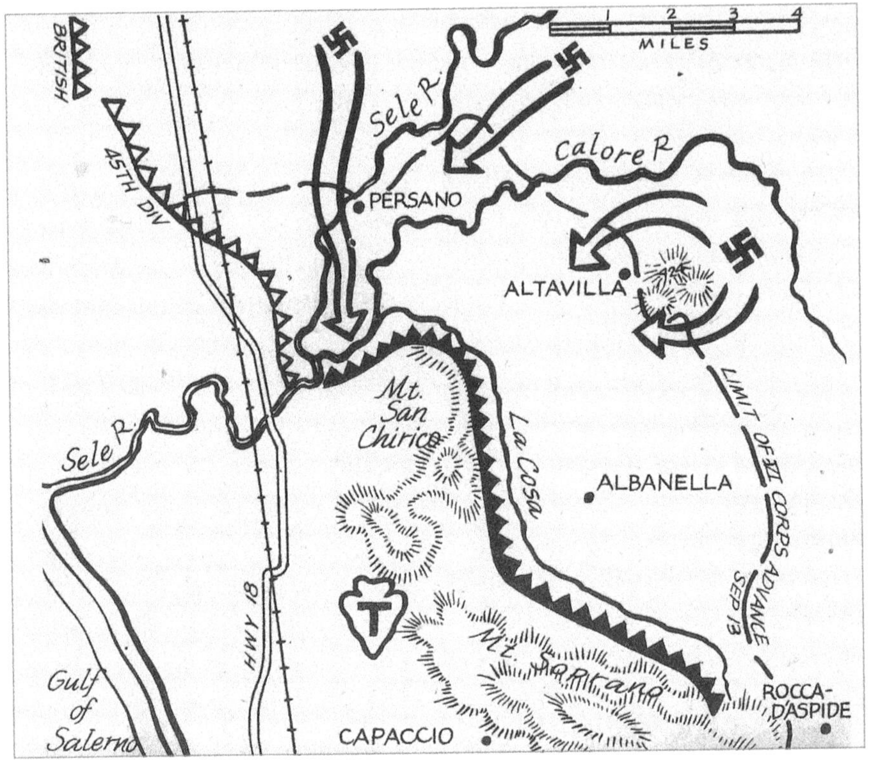

The German counterattack over the heights of Altavilla and across the Sele River nearly collapsed the American beachhead at Salerno.

the courage of the 36th at Salerno with, "In this manner our toehold on Fortress Europa was gained, and no soldiers ever fought more bravely than the men of the 36th Division".

1st platoon of Company C returned to work Sunday clearing the roads northwest of Altavilla of wrecked enemy vehicles and repairing damaged bypasses. Company A, doing what needed to be done with a demoralizing job, were assigned to bury the dead soldiers and civilians in and around the town of Altavilla. Although assisted by 3rd platoon of Company B, the process took two days.

The tired but proud Division was relieved by the American 3rd Infantry Division on Monday and moved into reserve for much-needed recovery time. While in constant contact with the enemy for twelve days, the 36th Division

Beat Off Fierce Counterattacks In Hard Fighting

(By Associated Press)

Allied Headquarters in North Africa, Sept. 15.—The Northwest African Air Force hurled every plane in their command over the Salerno bridgehead from dawn yesterday to dawn today in the biggest air attack in history in the Mediterranean flying. More than 2,000 sorties were made, concentrating on a few miles between Salerno and Eboli. Not a single plane was lost.

Ground troops beat off fierce counter-attacks but were forced to yield some ground gained earlier to straighten their lines. Savage, close-quarter combat raged along the Salerno-Agropoli front, with both sides throwing heavy reinforcements of troops and armor into the battle.

The British Eighth Army is speeding up the west coast to support the landing, and drove through Belvedere village, 67 miles from Agropoli, to close the gap between Allied forces to some 80 miles coast line by land.

The Nazis managed to bring up more troops in the Salerno sector despite the concentrated pounding of roads by Allied aircraft. Small pieces of ground changed hands repeatedly in the day's fierce conflict. The Germans made their heaviest and most determined attempt to drive the Fifth Army into the sea by sharp thrusts on the villages of Excevilla and Armoniana, on high ground overlooking the Allied foothold of the Sele River valley.

Hundreds of big shells poured into the Nazi positions, where troops were concentrated for the counter-attacks, by American and British cruisers and destroyers steaming close inshore despite hit-run bombing attacks, and strong counter-fire from German artillery.

Victory for Allies Changes Picture Of Battle in Italy

Adolf Hitler lost a great gamble Friday and the German army began a bitter retreat from the hills overlooking the American-British bridgehead at Salerno.

Outguessed by Allied generalship and outfought by Allied power, the Germans had spent much for the Salerno position where for a time the whole Allied plan was in danger.

The danger was averted when the American Fifth Army, half-American, half-British, united with troops of the British Eighth Army from the south to form a 225-mile line across the ankle of Italy, then smashed forward and captured three important towns on the Salerno front.

The union of the two armies came as the Fifth won the violent battle for its bridgehead and the British Eighth completed its epic 200-mile conquest of the Italian toe. It shattered the last hopes of the weakened Germans for establishing a defense line in that area.

Dallas Morning News September 16, 1943, and September 18, 1943.

sustained 267 soldiers killed, 679 wounded, and 984 missing or captured. The depleted Second Battalion of the 143rd was down from approximately 1100 men to only 208.

As October began, the VI Corps path across the uneven Italian soil, made deadly by the slowly retreating Germans, climaxed with the capture of Naples. This was a trophy in the face of heavy combat losses sustained by Allied forces. For just a few brisk moments as the Allies moved into Naples, a single, simple thought raced through each soldier's mind. The Germans were retreating. The worst was over. Italy was theirs. Yet this desire never materialized. In a sickening instant, as they approached the Germans' sprawling Winter Line, that optimism was shattered and flickered into an indistinct memory.

Friday 3 September '43

Left area this morning. Muley got a truck to haul our guns down the hill to road. Arrived Oran at 3 PM. Harbor full of ships. Got off trucks and walked 1/2 mile. Still hot and our equipment is heavy. Boarded the *Samuel Chase*.[6] Had trouble getting a bunk but am finally fixed. Too cool on deck. Went to hole and put our guns on half- track.[7] Sure hot down there. Boat full of men.

Sunday 5 September '43

Stayed on deck this morning. Pulled out at 1 PM. Stayed in harbor till 3 PM and then proceeded north towards Algiers. About thirty ships. We'll pick up more along the way.[8] Lots of destroyers with us.[9] Will maneuver around for five days and hit the coast of Italy below Naples. Maneuver is to fool enemy. Men all rearing to go. Sea very smooth. Stayed on deck till 12:30 AM.

Monday 6 September '43

2nd day out of Oran. Shot dice all day. Best game I've been in. Lost $47. One guy won around $1000. Lt. Beahler [Lee Beahler of El Paso, Texas] has showed us maps of what we (Division) are supposed to do. Take airfield etc. around Naples. G. 2 (intelligence) reports only older Italian soldiers there. Too old for good active service. One German panzer Division[10] around somewhere. Ships all have barrage balloons[11] up to ward off dive bombers. Expect very little resistance when we land. Still no picnic.

Wednesday 8 September '43

Picked up another convoy. Reaches out of sight. Close to 100 ships now.[12] Few friendly planes around as aircraft carrier is along. Two air raid alarms today. At 10 PM had another. Convoy on our left attacked.[13] We have to go below but I got on deck. Pretty night. Sky lit up with tracer bullets and shell burst. Lasted 30 minutes. News is that Italy has surrendered but not sure. Our plans are the same. We now expect stiff resistance as news cast stated the Axis are expecting an attack on Naples and Salerno. That is exactly where we are going!!

Thursday 9 September '43

Landing made on schedule. All hell broke loose. Lots of Germans in area. 141st Infantry made objective, 142nd met stiff resistance. Heavy casualties. Bomber came over ships this morning. Too high for fire to reach (about seven miles). Taking photos. Left ship at noon. Hit shore at 1:30 PM. Thirty German tanks were attacking 1/2 mile from us. 88 mm guns[14] raining hell. Messerschmitt planes giving us trouble. Lost 1-37 mm gun by tank fire but no men.

Friday 10 September '43

Bivouacked at pasture last night by Roman ruins. Moved to Company assembly area. Not far. Had three attacks by M.E. 109s on beach but no harm done to us. They sure are fast. Things are fairly quiet today as Germans have fallen back to mountains about four miles from beach. Move up closer tonight.[15]

Saturday 11 September '43

Moved into a place to be out of shell range. Another air raid on beach at 5 AM. At noon we started up front to blow bridge so a German Panzer Division couldn't cross. Too Late! Air attack on beach at 2:30 PM. Heavy barrage sent up. Do more damage than good as they shot down two British Spit Fires one falling 1/2 mile of me. One dived on half-track. Poured lead to him. Also a spit fire! Oh Oh.[16]

Sunday 12 September '43

Several attacks on beach last night so I slept in fox hole as shrapnel and bullets falling in our area. M.E. over this morning heading for home-just a streak. Moved closer to beach at noon. Spitfire shot M.E. down over beach. Pilot bailed out. Several bombs hit. Up to front this PM to remove mines. Artillery jeep hit one. Blown to bits. Several killed. Back to area at 10 PM.

Monday 13 September '43

Went up close to Altavilla (German occupied). Got caught in artillery barrage (88mm). Maybe you think we didn't take out in our half-track. They tried to knock out a bridge just ahead of us but we beat them by a hair. They nearly got us just as we crossed as a shell went right over us and hit a few yards away. Pieces of it hit our vehicle but that only speeded us up. You should have seen us go up that mountain road. Lightening de lux! Finally got out but sure was close. Heavy artillery battles all day. Tank battle late this evening. Don't know outcome. Saw three planes shot down, one ours down in flames. Can't tell who has who surrounded but looks like it is us on the little end. Germans breaking thru.

Clyde W. Couch.

Tuesday 14 September '43

Retreated at 2 AM this morning before it was too late. At 5 AM moved to left flank and set up defense. Well dug in. Machine gun set up. Ground very hard. Artillery shelled us all day. Battle was pretty hot till noon. Bullets and shells zooming all over. Quieted down at noon. Germans counter attacked this PM. Shell skimmed by me and killed Sgt. Couch.

Wednesday 15 September '43

Yesterday was our worse day. Sniper fired on me all day. Barrage finally settled on us. Germans nearly broke thru. Their tanks were all around, but our Tank Destroyers kept them off. Left shore at 8:30 last night as Germans retreated. A few new troops came up from beach. We needed them! The Germans nearly drove us back to beach. We won by a hand fight. Rested today as battle has moved away.

(Letter home concerning battle at La Cosa Creek)

Its funny how confident the people there (US) seem about this war being over soon. If they could really see a few things they might change a little. The Germans are not the type to give up and fight every inch of the way. And they are good fighters and smart. I know that to be a fact as I've seen them counterattack several times into what looked to me to be plain suicide. They've got nerve and good leaders.

I owe my safety to our artillery and Navy, who really handed it out and, of course, our air force was on the job. I laid in my fox-hole and watched the artillery hold them off for a whole day and thereby keep their tanks off of us. The tanks would sneak up a dry creek bed and get within a few hundred yards

Hopkins County Boys at Salerno

Associated Press dispatches reveal that the Thirty-Sixth Division of the U. S. Army is in the thick of the bloody fighting at Salerno, in Southern Italy, where the American forces are throwing their entire weight into the struggle to hold bridgeheads established in the Allied landings.

From information gained locally it is known that at least four Hopkins County boys are members of this division, but nothing has been heard from any of them since the division landed in Italy. The Hopkins County boys known to be in the 36th Division are:

Frank Pearce, son of Mr. and Mrs. R. A. Pearce, of Sulphur Springs.

Edward (Muley) Junell, son of Mrs. W. B. Junell, of Sulphur Springs.

J. P. Johnston, son of Mrs. Odessa Irons, of Sulphur Springs.

Arnold Glenn, of Yantis.

Sulphur Springs Daily News Telegram September 1943.

of me, but the artillery would drive them back. We had tanks, but the Germans had the advantage of cover and when our tanks moved up, they would let them have it. I noticed one crawl up on top of a hill and immediately a German tank made a direct hit on it. It burned all day.

It was nip and tuck all day, in fact the worst day we had, as they were determined to wipe us out. Later, I went thru the woods and area and there were Germans tanks scattered everywhere, along with equipment. I counted about twenty knocked out. If they had gotten through it would have been a bad spot.

A sniper shot at me all evening but was a bum shot. I finally got disgusted with him and got out to walk around. I never could locate him so let him shoot. The best he could do would be to kick up a little dirt about 30 feet from me, but most of the bullets would go over my head. After a while a fellow don't pay any attention to those things.

Thursday 16 September '43

No more retreating so says General Walker. It is now or never. 2500 air borne troops[17] came in yesterday. Went up to front last night and put up barbwire[18] in front of Infantry. Few shells hit but no rifle fire. I sighted a German out on patrol, but we avoided each other. Suited me! Got in at 3 AM. Went down to house and stole a fryer. A.A. shot down three M. E. over beach. Germans reported retreating. I hope so.

(Letter home concerning the air combat)

They would send a few Messerschmitt 109's over to bomb and worry us but soon found that costly. I saw a P-38 American plane[19] peel off from the formation and neatly blow one to hell and then pull back into formation as if nothing had happened. The M.E. 109 burned, of course, and flew quite a ways like a falling star. When they hit, it is just a big flash of fire. I saw quite a few of our planes bite the dirt too. I suppose this all sounds bad, but it's not so bad, in fact, I even found time to enjoy it. I really enjoy an air battle or anti-air-craft fire. It was so bad for a time that I slept in a fox-hole in order to avoid shrapnel and spent bullets as millions are in the air after the planes.

German Mark IV Tank destroyed in the counterattack. (U.S. Army Signal Corps)

Friday 17 September '43

Nothing for us to do today. Got dark on me before I got chicken cooked so had it for breakfast. Few air raids last night. All quiet in this area. One can imagine how bad it gets when Engineers are used for Infantry. We all came close to being wiped out. I can't say too much for the action of our Captain and one Lieutenant Yellow I call it. Scared to death. Hid in a barn.

Saturday 18 September '43

Another day with nothing to do. Enemy has retreated so fast we have lost contact. Contact was made with British 8th army on our right day before yesterday. They came up from toe of Italy.[20] Glad to see them. Don't know where 10th corps is on our left.

Sunday 19 September '43

Went up to where we had battle and built by passes over the river. That's all that saved us. They couldn't cross under our fire. Pulled Mark IV tank (German)[21] off road below Altavilla that broke thru and was knocked out. Burned. Dead cattle and a few Germans (dead) still around. Trees all shot to pieces.

Monday 20 September '43

Ran around all day. Tanks scattered everywhere our artillery etc. hit them. Went up to large factory and made estimate of lumber on hand. Italians very nice. Gave us some bread. Hard so soaked it in water. Also some dry cheese. People moving back in and digging out what they can. Roads lined with Italian soldiers going home. In rags etc. and carry big packs.

Tuesday 21 September '43

Looks as if our fighting is over as battle has moved completely away. Moved up close to Altavilla and bivouacked. The town we had so much trouble taking. Set up tent. Mosquitoes bad over here. Take atabrine[22] regularly. Gets dark over here at 7:30 PM.

Thursday 23 September '43

Moved up about 25 miles this morning to build a bridge. Passed lots of villages. People seemed glad to see us. Villages built high on pinnacle of rock. No way to get there except walk. Not me!! Bridge really blown. Take us two days to build another. Plenty of good springs along. British Eighth bivouacked next to us. German graves all along the way up.

Friday 24 September '43

Stood guard last night. Swapping C rations for onions and potatoes, peaches, etc. Bridge is completed. Going back to old area late this evening. Vehicles scatted along highway where Germans retreated and our planes strafed them. Got first "Stars and Stripes"[23] since being here. Interesting to read about ourselves. Altho a little on the side that people like to read. How brave etc. we were! We were all scared to death, but some good fighting was done. A case of have too!!

Monday 27 September '43

One of the half-track boys (Benedict) traded a pair of shoes for a turkey. I'm elected cook. Built an oven out of artillery case ends and mud. Dressed turkey and put him in at 9:45. Made dressing from C ration biscuits, two eggs, onions, bell pepper etc. All ready at 3 PM. Mashed potatoes and coffee. Best turkey I've ever eaten. Lieutenant Gautier and Lieutenant Beahler came by and helped us eat it.

Tuesday 28 September '43

Had exercises this morning and then went to map school and compass school this evening. Same old junk. On out post guard tonight 1/2 mile from Company. High winds came up with lightning and a down pour. Filled gun pit full in a few minutes. Our blankets and us were soaked and muddy. Rained all night. A very miserable night as it was chilly. No cover.

Wednesday 29 September '43

Early this morning I attempted to build a fire. Farmhouse close by. Italian farmer got some dry branches out of shed and built us a fire. Sun shone today so we got dried out. Kids hang around us but don't beg. We gave them "C" rations and away they go for home. Bought two quarts of wine off a kid for 50 lira (50 c). Not very good.

Thursday 30 September '43

Sick last night. Vomited several times. Lost my breakfast this morning. Probably the vino (wine). Baked two chickens for dinner and fried two for supper. Italians are hard to trade with. Too high. Want $1 for fryer. Swapped a pair of shoes for two chickens. Cleaned gun this evening. Old routine of exercise & drilling starting!!

4 NAPOLI

"Pitiful sight. People fighting over piece of candy or cigarette. Beg for meat. They brought out their babies and beg food. Hard to turn them down. We gave away everything we had. Destruction and disease and hunger. Civilized people gone mad."

On October 1 the 82nd Airborne Division entered Naples, the gem of the Allied invasion because of its seaport, reinforced by Lieutenant Colonel William O. "Bill" Darby's Rangers. Still, its capture was short of Allied hopes because it had been virtually demolished by Allied bombing and the retreating Germans. Departing German demolition teams eliminated or crippled all communications, water, and power sources. Ships that remained in the harbor were deliberately scuttled, adding, in addition to those already destroyed by the Allies, more obstacles to opening the port for use. Despite continuous German air raids and the damage done before they evacuated, the port of Naples was reopened to traffic in only a week.

The capture of Naples and the Foggia airfield by the British Eighth Army formally ended Operation Avalanche. During the fierce fighting, Allied troops had suffered nearly two thousand killed, seven thousand wounded and thirty-five hundred missing in action.

Slowly falling back, the Germans were now on the defensive and withdrawing behind prepared lines established to halt the Allied advance. The three lines, located twenty-five to sixty-five miles north of Naples, were the Barbara Line, the Bernhardt Line, and the Gustav Line. Collectively, they were called the Winter Line by the invading forces about to assault them.

The Barbara Line, located twenty-five miles from Naples along the Volturno River was breached by the Allies. Despite yielding the position to the Allies here, the German forces had followed Field Marshall Albrecht Kesselring's directions. One of the best and most respected generals on either side of the battling armies, Kesselring's orders were to hold here until the middle of October. This allowed his troops to use the extended amount of time to better prepare the defensive fortifications at the remaining two Winter Lines.

In the middle of the month, the skies of Italy introduced another enemy to the already-taxed soldiers: rain! Previously appreciated for its cooling break from the heat, the eleventh month of the year changed that perspective for good. The 36th Division was now pounded by rain, which made for sloppy, muddy conditions, and turned the fields and roads into quagmires. The cold weather also created new problems for soldiers sleeping in thin-walled tents or protected only by the soggy banks of their fox holes.

Friday 1 October '43

Baked a turkey for part of 1st squad. Bombers going over all evening headed north. Over a hundred making trip after trip. Probably bombing retreating Germans as we heard that Naples fell this morning. Hope it did as they have been trying to take it for several days.

Saturday 2 October '43

Arose at 2 AM. Got ready to move. Pulled out at 6:30 heading for Naples. First town of Battipaglia was in ruins. Nothing left whole. All day we were in populated places as one town runs into another. Salerno is quite a large place. Not hurt much.

Passed thru Pompeii. Shot up some. Then Naples. We traveled for quite some time before we reached the heart of Naples. Slow going as British Eighth and American Fifth moving up. All bridges blown and replaced by one-way Bailey bridge. Rained on us as we started into Naples. In Naples we went down by docks. All a twisted mess of wreckage and the buildings for blocks around a desolate mass of stones. People glad to see us. We stopped, and they mobbed us begging for food. Swapped "C" for wine.

Gave all our candy and cigarettes away. Pitiful sight. People fighting over piece of candy or cigarette. Beg for meat. They brought out their babies and beg food. Hard to turn them down. We gave away everything we had. Destruction and disease and hunger. Civilized people gone mad. Only saw one kid run over by vehicle but am surprised there weren't more as they crowd and push along the street. Saw Mt. Vesuvius.

Tuesday 5 October '43 [1]

Past two days we have been working at docks cleaning it up for use. Ships sunk all over the place and all buildings ruined. Water line set up by gate as Germans blew all lines and sewer.[2] People fighting for water. Lots of good-looking girls here. Some of the boys are doing alright but I don't care for them as they were for the Germans when they were here.

Wednesday 6 October '43

Drove jeep for Lieutenant Beahler yesterday and today. Went up into Naples yesterday and found curio shop. Bought vases and cameos for Iona. Went across Naples today to some barracks the Germans used and searched there for mines. Use to be an orphanage. All windows knocked out and messed up in general, so we couldn't use them. Lots of underground tunnels about twenty feet wide and thirty feet high. Went back up to top of city but didn't buy anything as prices jumped to unheard of heights. Coming down we stopped for a moment so Muley could buy something and a mine went off under the street about a block from us. Debris filled the air, big chunks of pavement and dust. Civilians running and screaming. No one hurt. Blew hole about fifty feet wide, fifteen feet deep. We're lucky.

Saturday 9 October '43

Left Naples yesterday and came back to area of Altavilla. Rained all day and night. On guard again last night but stayed in farmers shed. I have been broken out with bumps for several days which really itch. Fleas!! J.P. shot himself in the leg with a 44 pistol he got in Naples (yesterday). Not serious. Boys all got Italian pistols in Naples for $1 and up. People stole them from armory there.

(L-R) Pearce, Junell, Beahler, unknown, and Ellis in Naples, October 1943.

Monday 11 October '43

Nothing doing for half-track crew, so we just laid around and took it easy and cleaned our weapons. We have fifteen weapons on half-track we have accumulated. Everything from a 37 mm anti tank gun down to a 45 pistol. Two 30 cal. machine guns & two 50 cal. machine guns. Muley has an automatic rifle. Buildings still blowing up in Naples. Some 36th Engineer boys were killed by mines there. One use to be in this company (Weinstein). [George Weinstein of New York was killed October 10.]

Wednesday 13 October '43[3]

Fleas bothering me again. Made an eight mile hike this morning. My right foot is broken down so I had a hard time. Went to Albanella in half-track to try and buy vegetables. Got some hazel nuts (four pounds $1.00), ¾ bushel of potatoes ($3.50), quart of olive oil and a flat loaf of Italian bread. ($2.00) A few onions. Such prices are what we put up with.

Saturday 16 October '43

Going up to rejoin Battalion at Naples. Got up at 3 AM and racked tents etc. Moved out at 4:30. Went to Salerno and from there took a different route to Naples than before. People actually gave us some apples without asking for a thing. Bivouacked about ten miles N.E. of Naples. Been cold past two days.

Monday 18 October '43

Went about five miles up past a town of Qualiano to where bridge over railroad was blown. Checked area for mines. Signs of S mine but believe all set off by people or cattle.[4] Stayed in area this evening and read. Am reading "Anthony Adverse". Kitchen set up for first time. Had hot cakes for breakfast.

Wednesday 20 October '43

Stayed at camp but others went back to bridge site. Someone has to stay as the Italians are always hanging around and picking up stuff, especially the kids. Then went to Naples on pass. Sure changed. Streets full of people peddling wares. Water is on. Drank lots of wine. All kinds of people. Lots of prostitutes. Pimps everywhere. Streets and buildings are filthy. Never saw so many kids.

Thursday 21 October '43

Back to bridge site as air guard. Read all day. Lots of bombers going over (ours). Fighters so high they can't be seen but leave a trail of vapor like a cloud. Sky criss-crossed with them. At 7 PM air raid on Naples. Quite a few planes circle over area. One bomb fell ¼ miles from us. Lasted thirty minutes. Duds and shrapnel fell in our area. Lots of anti-aircraft fire.

Saturday 23 October '43

Back to bridge site. Sick this morning. Another raid on Naples tonight just after dark. Lots more anti-aircraft fire went up than last time. They are after the ships in the harbor. Drop flares to mark target and then circle and drop bombs. Search lights go on & off. Mainly to see if troops dropped.

Thursday 28 October '43

Another day at the bridge. Building a steel bridge and coming along very slowly. Had articles of war read to us again. Lecture on sex hygiene. Same old stuff. Quite a few boys have caught venereal disease in Naples. Went to Naples on pass this evening with Arnold Glenn. Bought a quart of rum and a quart of anisette. $4 a quart. Really got tite. It is worrisome there with the pimps hanging on your arm asking "Senorita or Spaghetti."[5]

Sunday 31 October '43

Went to Naples this morning. Missed truck at 1 PM back to camp so spent the day (intentional). Private Ellis and myself drank rum, cognac, etc. All on him. Had good time. Came in on 6 PM truck. Nothing said about it yet.

Monday 1 November '43

Got my pay this morning. $11.87. 67 cents was for longevity (3 years service) for a few days over 3 years. Draw more next time. Helped driver on half-track in motor pool. Show tonight in tunnel "Sea Hawks". Big air raid on Naples while in there. Could feel the jar as bombs hit in Naples twelve miles away. Didn't leave show.

Tuesday 2 November '43

Spent day in motor pool to get out of drilling. Did nothing. 141st boarded ship today.[6] May hit farther up coast. I understand there were lots of soldiers and civilians killed in last nights air raid. Biggest one on Naples yet.

Thursday 4 November '43

Back to bridge site. Rest of company (2nd and 3rd platoon) moved up to Volturno river. We finish job today and go up. Brought in an Italian on a stretcher today from house by the bridge. Some other Italian shot him in rear end with buck shot. Very painful to him.

Friday 5 November '43

Took down camouflage nets. Left area at 2 PM. Went back thru Naples and northeast about twenty miles. Bivouacked in plowed field. Air raid on Naples plainly seen from here. Sky full of tracers and air burst. Large flashes followed later by a big boom. Believe this is largest one so far. Lasted over an hour.

Saturday 6 November '43

Put up nets. This evening we went up to river [Volturno] about six miles away. Putting up rubber pontoon bridge.[7] After finishing it we tore it down. Playing soldier again. Came in at 5 PM. Brought in boats and Company goes out at 2 AM to see how fast they can put it up. On guard tonight. This practicing is boresome. Damn silly I say.

"MULEY" JUNELL AND FRANK PEARCE WRITE FROM ITALY

Finding time for their usual humor and jesting, Daniel E. "Muley" Junell and Frank Pierce, Sulphur Springs boys with the American Army in Italy, have written the following welcomed letter to The Hopkins County Echo. Both of these boys have been in action for considerable time, getting their first baptism of fire in the Allied invasion of Italy. Since then they have been in Sicily, Salerno and are now in Italy.

"Somewhere in Italy,
Nov. 6, 1943.

Hopkins County Echo,
Sulphur Springs.

What we would like to know is whether or not you are still printing The Echo. We have not seen one in six months. We believe a copy of The Echo would be nice to read while we are sitting in our fox-holes. It is very dull with nothing to do but dodge bullets and hope the next shell doesn't come in to keep us company. Through The Echo is the only way we can keep up on events in good old Hopkins County. We would like to know who is in possession of our favorite corner down in "No Man's Land." We will be glad to trade our corner in No Man's Land here for our old spot there.

We hope this letter will make our creditors breathe a little easier. We are still kicking, but if they have any creditors in Germany, they can charge it up to profit and loss column.

If possible, please send us a copy of The Echo, which will be greatly appreciated. Sincerely, "Muley" and Frank.

Pearce and Junell kept the folks back in Sulphur Springs informed on the progress of the war in Italy.[8]

Sunday 7 November '43

There was a grave by the river where the guy floated down and 19th Engineers pulled him out & buried him. "Ernest Smith Canton Ohio."[9] Killed during battle there. Finished my guard tour today and took it easy. Raining tonight.

Monday 8 November '43

Still raining so I laid around today. That landing of 141st was a trick. They unloaded on an island and boats went on up. Germans withdrew troops to rush up coast and our Infantry pushed up on this front. We were supposed to go up tonight and build bridge over some river on front so Infantry could take other bank. Our Eighth army broke across.

Wednesday 10 November '43

Moved out at 6 PM to new area about thirty miles north of here. Passed thru quite a few large towns, Caserta, St. Maria & Capua. Buildings looked more modern. Got to area at 8:30. [two miles west of Villa Volturno] Crossed Volturno River. Air raid at 3:30 AM. Three Bombs hit in Division H.Q. area, but most were several miles away after bridge over river. Put up nets etc and dug fox holes. Ground hard.

Private Ernest Smith.

Thursday 11 November '43

Six M.E. 109s came over area early this morning. Got thru the anti-aircraft fire heading for home. Three German graves just across road. Killed 10-12-43. On top of graves were Nazis symbols made from white pebbles and lime in center. Reveille at 6:15. Had calisthenics and close order drill. What a life, what a war.

(November 12 letter to Iona)

I am sure you appreciate more than a V letter every once in a while, although I find it hard to write at any great length. Yesterday I received two letters from you of Oct. 27th, and the Christmas package. The package only took one month to get here. A little mail must be expected to be lost. Am glad you got the picture. It was made by a street photographer and one of those quick jobs. That is Lieutenant Beahler I am with (of El Paso).[10]

Lee Beahler Jr. and Frank Pearce in Naples.

Italian mud. (ACME)

I got your vases right about where it was taken. Can't say just where but you can give a good guess [Naples on October 5]. I wonder where Marvin has gone.[11] I'm sorry he didn't get to come home before he left. Don't worry about him as he is in a good place and won't be in actual fighting. His worries will only be air raids and they are not too successful. And too, he will be a long way behind the fronts. Of course, it will seem like a big difference to you all, just knowing he is overseas. I feel like it will be another year before either of us get back home.

Sometimes as I ride along the roads and see grave after grave of all nationalities, I wonder if they are not better off than some of the living. Other people are taught to die for their country and we are taught to make them do just that. I can say tho, that we are faced with just that every day. I have seen very few fellows that do not show their bringing up. People think we are having a time doing whatever we please, but that is not so. We live just as much like we used to as we can, in fact I seem to be living a lot quieter and more decent life than I did there. It's because I can't help it, tho. Well, thanks again for the packages. Hope you all are doing alright. Take care of yourselves and I'll do the same.

Saturday 13 November '43

My birthday (28th). My dinner consisted of Vienna sausage & beans. I hate them. Out of a mess kit of course as I have been eating out of one for seven months. Back to Infantry again. Five boys in B Company hurt by accidental explosion of some caps. One had hand blown off etc. Raining tonight.

Sunday 14 November '43

No reveille today. Washed my dirty clothes. Laid around rest of day. Raining some today. Move up tomorrow night. Expect to have a little harder time as the mountains are full of Jerries and hard to take.

5 INCH BY AGONIZING INCH

"Sgt. Duncan went up and picked up Gus body. Carried it over to Div. grave yard. It seems the Grave Registration hasn't enough men to keep up so some bodies lie out quite some time."

For the second time in the Italian campaign, the 36th Division was thrown into battle. The Division, now part of the II Corps, moved forward to face a prepared, battle-hardened German army defending a fortified sequence of mountains known as the Bernhardt Line. Their commitment was in the Mignano-San Pietro section. This line of opposition, fifty miles north of Naples, included the Camino Hill Mass, Monte Maggiore, Monte Lungo, and Monte Sammucro.

The previous month, while Allied soldiers struggled across the crooked, bending, and weaving Volturno River—netting only twenty-five miles—the 36th refitted and prepared for the next operation. The 3rd Infantry Division had endured the specter of death since middle of September and the combat, rain, and cold had taken its toll. Moving up past these bone-weary soldiers, the 36th halted. On Clark's orders, the Fifth Army waited for two weeks to let its forces totally regroup for the planned offensive. There would be little time for rest in the upcoming months.

The new Allied attack was devised under the code name Operation Raincoat. The part of Operation Raincoat involving the 36th would be against a group of high points located on the Camino Hill Mass. This range of hills, six miles long and four miles wide, dominated the left flank of a low passage known as the Mignano Gap, which ran through the mountainous Bernhardt Line. Conspicuous peaks included a commanding point on Monte Camino (in the British X Corps field of operation) and two lower crests on Monte la Difensa and Monte la Remetanea.

Overlooking the gap on the far end of the Camino Hill Mass were the heights of Monte Maggiore.

First Special Service Force, an American and Canadian mix of six battalions attached to the 36th Division, advanced during the night of December 2-3. Working on the western side of the II Corps offense into the Camino Hill Mass, they captured Monte la Difensa (Hill 960) and Monte la Remetanea (Hill 907). They would only be able to hold the latter for a day before being driven back.

Monte Maggiore (Hill 630), at the far end of the Camino Hill Mass, was pried from the Germans in late afternoon on the third by the 142nd infantry. Immediately upon securing it, defensive positions were quickly set up to repel determined German counterattacks. Over the next few days, counterattack after counterattack was beaten back. The 142nd, with only the supplies they managed

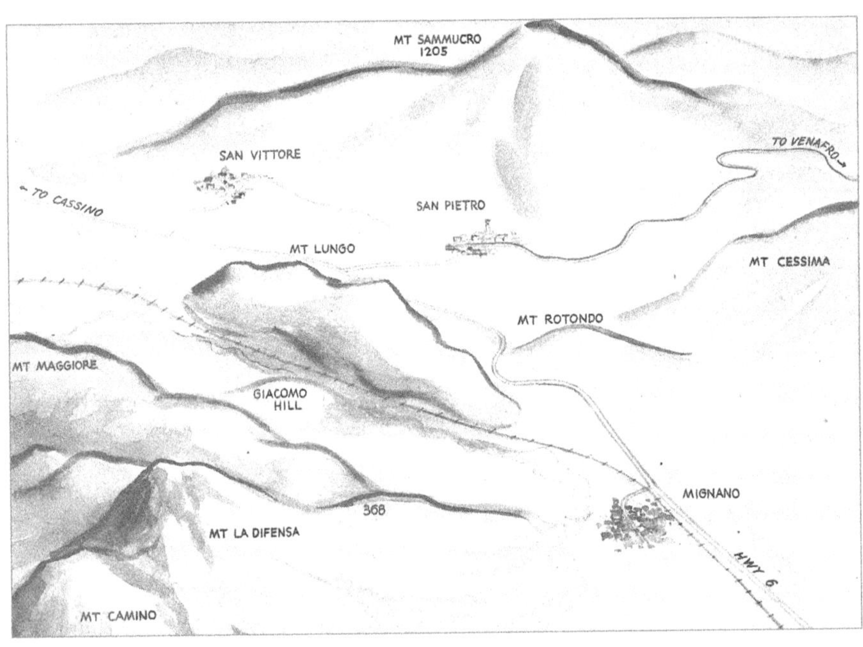

German troops used rugged terrain to make the Bernhardt Line into a strong defensive position. The small town of San Pietro Infine would prove pivotal to any American breakthrough.

to carry with them, and approaching the problem of limited ammunition, heroically held onto its difficult position.

First Special Service Force, despite losing Hill 907 on December 4th, retook it on the 8th and cleared it of enemy troops, ending organized resistance at this hot spot. Operation Raincoat was a success. Taking the Camino Hill Mass, which happened in a surprisingly short time, was only the first phase of gaining access to the potential "Gateway to Rome." Relieved by the British X Corps in the Camino Hill Mass, the 36th prepared for phase two. Starting on December 8th, with the sounds of battle in the Camino section only recently quieted, the second phase was timed to give the enemy no chance to recover.

During these operations, on December 4 and 5, several Engineers were damaged or killed. On Saturday, while Company C remained in bivouac, 2nd and 3rd platoons of Company B moved up Monte la Difensa to do demolition work preparing mortar and machine gun emplacements for 1st Battalion of the 142nd. Using the only trail available, they were brought to a jarring halt by German shelling. With little protection from the artillery storm, John A. Bettis was cut down. Willie R. Smith of Port Arthur, Texas, bashed by the same shell, received life threatening wounds to his left arm, legs and abdomen forcing his evacuation. With the death of Bettis, who was the squad leader for 2nd squad of 2nd platoon, the mission had to be abandoned.

Sunday was horrible for all three companies of the combat engineers. Company C had a job building two Bailey Bridges three miles southwest of Venafro on the road to San Pietro. 1st and 3rd platoons had to put up a Bailey bridge each, constructed six hundred yards apart. 2nd platoon's mission was mine detection and furnishing security against ground attacks. Pearce's platoon completed most of its bridge by midnight, but 3rd platoon's efforts faltered. Well-directed Nazi shelling necessitated a removal of the platoon without completing its assignment, and with two men downed. Andy Bochusz of Windber, Pennsylvania, received a left shoulder injury and Walter Wosik of Hamtramck, Michigan, was slightly wounded in the enemy's final salvo.

Company A's 1st and 2nd platoons put in a day's work repairing a bomb crater filled road two miles from Venafro. As the soldiers prepared to spend the night near the area of their assignment, six artillery shells found their mark. When the deafening sounds had ceased, the bodies of Charles George of Niles, Ohio, and

Milary King of Oak Park, Georgia, were sprawled on the bloodstained ground. George suffered a lethal head injury while King was seriously hurt.

For phase two, the 1st Italian Motorized Brigade, attached to the II Corps, drive on Monte Lungo's highest peak (Hill 343) was coordinated with operations to the east on San Pietro, Hill 950 and Hill 1205 (Monte Sammucro). The 6:30 AM advance up Lungo, on December 8, resulted in heavy casualties and a forced retreat by the Italians. With more than 350 Italians killed, wounded, or missing, the strategic German outpost overlooking San Pietro from the west still posed a major obstacle to taking that city.

In the center of the harmonized advance was San Pietro. The 2nd and 3rd Battalions of the 143rd crossed their lines of departure and moved toward this village on the slopes of Sammucro. Even with both battalions committed, the assault never progressed more than six hundred yards. Two more attempts to spring forward resulted in the same: no gain with heavy loss of life.

Failure by the Italians on Monte Lungo allowed the Germans to use machine gun and mortar fire from there to pound the Americans moving in the valley below towards San Pietro. Like Monte Lungo, San Pietro remained in German hands. On December 9, the 2nd and 3rd Battalions moved back to their original pre-advancement position.

Success did arrive during a tedious five-hour climb for the men creeping, crawling, and inching up Monte Sammucro. At 1205 meters it was one of the steepest heights scaled by Allied troops during the entire war. Despite the physical difficulties of the climb, at dawn the 143's rugged 1st Battalion overwhelmed enemy troops atop Hill 1205 and secured a foothold on its crest. To the right of Monte Sammucro, the 3rd Ranger Battalion, after failed attacks and heavy casualties, finally took Hill 950 on December 10. The result of the second phase ended in failure for two of the four attacks on the Bernhardt Line.

Still, the Mignano Gap was slowly moving into the Americans hands. Two major aims remained—Monte Lungo and the shattered remains of San Pietro. The most important was Monte Lungo. Because it held out in the attempted takeover by the Italians, its firepower was free to be loosed upon the Americans. Those forces, moving below its heights towards San Pietro, took the hit for the Italians' failure.

Things changed quickly when, on the night of December 15th, the 1st and 2nd Battalions of the 142nd (with Company B's 1st squad of 1st platoon available to remove mines) surprised a sleeping enemy on Monte Lungo and, in a moment of stunning swiftness, took over the mountain. Viewing the valley below by light of day, the Americans realized what a line of fire they now had on the German forces below in the San Pietro area.

The engineers' support had been valuable for the 142nd. Using six mine detectors, they had cleared out twenty-four "S" mines and twelve booby traps, armed with Tellermines or hand grenades.[1]

Before the conquest of Monte Lungo, American aggression at San Pietro on the 15th achieved the same as previous results.[2] Efforts by elements of the 141st and 143rd gained limited ground until forced to halt under a withering enemy fire. Yet with the loss of the critical positions on Lungo and, earlier, the Sammucro peaks, the Germans hastily prepared to retreat from their previously tenacious positions in front of San Pietro.

A German counterattack, to cover its retreat out of San Pietro, was blunted and fighting ended after midnight on the 17th. San Pietro fell to the 143rd, but they had little time to enjoy their success. The 143rd, astounded by the German retreat, pushed forward to reestablish contact with the enemy. Contact was almost instant as the Germans were determined to retain control of the lower southern and western slopes on Sammucro. Fierce combat continued for a week until a rested 1st Battalion of the 143rd, with help from First Special Service Forces and the 504th Parachute Infantry, succeeded in punching the Germans out of their holdings on December 25-26. With the Mignano Gap now in Allied hands, the 36th Division received a much-needed refitting/rest period.

The 36th Division's total battle casualties for December were 1,169 killed, wounded or missing. Another 2,168 were non-combat losses caused by disease or injuries. Due to the large number of losses, the original Texas Division's ranks now included only forty percent of its men from the Lone Star State. After midnight, the entire II Corps artillery fired three rounds per artillery piece at German targets on what became known as the "New Year Shoot". The Germans, not wanting to waste needed ammunition, celebrated with a return fire of considerably less bulk.

The remains of San Pietro after the Germans retreated. (ACME)

The effectively adolescent soldiers that scrambled across Italian beaches in September had now developed into a mature fighting machine. With each passing day it became alarmingly obvious to the German commanders that they were facing the best fighting men in the world. Quick to learn and eager to fight, the citizen soldier had now become the trained professional. The end of 1943 promised much more upcoming success, maybe even a glance at the possibility that the end of the war would come in 1944.

Monday 15 November '43

Moved out at 11:30 AM. Came about 27 miles about five miles from front. Biggest rain yet came up at 1 PM and I got soaked. Some hail. Area a sea of mud. Had trouble getting tent up. On guard!! Shells fell fairly close to us, but we are under a hill, so they go over.[3] Our artillery blasted all night. 143rd moved up. Mud knee deep.

Tuesday 16 November '43

Laid around between guard reliefs and tried to get tent better fixed. Just had to put it up over mud. I'm still wet. We have to maintain roads, so it will be a mess. Heard 27 men were killed in 3rd Division area by shelling last night.

Wednesday 17 November '43

Got up at 5:15 and drove jeep for Lieutenant Beahler. Went up to front to build a bypass at foot of mountain occupied by Jerry. Were shelled off and on all day. Like to have got me once.[4] 142nd relieved 3rd Division boys. They looked like a corpse after being in this weather. Rain all day. Came back after dark. Use no lights. Over mountain worst drive yet.

Thursday 18 November '43

Went back to same job. Carried half-track. Rained this evening. Artillery on both sides very active. Going over me today. Our artillery shelled mountain all day. Infantry using Phosphorus mortar shells. I had ring side seat. Had hard time getting back as it was dark & raining. Can't see your hand in front of you. Concussion from guns nearly jar me out of bed.

Saturday 20 November '43

Rained today. Muley & I went into town just above us (Presenzano) to look for Jones [Clyfton N. Jones of Wilmington, North Carolina] who has been missing two days. No trace. I went all thru it. Streets narrow & filthy. Town very old. So steep the streets are built in steps. A good place to be done away with. Missing guy showed up tonight. Been to Naples.[5]

Wednesday 24 November '43

Went up toward Venafro to where we are fixing road. Could see phosphorus shells hitting on mountain [Sammucro] around Venafro. On guard tonight. Four hour shifts. Go on from 9 to 1 etc. Artillery still going at intervals. Must be lots of it here in this valley as the whole valley can be seen by the gun flashes. Raining off and on again.

Thursday 25 November '43

Truck turned over in ditch last night just below my post. No one killed. Two boys had leg broke. Today is Thanksgiving. Also my 3rd anniversary to be in the army. Turkey supper. Big rain so had turkey and water. Chaplin came down. Several shells came in last night and hit close. Usually I sleep right on. Don't believe they can hit us on account of the mountain. Could be mistaken!

Friday 26 November '43

Had to go out last night with Company to work on bypass so artillery could move up. Mud and slop knee deep. So dark one couldn't see. Had to reroute artillery as we couldn't fix it. Came in at 12 o'clock. Caves dug in side of mountains by Italians. All old. Most are booby trapped by Germans. Company A boy killed couple days ago upon entering one. [Stanley S. Dardginski of Newark, New Jersey, on November 22, triggered a booby trap placed near a road to Lecave and died on the spot] Sun today! Air raid to the south tonight about Caserta.

Saturday 27 November '43

Finished bypass yesterday. [two miles northeast of Lecave] Heavy barrage by our guns last night. Went out today to the bypass and worked on it some more as traffic is heavy. Came in after dark. These black out drives over the narrow mountain roads are nerve racking. Few shells fell close to us but couldn't quite reach us on account of mountain.

Sunday 28 November '43

Went back to maintain bypass. We carried half-track so didn't work. Got in before dark. British buried a guy up there today. Procedure: as he was stiff they tie his arms across his chest. Also legs. Dip water out of hole and put him in. All bodies are usually buried in blanket or bed sack (in our case). Cross marks spot with name, organization. Artillery so loud tonight it even disturbed me. Have set up some 8 inch guns about 400 yards down the hill. What a bang. Hate to be on receiving end.

Wednesday 1 December '43

Loaded gravel this morning. Cut poles this evening. Lots of air activity. Saw about eighty of our bombers[6] go over and bomb German positions. Could hear concussion. About forty P51s and spit fires buzzing around.[7] No Jerry planes came up to argue.

Thursday 2 December '43

Cut poles this morning. Nothing doing this evening. Artillery started its heaviest barrage at 5 PM. Went up to front with truck driver with gravel for road. On mountain there was the damndest concentration of fire I have seen. Just a ball of fire from artillery and machine gun tracers. Steady roar.[8] Lots of bombers went over today.[9] First freeze last night.

> [Editor's note: The engineers, because of the "Mignano mud", constantly put gravel on the roads while at other impassable spots the engineers lay poles cut near the Volturno River. Wednesday, it was Company C who did the cutting. They labored all afternoon and produced fifteen truckloads of "corduroy poles" for road use. Thursday the company did more sawing, chopping, and cutting of trees near the Volturno River. This time thirty-five trucks were filled with wood to help improve the quality of transportation on Italian roads.]

Friday 3 December '43

Rained all day so did nothing. Canteen supplies today.[10] Understand we took a couple of hills last night. I don't see how anything can live under fire like last night but one can. Sure tiresome trying to eat in rain. No shelter and mess kit fills up with water. What a life.

Sunday 5 December '43

Went up past Venafro and built a bridge (Bailey). Germans had observation on mountain and shelled us all day off & on. Finished at midnight. Shelled us heavy about then. We had two men hurt by shrapnel. (Wosik, Bochusz). Company A had a Sergeant killed. [John A. Bettis] As bad a spot as we have been yet. To bed at 2 AM

Tuesday 7 December '43

Laid around today as no job for us. On guard tonight. Bunch of Italian soldiers bivouacked below us.[11] Go into action soon. Don't believe they will be worth a damn. Also Goumiers from Africa are on front.[12]

Thursday 9 December '43

Went back above Venafro this morning. Heavy fighting on mountain. [Sammucro] Ambulances and jeeps bringing out lots of wounded and dead. Really having hell up there. Mortars doing lots of damage. Boys sure look tired and dazed. Watched 24 of our A-36 planes dive bomb Jerry just over mountain.[13] All came out of it O.K. What a racket.

Friday 10 December '43

Went back to bridge site and finished it up good. [Bailey bridge of December 5 was open to traffic by 9:30 AM] Not too much going on. Occasional gun fire and mortar fire. Rained so mountain was hid by clouds. We are not making much progress as it is hard to root them out of these mountains. They are always looking down our throats. Cost in lives heavy.

Saturday 11 December '43

Went up to bridge to get surplus material. While we were working we were suddenly attack by about ten Jerry planes. (F.W.190s)[14] They came in low and high speed. Caught us flat footed. Dropped two clusters of bombs. Landed above us about 300 yards in 82nd airborne area. Killed and maimed quite a few. One of our men slightly wounded. [Eugene E. McDonald of Coldwater Branch, Michigan in left leg]

Monday 13 December '43

Been on front for a month today since our rest period. Moved today north of Venafro. Mountain is ours now. Fair day. Set up machine gun for air protection.

Pearce prepared for the Luftwaffe.

Tuesday 14 December '43

German planes swooped over mountain and bombed artillery position about one mile to our right. I've never seen so much flak and machine gun fire go up. I got off a belt myself. Our planes have been giving them hell. Can see German flak etc. from here as only a mountain separate us. Dug hole big enough for two and put tent over it.

Wednesday 15 December '43

German planes over again but didn't stay long. Too hot for them. Today has been a noisy one as we are advancing. A tank battle was fought just over the mountain. They say we won. Our planes have bombed and strafed them all day. Seems like everything is going at once. Noise terrific. Counterattack on mountain tonight. Quite a battle for a hour. Guess we held.

Thursday 16 December '43

On guard tonight. 4:30 PM to 8:30 and 4:30 AM to 8:30. Another battle on mountain. We are at its foot. Germans trying to take it back. Mortars going all night. Artillery going strong. The Germans are really getting it put to them.

Saturday 18 December '43

San Pietro on other side of mountain is ours. Went up to San Pietro. Worse torn up country I've seen yet. Still lots of bodies scattered around. Saw one Jerry with head blown off. Also an Italian civilian. All been dead some time. Smell not too good. Germans had elaborate dug outs with tables & soft chairs. Found one booby trap which I nearly got into. Found two wounded Germans in cave. One bad with head & arm all shot up.

Sunday 19 December '43

That tank battle was costly. I saw twelve tanks scattered around San Pietro all ours knocked out.[15] Only sent up sixteen. 88 mm go thru them. I didn't go up today. Had one squad up there and planes bombed them. Killed Felix Gus, Lieutenant Evans, wounded Jaeger (hand off), Rabb, Cope, Anderson and more. Gus was one of best liked boys in platoon.

> [Editor's note: Seven German planes sped in from the east at 9:43 AM shielded by the bright morning sun. Bombs loosened and machine guns blaring, the planes stunned the startled men of Company C's 1st and 2nd platoons, working to clear debris in San Pietro. With their visibility nil because of the sun, the suddenness of the strafing allowed them no time to secure adequate shelter. Felix Gus of Windber, Pennsylvania, and James Evans of Lafayette, Indiana, were killed. The causality list of wounded included Joseph Jaeger of Redondo Beach, California, Glenn Rabb of Waynesville, North Carolina, Willie Cope of Sparta, Tennessee, Charles Anderson of Long Branch, New Jersey, Kenneth Hand of Louisville, Kentucky, Richard Nims of Avenel, New Jersey, Anicet Fournier of Fall River, Massachusetts, and medic Leroy Gloor of Gonzales, Texas.]

Monday 20 December '43

Lieutenant Evans had only been with us a few days. Had his arm blown off. A fellow hasn't a chance with these planes dropping out of sun. Gus was my tent mate in Africa long with Rabb & Cope. Rained today. Nothing doing and quiet today. Gets dark at 5 o'clock. No lights allowed but we manage to cover ours up so can read.

Tuesday 21 December '43

Nothing for us to do today. Sergeant Duncan [Charlie Duncan of Leonard, Texas] went up and picked up Gus body. Carried it over to Division graveyard. It seems the Grave Registration hasn't enough men to keep up so some bodies lie out quite some time. Can't be helped. Any of us are liable to get it any day but we never worry about that anymore.

> [Editor's note: Removing the dead under German fire was slow as well as risky. With the weather cold, many men were left near where they fell until there was enough time or it was safe to recover their bodies.
>
> Mourning a lost friend crashed down hard on men during combat. Thousands of soldiers witnessed the deaths of those they had come to love. Duncan and Gus, each from different sections of the country, had established during their military careers a mutual bond only soldiers share. Duncan lived to return to his hometown of Leonard, Texas, while Gus would remain on the peninsula. He was buried at the Sicily-Rome American Cemetery in Nettuno, Italy.

Left: Charlie Duncan. *Right*: John Bettis.

This same relationship can exist throughout entire squads. On December 11, Company B received saddening news that the body of Sergeant Bettis, killed on December 4, had not been removed from the side of Monte La Difensa. The entire 2nd squad of Company B's 2nd platoon, of which he had been the respected squad leader, returned to the mountain trail to rescue the body. Once discovered, it too was turned over to Grave Registration for burial. Then they trudged back to the front, warmed by the fact they had honored an extraordinary man who was much more than just their leader.]

Wednesday 22 December '43

Rained all day. Didn't go out today. Put up big tent. Each platoon has one for recreational purposes. Played more poker and won tonight. I feel sorry for the Infantry boys who have the hell in this war. Cassino is next town of any size. Be hard to take.

Friday 24 December '43

Went out this morning as air guard on job but saw no planes. On guard tonight. Lieutenant Beahler gave me a shot or two of alcohol he got from medics. Mixed with orange and grapefruit juice which made me sick. On guard from 12:30 to 4:30. Hardest one yet as I am sick. Didn't get any sleep.[16]

Saturday 25 December '43

Got up at 11 o'clock and ate dinner. Had stew. Back on guard at 12:30. Fair day but is cool. Turkey for supper. Three years ago I was on guard on Xmas back in Greenville at armory. Quite some difference now. Will be relieved soon as Infantry is low on men. Some companies have as few as eighty men.

[Editor's note: Early Sunday morning, two boys of Company A, while they slept, were seriously injured by a reconnaissance car parked carelessly on a terrace above their tent. By an act of God or ignorance of a trooper, it slipped out of gear and careened down on top of them. The rolling vehicle hit both sleeping men in the tent. Kenneth Wagner of Oxford, Nebraska, survived, but Walter B. Scott of Keansburg, New Jersey, died two days later. As illustrated with this incident, the dangers of war weren't always about having to dodge mortar fire, disarm booby traps, and defuse mines.]

Tuesday 28 December '43

Took down tents etc and moved out at 11:00 AM. Wire shorted on half-track. Came thru several small towns and ended up out here in the mountains close to Piedimonte. [three miles northwest of Alife] Pyramidal tents already set up. Made me a bed and am all fixed up. Not too far from front.

Wednesday 29 December '43

Made a stove out of oil can. Works fine. Muley went into town and bought back a half gallon of cognac. I gave him the money before he left. Ten bucks for it. Been sipping it all evening. About like corn whiskey. Nothing doing today.

Friday 31 December '43

Bad day.[17] Rain. Went on wood hunting detail this evening. Really scarce. Muley got off in town and got a gallon of cognac ($20) for New Years. Split up cognac with others. Played poker and drank until 1:30 AM. Lost $33. Didn't get too tight. Don't trust the stuff as so much of it is made from wood alcohol. Weather is fairly cool but mostly wet and disagreeable. Pay day. I drew 13.70.[18]

6 NECESSARY LOSSES?

"Saw the prettiest sight I ever expect to see in war. Clear day and in groups of 24, 143 Flying Fortress came over and bombed the Monastery and Mountain above Cassino. Later 36 B 25 came in and this evening 36 more. The Monastery just a shell now. Most terrible implement of war!"

While the troops rejoiced at being relieved from the front so they could enjoy some rest and relaxation, there was also a moment to reflect on their accomplishments from 1943 and remember friends lost. Whether it was splitting cognac in a breezy tent or resting with eyes closed and reminiscing about home, it was still Italy, not the USA. There was more war ahead, heroics to take place, and men to pay the ultimate price for friends and loved ones.

New Year's Day also saw Mother Nature, with other ideas for the present, blast the troops out of their glowing memories and into warm clothing. A huge storm with heavy winds pelted the recuperating men with rain and snow. What next? Within three weeks that answer would be stamped in the annals of 36th Division history—the Rapido River.

The Bernhardt Line campaign, which started in mid-November, ended in mid-January. Fifth Army's attempt to drive the Germans out of southern Italy had forced the enemy back into the Gustav Line, a third well-prepared German defensive front sixty miles north of Naples. Monte Trocchio, the last obstacle east of the Gustav Line, fell on January 14. A solitary hill almost one mile from the Rapido River and over four miles northwest of San Pietro, it was overrun by the 34th Division while receiving no enemy opposition. There was fighting for a smaller bluff on the southern slope of Trocchio but was soon taken by the 141st.

William J. Jones.

The snail's pace that gained them ground thus far—and at a costly price in men—now seemed a distant memory as a view of the Liri Valley area promised that great things would quickly follow. Sadly, their initial speed quickly digressed; swift maneuvering was hobbled, then stopped, and the hope of an unimpeded strike faded into disappointment.

After the brief rest period, the 111th moved into position in preparation to drive up the Liri Valley. Company A and the 141st relocated on January 12, with the other two companies settling in bivouac two miles south of Mignano on the 16th. From here, they carried out the critical tasks of preparing roads for travel, eliminating the threat of mines, and reconnaissance of roads, bridges, and minefields facing the Americans.

Typical of their workload over the next few days was the reconnaissance duties of Company A on the sixteenth. Four engineers assisted two patrols from the 141st on a night mission. The engineer's purpose was gathering information as well as helping the patrols with reconnaissance boats needed to cross over the Rapido River to scout the enemy side.

Well-hidden Nazi machine gun blasts from the far bank halted one patrol's attempt, but the second, near what was left of the little town of Sant' Angelo Theodiche, achieved its purpose. Paddling quietly over the rapid water, they landed and advanced over eight hundred yards into enemy infested terrain collecting key details. Like the other patrol, during movement back it came under heavy enemy fire. The patrol's causalities were three reconnaissance boats lost, several infantrymen killed and two wounded. During the firefight, two pursuing Germans were eliminated, and an unknown number wounded.

The unsung hero, of this encounter across a section of the forty-foot-wide Rapido River, was Company A's Sergeant William J. Jones of Flint, Michigan. After their mission ended, Jones and his companions aided the two wounded infantrymen until medical help arrived and then, being wet, cold, and tired, prepared to return to their bivouac area.

Suddenly, ringing across the darkened landscape, came the painful screams of other infantrymen. The sounds were from GIs who had stumbled into an unmarked minefield and triggered the deadly devices. Led by Jones, the engineers blatantly maneuvered over the muddy grounds, incredibly avoiding live mines and shrapnel from artillery shells, to rescue the soldiers. After moving the wounded to safety, they signaled for medical aid and remained to help the men be evacuated. All in a night's work for such champions as a mud splattered Jones and friends.

January 17 and 18 saw more infantry/engineer patrols evaluating the river's edge, charting the numerous minefields, and getting a first-hand view of the road structure leading to the front. For all the missions attempted and all the German shells aimed at stopping them, the engineers experienced only a single casualty. Frank Calabrexe of Hartford, Connecticut, was wounded by mortar fragments during a reconnaissance mission near Sant' Angelo.

The 36th now prepared to enter the blackest moment in its history. A Rapido River bridging by the Division, despite overwhelming odds, was a part of a Fifth Army scheme named Operation Shingle. Directly helping the 36th, the British X Corps would ford the Garigliano River in two spots while the II Corps, on the twentieth, made a thrust over the Rapido.[1] This would be followed by an amphibious assault behind German lines at Anzio on January 22. Clark, in command of the entire operation, hoped the river crossings would draw German reinforcements south from Rome and away from Anzio. The combination attacks were expected to force an end to the Gustav Line and free the Allies to advance all the way to Rome. In retrospect, it was a war plan filled with crater sized holes and when executed, achieved little.

Call the order crazy. Scream that it was stupid. Yet no matter how you label it, the order to cross the Rapido River, at the point selected for the 36th, snuffed out the candle of life of so many fine American infantrymen in a ridiculous fording of a heavily defended stream. Experienced fighting men were sacrificed, and important leadership wasted in the two attempts to take up positions around Sant' Angelo.

Even Clark, who had received instructions from his boss, Sir Alexander, to make a thrust at the Gustav line to tie down the Germans, knew the cost would be high. He wrote " . . . it is essential that I make that attack (across the Rapido), fully expecting heavy losses, in order to hold all the German troops on my front and draw more to it, thereby clearing the way for Shingle. (invasion at Anzio)"

Clark's problems were bigger than the necessary loss of a few men at a narrow riverfront. His attention stretched like elastic in multiple directions. Therefore, he had a wide focus view of the Rapido crossing. The men of the 36th needed fine focus. The division, on orders by Clark and initiated by II Corps Commander Geoffrey Keyes, were ordered to cross the Rapido River in two spots near Sant' Angelo and establish a bridgehead.

Due to tremendous losses thus far in Italy, the Division received more than 1100 new men in the two weeks prior to the Rapido River crossing. The 141st alone added thirty-five officers and 694 enlisted men. Most were soldiers limited to seventeen weeks of infantry training, while the officers were officer candidate school graduates with little or no combat experience.

The flooding mountain stream, swollen to about two football first downs wide, was cradled on each side by steep banks. Depth, at this site, of the swift ten miles per hour icy river was approximately twelve feet. On the west side the 15th Panzer Grenadier Division, one of the best in Italy, armed with artillery, tanks, excellent defensive positions, and great observation points overlooking the river line, opposed the division. The near east bank of the Rapido River was heavily mined and frequently patrolled by the Germans. Therefore, the approach to the river was not completely under American control, thus creating problems of getting to the river, crossing the fast-flowing water, and gaining control of the German riverbank.

Strike one dooming the 36th came from the British. A British X Corp's attempt near Sant' Ambrogio was designed to create a bridgehead over the Garigliano

River and secure heights overlooking Sant' Angelo. Only a few miles to the left of the T-Patch strike point, the plan was for the British to eliminate the German's ability to counterattack the exposed Texas Division flank. The British planned to attack on January 18, delayed a day, and in what became a half-hearted effort on January 19, was completely stymied. With this failure, the 36th attempt, moving east to west across a river surrounded north and south by commanding heights, seemed foolhardy. Still, Clark demanded the plan go on.

Keyes, to his credit, requested a one-day delay for the 36th giving the British two days to do their job. Clark, more concerned about his Fifth Army control of the Anzio invasion, refused. The overall strategy of the campaign dwarfed the realities of a single battle. If American blood was to be shed in quantities, it would come from the thousands at the Rapido and not the tens of thousands on the beaches of Anzio.[2]

Strike two then, dooming the 36th, could be placed at Clark's feet. It was his choice of where to grind out the II Corp's break through. The idea of punching past the Germans holding the river's edge and into the valley beyond seemed like a fantasy.

Finally, strike three of the near destruction of the 36th Division was the butcher's bill of this operation. On this wild ride into military insanity, in forty-eight hours of courageous fighting, under impossible conditions, the 141st and 143rd lost 143 men killed, 663 wounded, and 875 missing in action.

Even so, the command followed orders to the best of their ability. In early January, Walker had Oran Stovall evaluate, estimate, and recommend what the engineers needed to get the infantry to and across the Rapido. Like the past, as well as in the future, Stovall presented realistic questions and sought answers from his superiors. In this case, he observed "an appalling lack of basic engineer supplies available". Unless major supplies of equipment were added, the attempt would be impossible.

Stovall was informed he would not only receive the needed equipment to ford the Rapido, but also help from the other sources. Manpower from the 19th Engineer Combat Regiment and the 16th Armored Engineer Battalion were added to the pending attack.

Two companies from the 16th Armored Engineers teamed with the three companies of the 111th to do the dirty work of getting the battlefield ready for advancement. They were to clear mines and mark trails to the crossing sites, construct approaches before, during and after the attack, and provide bridges over the Rapido after the enemy was dislodged.

On January 19, the 19th Engineer Combat Regiment gave the 36th two battalions, less a company each, to be attached to the infantry. 2nd Battalion of the 19th would work with the 141st, and the 1st Battalion of the same was assigned to the 143rd. Their job was getting the actual equipment to the river's edge and then assisting in ferrying the men over the freezing water to the west bank by boat and bridge.

Despite all the hard work on roads, time consuming nighttime removal of mine fields and congregating all the equipment needed, things went wrong. The two battalions of the 19th, due to road conditions, decided they couldn't get the equipment up front by truck, so it was left a mile or more back near Monte Trocchio. Inexcusably so, the infantry, not the engineers, added to their individual load the weight of this poor decision. Men primed to fight became cargo bearers for the equipment.

Nearing the river, the 19th Engineers were to guide the infantry through minefields cleared by the 111th. Tragically, before the troops got to the river's bank, there were already heavy losses. With the ear-piercing whine of numerous sharp crackling blasts blanketing the approaches, the German artillery, mortar fire, hidden mines and booby traps shredded the slowly moving soldiers.

The troubles stacked up. The valley was obscured in an unforgiving fog and, coupled with smoke screens, dropped visibility to nearly zero. Seas of soft mud covering the landscape, and landmarks through the minefields became obliterated by incoming shell fire, creating disaster. The guides became lost and confused and stumbled into minefields, whittling away the troops before even beginning the cross-river assault. Once at the banks of the Rapido, the boats, bridges, and tangled up men faced more chaos. It was a scene from Hell. Detailed planning by Stovall, combat ready engineers, adequate supplies, and courage could not overcome the choices made of by higher command.

Between 7:05 and 8:00 PM on January 20th, the infantry jumped off. The 36th part involved a two-pronged operation. The 143rd attack point was south of Sant' Angelo while the 141st crossing spot was north. The 142nd was held in reserve.

Preparing to move to the front, a group of litter bearers take cover from sniper fire seven hundred yards from the Rapido.

In the north, the 141st managed to get more than a hundred men to the west side of the river. Unobstructed German fire quickly pinned them down and rendered them ineffective. They were trapped there all day, but no help could reach them. All were killed or captured.

Farther south the 1st battalion of the 143rd got entirely across by 6:00 AM on the twenty-first. They advanced about one hundred yards before grinding to a stop. To keep from being completely wiped out, they retreated to the east side of the river by 10:00 AM. The first try to ford the Rapido River came to a bloody halt. Rifles just didn't match up against artillery, mortars, and dug-in defenders.

Phase two to cross the river would be just as costly. A crisis immediately existed in the south during the second phase of the river crossing. The 143rd, with the river heavily smoked for concealment, moved forward at 4:00 PM on January 21. Despite a maximum effort to extend farther inland, they were quickly hacked to pieces. With ammunition short and their losses staggering, all retreated to safety.

Just 100 yards from the Rapido, infantrymen take cover behind rock-constructed stable.

The 141st, lurking in the darkness of 9:00 PM on January 21, got parts of two battalions across the river and drove ahead several hundred yards, but by daybreak on January 22 they came to a standstill against stiff resistance. These brave infantrymen were given the order of no retreat despite the dire conditions they were encountering.

German counter attacks increased, extracting their toll in the north. Sadly, by 11:00 PM an ominous silence ricocheted across the river valley. All the men of the 141st still on the west side of the river in this grotesque garden of death were killed, wounded, or captured. In small groups or individually some forty to fifty survivors managed to struggle back across the Rapido to its east bank and safety. As phase two failed miserably, a dismembered 36th Division tried to shake off the shock and despair it had experienced in such a short period of time.

The 142nd received their first taste of the Gustav Line when they suddenly moved from the reserve toward the north as reinforcements. Earlier the 34th Division, bridging the Rapido River on January 26 several miles north of Cassino, established a front and managed to hold it. Between January 28 and January 31, the entire 142nd was across the Rapido River, stationed on or by Hill 382, prepared for combat. Company B, at 6 AM on January 28, moved out to join the 142nd. The engineers started in vehicles, but rugged terrain forced the final portion to be on foot. After the thirty-eight-mile adventure, they began support operations with the 142nd.

The 141st and the 143rd were still woefully under manned, physically spent, shot up, and feeling betrayed over being sent into the meatgrinder with little hope of success. Even so, the shattered units, still without the replacement of fresh troops, drifted north on February 5th to aid in the breakthrough forged by the 34th Division.

The next fight came shortly thereafter. 141st and 142nd, despite the swirl of a snowstorm on the morning of February 11, attacked south of Monte Castellone pushing to acquire the northern heights behind the Abbey. The advance in some places was productive, but due to weather, German fire, and nightfall, they were forced to a gloomy stop. The 143rd, due to losses at the Rapido River, was too short-handed to advance. They were utilized for defensive purposes on Monte Castellone.

On the following day, the Germans made several desperate counterattacks to recapture parts of Monte Castellone, but elements of the 141st, 142nd and 143rd beat back attempts to take the mountain and those surrounding it. Although the GIs retained ownership, their loss of wounded and killed was too big a burden to entertain any thoughts of resuming the offensive.

Once again, the infantry and its support units had shown the true character of the American fighting man. When the attacks halted in late afternoon, the occupied territory across the Rapido River was still safe in Allied hands. When the Germans fell back into their own stout defenses, Keyes called the battered 36th off of the line to regroup and fight another day. A stalemate ensued around Monte Cassino.

The 111th suffered as well. Commencing on January 27 and ending on February 14, the enemy rattled the engineers with exploding mines and precise shelling wounding twenty-seven and killing two. Spared losses during the first Rapido River action, mayhem began with the 3rd platoon of Company A during a mine sweeping assignment north of Sant' Angelo during the second attempt.

Things turned ugly when an exploding mine sent fragments slicing through the left leg of Harry Rutzisay of New York, New York. First aid was being rendered when another mine exploded. Rutzisay died from the second blast.

The rest of the platoon bore the impact of the flying debris. Raymond Nichols of Jefferson, Texas, John Rogers of Campbellsville, Kentucky, Albert Lubin of Detroit, Michigan, Okey Edge of San Leandro, California, and John Tekus of Cleveland, Ohio, were hit. Added to this growing list of wounded were nine other platoon members suffering from shock or concussions.

During these dark times, Company C's Melvin J. Bunkers of Del Rapids, South Dakota, stepped on an S-mine and survived despite the swarm of shrapnel. D. B. Mainord of Point, Texas, was slightly injured in the same explosion.

There were other dangers. Before sunset on February 5, German aircraft were spotted approaching overhead. Anti-aircraft units put up a stream of flak to eliminate the threat. Some of the ammunition didn't explode, and ended up bringing destruction down on Company C. John J. Malauskas of Downers Grove, Illinois, Roy E. Staton of Gonzales, Texas, and Clyfton N. Jones were all hit by shell fragments. Continued anti-aircraft fire, producing a dud round, also fell on top of first platoon of Company B. The heavy round added another wounded man to the friendly fire list in Thomas A. Cooney of Lilly, Pennsylvania.

As all combat soldiers know, death never takes a holiday during wartime. Company B endured harassing fire from German gunners for over two weeks while in close support of the 142nd actions. Until the fourteenth, only a few engineers received a Purple Heart from the constant shelling. Then happenstance took its toll on the forward slopes of Monte Castellone.

Late in evening, after limited battering during the day light hours, a few rounds were fired at random to keep the Americans on the mountain alert. Unfortunately, Willis Bell of Cambellsport, Wisconsin, sheltered in a slit trench, received a direct hit and was killed. Only the penetration exactly on top of his position could have been life threatening.

Day after day, the shell-weary soldiers believed the Benedictine Abbey, 1,703 feet above sea level on Monte Cassino, was being used as a German observation post directing fire down on them. It became a source of frustration as more men lost their lives to German artillery and this important religious and historical landmark remained untouched. To let it stand seemed a crime against each muddied, bearded warrior facing it. Politics and history meant nothing to the men who were living and dying underneath its glare.[4]

That soon changed. On February 15, more than 220 planes dropped 450 plus tons of bombs leveling the Abbey. Was it used as an observation spot by the Germans? Historians debate that question. Clearly the Germans were in the neighborhood if not taking shelter in the building itself. The destruction was, however, a morale boost for the Americans who had bled trying to take the Abbey.

On February 17, Allied artillery opened on Cassino and surrounding area about 9:00 PM and went nonstop for five hours. In the early hours of February 18 another attempt to seize Cassino, sans the 36th Division, was tried. For four days the 4th Indian Division attacked Monte Cassino, but as with its predecessors, these failed. The 2nd New Zealand's approach, at the same time on the town of Cassino, also gained no ground. With heavy losses and no substantial gains, the Allies again called off the attack. Cassino remained in enemy hands. With the break in the action, both sides regrouped.

Saturday 1 January '44

Had storm last nite. High wind about 4 AM to 7 AM. Blew lots of tents down. Real cold and raining and snowing. Snow on all the mountains. Slept to 11 AM. On guard tonight. 8:30 to 12:30. Won $7 at poker tonight. Had one meal today as kitchen blew away. Turkey.

Monday 3 January '44

Nothing doing today. Passes being given to go to rest camp in Naples for five days.[5] Five men every five days. Won $5 in crap game. Went to a show tonight. Went up to Piedimonte by truck.[6] "Dixie Dugan" playing. Had it in a regular theatre which had escaped bombs. Had to stand up as very crowded. Enjoyed it very much.

BRONZE STAR IS AWARDED CPL. J. P. JOHNSTON

The Bronze Star Medal for gallantry in action has been awarded Cpl. J. P. Johnston, son of Mrs. Robert Irons, city, according to information received here.

A citation regarding the award, written by Fred L. Walker, Major General, U. S. Army, reads as follows: "J. P. (10) Johnston, Corporal, Company C, 111th Engineer Combat Battalion, for gallantry in action on 2 February 1944, in Italy. Corporal Johnston, under constant threat of hostile fire, assisted in clearing three pathways through an enemy minefield near a treacherous river essential for the advance of infantry troops. Because he was in advance of friendly outposts and within range of enemy observers, he was forced to work on his hands and knees, sometimes crawling forward on his stomach. In searching out the mines, which booby traps and connecting trip wires rendered more deadly, Corporal Johnston had to employ the tedious and dangerous probing method. In spite of all dangers and difficulties, he worked tirelessly and efficiently until the paths were successfully cleared of mines and safe for the advancing infantry."

Cpl. Johnston, who is only 20 years of age, has been in the service for the past four years and has been overseas during the past twelve months. A recent letter from him states that he has five "Jerry" prisoners to his credit and that he very definitely is not hunting any more medals. He is a member of the famous 36th Division participating in the Italian campaign.

Sulphur Springs Daily News Telegram, date unknown.

Tuesday 4 January '44

Had assembly at 8:30. Exercises & drilling will be started. They call this a rest Camp? Cleaned guns today. Inspection tomorrow. Had a stage show this evening. All soldiers and it was really good. All actors & radio performers. Won $5 in crap game. Won $38 tonight at poker. Raining tonight.

Wednesday 5 January '44

Laid around this morning. High wind. Schedule called off. Ate dinner at 11:00 AM. Went to Piedimonte to the delousing area. Turned in clothes and took hot shower. Got new clothes and pair of boots. Wind increased tonight to a gale. Lost my roll at poker tonight. What a game. Hope tent stays up. Cold.

Saturday 8 January '44[7]

Went to see Doctor at dispensary about my foot. He taped it up. No help as my arch is down. Gas mask inspection today. Passes being given to Piedimonte, but I don't care to go. Physical inspection (venereal) and also teeth and foot. Routine stuff. Really not looking for bad teeth or feet. No more passes to Naples. Typhus they say but the real reason is the high rate of venereal disease.

Monday 10 January '44

Went back to dispensary this morning. Had promise of them trying to get me an arch support. Laid around all morning as I don't intend to do any working. May get away with it. Went to first town (Alife) by truck this evening and saw a show "My Heart Belongs to Daddy." Saw it in States. Still good.

Tuesday 11 January '44

Laid around today. Went to 142nd area this evening to see Humphrey Bogart but it isn't till tomorrow. I was up again for Private First Class, but Captain turned it down (4th time). He won't give a guy another chance that has messed up. I see no need in toeing the line if no advance is in view.

Wednesday 12 January '44

Went to dispensary this morning. Suppose to go to Piedimonte to get shoes fixed but didn't get to go until this evening. Left pair of shoes at a G. I. shoe shop. Go back Friday. They said they would try to fix me some arch supports. Didn't seem too interested in it. That's the army tho!!

Thursday 13 January '44

Cleaned machine gun today as it was fired on the range yesterday by crew. Sure dirty. Had inspection this morning at 11 o'clock. Went to Piedimonte tonight to show. Had stage show. Some Italians. Darn good. Spoke very little English. Girl sang "Star Dust" in English. Really good. Picture was "Follow the Band."

Friday 14 January '44

Did nothing this morning. Went to Piedimonte this evening and got my arch supports. Made of leather. Not too good but believe they will help. Worth a try. Fried chicken for supper. Mighty good too.

Sunday 16 January '44

Took down tent and cleaned up area. Left area around 9 o'clock. Moved about ten miles. Bivouacked about ten miles from front. Town of Mignano just up valley. We still have our guns on half-track as no one else will have them. Had a good dog fight above us this morning. Above clouds with occasional glimpse of planes. Gun fire and motors very loud. Two fell but don't know where.

Thursday 20 January '44

Ice this morning. Went with Lieutenant Beahler on road reconnaissance up close to front. Our bombers over the German lines. Lots of anti aircraft fire. No shells fell on us so had quiet trip. Got four German blankets and two shelter halves. Infantry making effort to cross Rapido River tonight. We go up to construct roads after they cross. Be bloody battle.

Friday 21 January '44

Came in at 3 AM. Didn't do any work as the crossing didn't hold out. Infantry had to withdraw. Like to have frozen as it was cold last night. Slept till 2 PM. Company going back up as the Infantry is going across again in effort to take Cassino. Artillery was active last night but not much Jerry shells hit around us. On guard tonight.

Saturday 22 January '44

Back on guard from 9 AM to 1 PM. Infantry not doing any good as they keep having to fall back. Can't get bridge in as Germans are shelling too heavy. Hot battle and lots of causalities. 1st and 2nd platoon are staying up there to be on hand. 16th Engineers are supporting Infantry. P38 fell over our area at 5 P.M. German anti aircraft hit spit fire so it's pilot bailed out.

Sunday 23 January '44

As platoon was out the half-track crew had to guard area, so I was on guard again last night. Was funny how the guys took off when that plane fell. It came screaming down and the boys thought it was a bomb and hit for the ditch. 45th and 3rd Divisions made landing close to Rome yesterday.[8] Hope they can cut Germans off. Still on guard.

Monday 24 January '44

Nothing doing this morning. Muley came back and told us to get ready to go up front so we went up around 2 PM.[9] About one mile from river which is front. Staying in a house that had one good room left that artillery failed to wreck. Found a jug with about three gallons of white wine in it.

Tuesday 25 January '44

Didn't sleep too good last night as artillery was busy. Could hear machine gun and rifle fire on river. Screaming meemies[10] coming over. We barred the door to room and went to bed. Didn't do anything today and came back to area about 3 PM. Don't know why we went up!

Wednesday 26 January '44

Rained this morning. Had canteen supplies. Two bars of candy. Read this evening "Mutiny on the Bounty." Cleared off this evening. Battle still going although we are just holding now. Had three hour truce yesterday (2 to 5) to pick up wounded.[11] We have really lost heavily. At least two out of three. Sergeant Glenn brought me bottle rum.

Thursday 27 January '44

On K.P. today. Not much to do. Drank bottle of rum Sergeant Glenn got for me in Caserta. Pure poison. Must have been made out of fuel alcohol. 142nd Infantry transferred over to 34th Division area south of Cassino. Can't cross river in this area. Battle at a stand still

Friday 28 January '44

Went out on half-track to be air guard. Platoon loading gravel for use on roads. Helped this morning. Our planes have really worried Jerry today. Bunches of twelve go over and dive bomb. Go straight down from high altitude. Real pretty. Lots of anti aircraft going up but they just made thru. Lots of screaming meemies today. One man in A Company killed by mine.

Saturday 29 January '44

That A Company boy was killed by mine Thursday night and five more wounded. They were on front hunting out mines. Went back out on same job today. Not much air activity as valley was all smoked up again. Not much action in this particular spot.

[Editor's Note: Most of the mine removal occurred at night because of the Germans' observation points on the surrounding heights. Any daylight work brought down heavy fire with deadly consequences. The engineers, since all mines were not made of metal, couldn't always count on mine detectors. This problem made the poke and dig process the most common way to search for the deadly devices.

Probing with metal wire, drift pins, and bayonets could be lethal.[3] The trained engineers, checking every square inch in the direction the soldiers were moving, found the work extremely tiresome and at times gut wrenchingly unnerving. A simple miscue meant a gruesome death.]

Sunday 30 January '44

Back to same job. No air activity at all but could hear machine gun fire on river. Valley smoky. Noticed two 40 MM gun set up (about 9 inch). They opened fire tonight at 6 on San Angelo for thirty minutes. Biggest guns we have. Artillery really going last night on left flank.

Monday 31 January '44

Nothing doing today. Pay day. Paid this evening at 1 o'clock. $13.70. Put up one pyramidal tent for platoon use. Hooked up light from half-track. Played poker till midnight. Won enough to get me out of debt from last month.

Tuesday 1 February '44

Went out on half-track up close to river on road job.[12] Very foggy all day. No planes. Quite a bit of shelling on our left and also the screaming meemies. Came in this evening as I am on guard tonight. Slightly chilly today.

Saturday 5 February '44

Took down tents etc and moved closer to front this evening. Bivouacked in valley across from San Pietro. Also can see San Vittore. Very muddy getting in. Just before dark while having chow air raid took place. Anti aircraft dud hit about twenty feet from line and wounded three men. Not bad.

Sunday 6 February '44

Lots of air activity on both sides. More Germans planes than I've seen in some time.[13] Cold last night. Moved again about dark. Came up thru San Vittore which is in ruins. Bivouacked on high ground about three miles east of Cassino. Battle still going for Cassino. Artillery pounding her. Can see it plain from here.

Bombing of the Abbey.

Monday 7 February '44

Did nothing today. Watched battle at Cassino from hill thru glasses. Going out tonight over close to Cassino to build a jeep trail. Have to use poles etc as Germans have flooded area.[14] Driving jeep for Lieutenant Beahler as driver is gone.

Tuesday 8 February '44

Out all last night. Really was cold and miserable. Where we were, there was dead every where, all ours. Lots of tanks etc buried in mud. 2nd platoon man stepped on mine and blew foot off. Battle going on mountain and Cassino. Went back up for short while tonight.

Wednesday 9 February '44

Rained last night. Went up to river this evening on road reconnaissance. Road muddy. Went back tonight and came in at 12 midnight. All quiet. Both sides shelling Cassino. Our infantry dead is scattered all over this area. Pitiful sight. Germans shells going over our area tonight about 500 yards.

Thursday 10 February '44

Didn't go out today. Germans shelling this area all day. High velocity stuff. Could hear report of gun and at same time shell hit. Piece of shrapnel knocked spoon out of Headquarters cooks hand. Raining this evening and tonight. Tent is sure leaking. Other platoons out at river tonight. On mountain behind Cassino is the old Benedictine Monastery built in 530 A.D. Germans using it for observation etc. So far we have spared it as the Pope has asked.[15] It has cost us heavily in men as they can see all activity. Immense building with eight foot thick walls, seat of first recorded progress of civilization. We gave them warning!

Company C's Manuel Hovey of Hart, Michigan, and J.C. Roberson of Dallas, Texas, living quarters during Rapido River engagement.

Friday 11 February '44

Heavy barrage of artillery on mountain above Cassino this morning.[16] So far the abbey has been spared. Heaviest I've seen in sometime. Went out tonight to work on river road. Terrible traffic jam as Indian troop were moving up. (Gurkhas). Mules, vehicles and men. What a mess. Got in at 3 AM. Cassino battle still raging.

Saturday 12 February '44

Awaken about daylight by shells landing in this area. Was so warm and comfortable. I refused to get up as I can think of no better place to die than in bed.[17] Went up to 142 Infantry Command Post. this evening on reconnaissance with Lieutenant Pfister. [Charles E. Pfister of Terre Haute, Indiana] Shelling area tonight.

Sunday 13 February and Monday 14 February '44

Nothing doing for us yesterday or today. Part of Infantry has been relieved. We will be in few days. Probably be quite a while before we see action again as the Infantry is about wiped out again. Take some time to train more. Still can't take Cassino. Germans are making determined stand. Hell over there. Cold and clear tonight.

Muley Junell and James Jacobson of Chicago, Illinois, with half-track in Italy during break in combat.

Tuesday 15 February '44

Another day of in activity for us. Saw the prettiest sight I ever expect to see in war. Clear day and in groups of 24, 143 Flying Fortress came over and bombed the Monastery and Mountain above Cassino.[18] Later 36 B 25 came in and this evening 36 more.[19] The Monastery just a shell now. Most terrible implement of war!

Wednesday 16 February '44

Area shelled last nite. Got close but I stayed in tent. Rumors are we're going to England or States. No work today. This evening the abbey was dive bombed by A36 planes. Used glasses. Could follow bombs down. Direct hits. Also strafed. Several attacks till dark. Place a pile of rubble. Germans hold on!

Thursday 17 February '44

No work today and a quiet day. Abbey dive bombed again late this evening. Went up close to Cassino tonight where we built road. About 8:30 the artillery opened up and still going on a fast rate (10:00) British attacking tonight. Machine guns etc. really going. Quite a noise. Cassino still holding us up.

7 A REFRESHING BREAK

"Simply put the liquor in a bottle of Dill pickles after draining off the vinegar. The pickles do not hurt it at all and looks O.K."

Few American divisions suffered more losses while on the offensive than the 36th in the Cassino campaign. Veteran units sprinkled with brave but inexperienced recruits pushed ahead against smothering enemy firepower more than equal to their own. The loss of such spirited young men was devastating. Due to bad management, not courage, the original 36th Division was literally destroyed on the banks of the Rapido River. Then, without much needed recovery or restocking, they were ordered north. Having to reach deep inside themselves to produce more offensive output on the steep, rocky slopes there, they continued to give their all. Now it was time to rest. Cassino remained in German control, and the door to Rome through the Liri Valley stayed locked. While the battered 36th took time to rest, relax and refit for future action, the taking of Cassino was handed over to other Allied forces.

Back home, Elizabeth Iona Pearce was typical of many Great Depression women. Absorbed in family finances during the Depression, there just never was a right time to break away and create their own families. They eventually grew to be old maids because of their faithfulness and devotion to father and mother. Iona spent her life working hour upon monotonous hour as a sales lady at Perkins Brothers' Department Store. In between, she spent her Sundays as the secretary for the youth classes at the First Methodist Church in Sulphur Springs.[1] But, in 1944, Pearce just hoped her devotion to him would strengthen her resolve to send him some nostalgic hometown booze disguised as pickle brine.

From the privates to the officers, alcohol was the most effective release from trying times. Pulitzer Prize winner Bill Mauldin, in his book "Up Front," stated the following: "I'm not trying to say the American army is a drunken army. Yet there have been times over here when I have tied one on because I was homesick, or bored, or because I was sitting around with a bunch of guys who had a bottle, and when it came to me I just naturally took a belt of it. And there were many times I guzzled wine because the water was questionable. I don't think I'll carry a confirmed drinking habit back home with me. But until they send me home or send my wife over here, or until they ship over portable soda fountains, I'm going to do a little drinking now and then."

The thought of purchasing alcohol, even for a brother at war, didn't register very high on Iona's character meter. Sulphur Springs was a dry city and the nearest alcohol, not including the local bootleggers, was seventy miles away in the swinging little East Texas town of Gladewater. Add to this that gas was rationed, tires scarce, and a family car that had little hope of traveling that far without problems made Pearce correct. Iona would be embarrassed to be seen frequenting any of those liquor establishments. When the pickles finally arrived, it took only a quick twist of the lid to reveal dill pickles, bathed in vinegar and not liquor. It was appreciated, but not with the appreciation several gulps of Texas liquor would have brought.

Returning to bivouac from road repair near Caira, Company B found the air full of incoming artillery. When the attack lightened, there were two casualties. Omer Fortier was seriously hit in the arms, chest, and face while Vernon Bright of Columbus, Ohio took shrapnel in his right hand.

Vernon Bright.

Iona Pearce standing on the southwest side of the Sulphur Springs town square, 1944. Behind her is one of the three movie theaters in town, the Carnation Theater. Today a monument naming and honoring the military veterans of the county, including Frank and Marvin Pearce, stands where Carnation Theater once was.

The period of March to May was used to rebuild ground forces for a final push to Rome. During the ensuing time, the Mediterranean Allied Air Force began Operation Strangle on March 11. The operation ended May 11 after dropping over 33,000 tons of bombs on roads, railroads, and seas routes. That night, the beginning of a total Allied offensive in Italy began. The spring operation, called Diadem, had two aims. The first was trying to tie even more Germans down in Italy so they could not help when the Allies invaded France in June, and the second was to capture Rome. The opening phase was against the Gustav Line. Having failed three times since the start of the year, fresh reinforcements and good weather were in the Allies' favor this time.

With successful Fifth Army attacks, the Germans along the Gustav Line began to disengage and retreat. While the Americans had broken the Gustav Line at several places, they had lost another three thousand casualties. Meanwhile, the British 4th Infantry Division, on May 18, took the rubble that once stood as the town of Cassino. The wreckage was loaded with mines and booby traps, but it was free of the fleeing Germans. On the same day, the Polish 3rd Carpathian Division occupied the Abbey on Monte Cassino. The Germans, after months of stiff resistance, simply gave it up without a fight.

Friday 18 February '44

No work. They say the Gurkhas are at the abbey and have Cassino. Drive this evening. Artillery threw hundreds of smoke shells in and around Cassino for cover. Terrific noise. May lose Cassino as not too many troops there. Am going to Caserta tomorrow for five days to the rest camp. So many men go every five days.

(February 18 letter to Iona)

Will answer so as to lay low any idea you have that I am holding back anything. I'm sure there are some of my letters that do appear to you that something is bothering me. It is just the mood I happen to be in which creeps into my writing. There are times when I am low, generally after some experience or certain things I see which is best you don't know about. I used to think I knew war and its results, but one can never know until one actually sees it firsthand. To me it is something terrifying although not in a physical sort of way. It is the mental side that hurts. Physical wounds will heal but the mind retains its injuries. I don't mean that to shoot at a German injures ones mind, in fact it helps heal it. I have no horror of any physical wound, even up to losing a limb as that is expected. It's the things one comes in contact with that affect me at times. Probably that has sneaked in some of my letters after such a case.

It is just that I can see no sense in civilized people trying to kill each other. If facts were to be known I don't imagine either we or the opponent desires to do it. It is just that it is the feeling that if I don't beat him to it he will get me.

I didn't really intend to hold back about my foot as I didn't consider it important. It still bothers me quite a bit. I didn't know whether you remember about me complaining about it several years ago. If you remember it gave down on me back in '36 at the Dallas fair. [State Fair of Texas] I hurt it several times afterwards and if you remember I had trouble wearing new shoes, especially tite ones. It is my right foot. I have been able to get a pair of leather supports made which help a lot. It seems the bones in the ball gets out of place and sore. But it is not serious although I'll have trouble from now on with my shoes.

As far the question about any promotion I can say I have not been disappointed. There is definitely none in sight for me and I am not sorry. It is only the better pay that counts. Yes, there are reasons for it being the way it is. No, that Lieutenant is not with us now but there is someone else with the same make up. People there seems to think a guy is dumb etc. if he is only in the lower bracket. It would be nice socially to be up on top. Well this is no social affair. The buck private is the one who will win this war. I'm only trying to do my part and then get out. To me the most important thing is to get this over as soon as possible.

Back in the states the only thing to look forward to was getting a little higher in rank. Yes, I know it looks good in print that so & so has been commissioned to so & so. Over here it is different. Generally, if a commission is given, it is deserved thru hard work and proven courage. Those men have my respect. Some of your spic and span nattily dressed brass wearers there do not have my respect as their right to wear them has not been proven and in lots of cases will never be. Do you understand what I mean!?

I am not trying to justify my own feelings because I am a buck private. I've seen men's courage leave them. They are not cowards, but it is that mental injury that gets the upper hand. So far my nerves have weathered it all and I still feel no great amount of fear. To say I feel no fear would be an untruth. All men fear something but not the same thing. More heroes are accidentally made than on purpose. It is the long training and the impulse of the moment that comes out in an emergency. I am perfectly satisfied to be one of the majority and plug along doing what I am told. Don't think I am grieving about it. As I said, there is lots of difference in the social side there but not here. I'm sure you would be a lot prouder of me if it could be Lieutenant Frank Pearce writes an interesting letter. That would make you feel like you had more friends in society. You see I know society in our small town. To always live beyond your means, publicly doing big things, (which you don't give a hoot about) and having your off spring or kin above the average working man and always having their finger in the ruling class. Now since they were about to be caught in a draft they pulled all sorts of political vines to get their boy his respected place and then proudly shout "my boy who is a Captain etc says!"

The papers are really giving the dope about Cassino & vicinity? I suppose there was some comment on the bombing of the Monastery. I think that in this spot is where the Americans learned that the Germans can wage war. Seems to me they are determined to hold and not let us take Rome.

Again, I'm proud I am in the engineers instead of something else. To say our work is not dangerous would be a feeble attempt to fool you but I still say the infantry is the ones who bear the brunt of the war. At least I feel like I have a better chance to come thru it all.

Yes, Muley, J.P. and Arnold are still in here pitching. I know Muley doesn't write much so if it will make Mrs. Junell feel better you can always call her up and let her know. I would let you know if it was otherwise.

I'm looking forward to receiving the packages. Now I know you don't want to send me any booze, either because you are afraid you might be embarrassed or because you don't want me to have it. I think it is the former. Here's a fool proof method that is working for the other guys. Simply put the liquor in a bottle of Dill pickles after draining off the vinegar. The pickles do not hurt it at all and looks O.K. Suit your self about this but I would like to have a jar of Dill pickles and some stuffed olives and you might slip in some good fresh crackers. Anything else that you think I might like. Oh yes, a box of Chili pepper.

I can see mother puttering around with the flowers. I do hope they are a success. And swapping chickens at her age! [Daisy Pearce was 63] I bet the neighbor got skinned. Good old American customs. Boy I sure would like to walk down a street that was all there and lite up (and me too). No noise and no worries. That is my idea of heaven.

Saturday 19 February '44

Left for Caserta at 11 AM. Two hour drive.[2] Fair place. Large stone barracks. Used for Royal guard. Got new clothes. Went up town and got cognac etc. Had hard time finding food. Finally two M. P.'s took us to place and told them to feed us. Three women run it. Had two fried eggs & potatoes. Had good time as it seems war is just a dream here.

Sunday 20 February '44

Really slept good last night. Have shower etc. here. Chow fair. Went downtown and got shave and haircut. Ate three eggs & potatoes at same place. Eggs are 50c apiece. Came back and went to evening show. Then had U.S.O. show tonight. Not much. Another picture. They really rob a guy here. Everything sky high. All liquor is fuel alcohol.

Monday 21 February '44

Went to Naples (20 miles). It is off limits to us. May get in trouble as have bed check and I spent night there. Good soft bed and sheets and that ain't all. Toney [Warren Toney of Eau Claire, Michigan], Sampler [Jesse L. Sampler of Wichita Falls, Texas] & I. Eat, drink and etc. We spent $70. Met Billy Young there. Was I surprised. Cognac, steaks, & women. Really had a time. Hope nothing happens.[3]

Tuesday 22 February '44

Got back to Caserta about 10 A.M. What a night we spent. Hope everything is O.K. Biggest trouble over here is venereal diseases. Naples looks like N.Y. now. Streets full of wares & people. Traffic & street cars. Scare a guy at first. Show this evening & stage show tonight. Real good. 21st special service company.

Wednesday 23 February '44

Turned in blankets and went to town. Swapped carton of cigarettes for two bottles of cognac. Truck came at 1:30. Raining hard all way back and English convoy on road so it was 4:30 before getting here. Had several letters here. Glad to get back. Company still in same place. Say we'll be relieved in few days. I doubt it. Same situation.

Saturday 26 February '44

Packed up and moved out at 10:45. Rained all night and today. Back a few miles from our last rest period. Muddy as hell and a wide open place. [two miles south of Ailano] Bet we get a belly full of drilling etc. Fixed me a bed up off ground. Don't think I'll enjoy this back here. Cassino wasn't bombed on account of bad weather.[4]

Monday 28 February '44

Company meeting in which we were told our schedule. Reveille at 7 A.M., exercise 7 to 7:15, close order drill at 8-8:30 etc and retreat at 4:30. Move gravel shoveling today. Retreat this evening. Show at Division headquarters tonight about two miles from here. Trucks furnished. "Thank Your Lucky Stars". Really good. Oh my!

Thursday 2 March '44

Arnold, J.P. and I ask Captain for pass to Naples to see Billy Young. Got pass to Naples until 7 P.M. Missed truck so spent night. J.P., Arnold and Jeffries. [Robert W. Jeffries of Austin, Indiana] blew it out in a big way. Spent night at 154 Via Rama with old man who spoke English. He had plenty to drink and he cooked for us. Bill-$18.00. Oh at the pretty gals! Three air raids on docks.

Friday 3 March '44

We are now A.W.O.L. Spent the day cruising around in a horse taxi. Really got drunk and didn't get back to camp. Left Jeff in Naples and we went down to Caserta and spent night at rest camp. Oh but we were tight. Another day of hell raising. Didn't eat today. Oh my head!

Saturday 4 March '44

Left Caserta early and started to camp. Been raining every since we left. Got wet and muddy but got to camp about 9:30 AM. Reported to Captain. Got a lecture and restricted to camp for a week. Not bad! Issued three coca cola today (6 c). First since leaving states eleven months ago. Saw Billy Young while in Naples. Muley says I was up for Corporal until I was A.W.O.L. Oh my!

Monday 6 March '44

Rained all night but pretty today. Tore down tents and cleaned up and pulled out at 11:05. Looked like bunch of gypsies with our beds, stoves etc piled on trucks. Came thru Caserta and ended up about ten miles from there in the edge of Maddaloni. Put up tents, beds, etc. Soft field and muddy. Cold tonight. About twenty miles west (?) of Naples.

Tuesday 7 March '44

Went out on truck looking for hay but found none to sleep on. Then shoveled gravel all morning as we have to build roads into area. This P. M. I helped Private Ellis on demolition work. Breaking up a big rock about as large as a tent as it is in our way. Using pneumatic drill and T.N.T.[5] Didn't finish. Rained this A.M. Good meals now. Sgt. McDonald [Eugene V. McDonald of Wolfe City, Texas] & Muley going to Headquarters Company on the recon. squad.

Sunday 12 March '44

Raining. No reveille today and no duties. Private Ellis and I went on pass to Maddaloni. Could find nothing to do as most places of vice are off limits. Cognac here pure poison. Champagne no good. Ended up in some small town and drinking red wine. Oh my head etc. Got drunk of course.

Monday 13 March '44

Ate early as Private Ellis and I have to give Infantry instructions on building barb wire entanglements etc. Feel like hell and woke up several times last night dying for water. Drank plenty too. Finished at noon and slept this evening. This goes on for a week. Received package yesterday and one today. Got some straw for bed.

Tuesday 14 March '44

Raining hard this morning so Infantry schedule training was called off. About middle of morning sun came out. Had lecture on military courtesy by Lt. Kilby (Foxhole Joe) [William Kilby of Ysleta, Texas] and one by Captain. Suppose to go out this P.M. on problem but I dodged it. Went into town to show tonight. "Wild West."

Wednesday 15 March '44[6]

Big air raid on Naples last night. Out this morning lecturing to Infantry. Hundreds of big bombers going over. Must be headed for Cassino.[7] Went to stage show this afternoon. Italian actors. Band and bunch of the beat up-ish bitches I've ever seen. Battle scarred we say. Not too hot.

Friday 17 March '44

Finished classes with the Infantry today. Sure glad. Laid around this evening. Dodge details. Played volleyball this evening. Joined a little party up at Sergeants tent tonight. Wine, alcohol, cognac, champagne. Oh my head. What a noisy racket.

Saturday 18 March '44

Back out with Infantry on a little demolition. Felt like hell today. Cleaned out half-track and threw away Italian rifle as it is to be turned in tomorrow. Played volleyball this evening. Show tonight. "True to Life". Vesuvius putting out a high column of fire tonight. Small eruption about 20 mi. away.[8]

(March 18 letter to Iona)

I have trouble writing only a V-Mail, so I don't know how this will come out. One more thing I might enlighten you on is the conditions under which you presume I write. They are not as bad as you seem to think. I have written quite a bit under constant shelling, which is landing in our area, but heck, that ain't so bad as long as they don't come closer than a hundred yards. After a day or so one can tell just about where to expect them to land, as there are dead places that is impossible for them to hit. So we set around and listen to them. Of course, we have been wrong, so we always have a good foxhole. You have no idea how fast I can get underground. A prairie dog is a piker! (I've asked all the fellows how to spell prairie and we can't agree). So don't think I live like a rat.

Even on the front we have it pretty good. We are usually a mile or so back of the main line, so we can have our pup tents, etc., set up and our kitchen too. We ride up to our work, which is generally night work, and clear out before day. We have been lucky not to contact any enemy patrols, but we have to lay our firearms aside to work. And in the darkness anyone could infiltrate right in with us as it is hard to distinguish men apart.

I can't help but feel a prickly sensation on my neck when I go up ahead of the job with Lieutenant Beahler on a reconnaissance on a river, etc. That feeling of knowing you are at a disadvantage to anyone laying in wait and too, there is always the sign of violence, equipment scattered, knocked out tanks, and the smell sometimes is sickening, as there are those who are not coming back.

I can look upon a German body without any feeling of pity or remorse, but others affect me differently. I catch myself wondering about families of these boys and then find myself looking to see if by any chance I know them. I can see no glory in war.

I'm sure the papers give vivid details of the fighting, especially around Cassino. It is hard to realize how men can live in such a hell. Ernie Pyle does a fair job in his column. His column is in the Stars and Stripes, which we get six days a week. It burns me up to read or see in a short film the goings-on back there in the canteens and social world. Those guys are living the life of Riley.

The war in the Pacific gets a large play. People think this is easy compared to the Japs. Let me tell you a few facts. First, if it were the Germans there in the jungles instead of the Japs, the boys would not pass thru! There is no comparison between the two. There a battle is fought with ten to thirty casualties. Here there are hundreds. We have to compete with real, modern equipment and soldiers who don't uselessly give their lives. I occasionally read where some guy says he wished he was fighting the Germans instead of the Japs. The big thing they are fighting is the jungle itself, which has advantages over this mountain fighting, where a guy is always under direct observation. Don't misunderstand me. I realize they have lots to deal with that we don't. What I mean is that we have the best fighting man opposing us with equipment as good as, and in some cases better than ours.

You are misinformed about just what a rest period is. It is definitely not a vacation. It is used for training and reorganization. We have time to play ball, etc., but is more like life in a camp in the States. Then there are passes to town or points of interest. It is usually well appreciated as it gives us a chance to clean up and gain back a little weight and see a few movies. Well, I seem to have run out of material, so will have to sign off. I do hope you all are getting along fine.

Monday 20 March '44

Benedict has to go up to Cassino tonight with flame thrower. A dangerous job. May be a good thing I am on guard. Finished guard at 4:30 PM. Vesuvius really active. Can see lava spouting up and flowing over from here. Beautiful last night. Great column of smoke. Had a time keeping the Italians out of area at mealtime. Kids on up with buckets to pester men. Had to get a little rough. Show tonight "Three Hearts for Julia."

Tuesday 21 March '44

First day of spring. On K. P. today. Really had a job as there were hot cake griddles to clean and cake icing and meat loaf pans which are always stuck. Italian women & kids nearly mob me when I carry out a container. One old woman promised me a gal tonight if I would fill her buckets. Of course I did and she didn't.

Wednesday 22 March '44

Went to Pompeii today. Went thru ruins. In town itself, I went thru the new Cathedral. Beautiful. Vesuvius was shrouded by smoke and rumbled like thunder. Cinders falling in Pompeii. Went to another town where all the gals are. Got tite as a jug. Went in kitchen and in a discussion Sergeant Downing [Max E. Downing of Campbell, Texas] pulled a butcher knife on me. Have decided to let Downing get away with what he did this time as I would be on the little end. Private vs. Sergeant. There will come another day and then we'll see. Really hurts to let him go.

Friday 24 March '44

Last night Vesuvius was really blowing out. Lightning flashes all around it and in the smoke column. It is quiet tonight. May be quitting. 1st platoon and me spent the day practicing putting up and dismantling a Bailey bridge. Show tonight. Cheap one "Make Way for Tomorrow."

Saturday 25 March '44

Well today was called up to Command Post and Lieutenant Beahler ask if I would like to be his jeep driver. So I accepted. Gets me out of company duties but no snap. Went out to area where training is going on. I do nothing but drive. Believe Vesuvius has settled down.

Sunday 26 March '44

Didn't get up until 10 A.M. Very windy day. This evening took Lieutenant Beahler, Sergeant Duncan and Technical Sergeant Bruce in jeep out on what is known as a road reconnaissance. We went to several little towns fooling around and drank a little Vino. "That's" what I like about this job.

Friday 31 March '44

Drove Lieutenant up into Maddaloni where he picked up payroll from Quarter Master. $4857.75. Stopped in at hospital (64th) and paid some boys. Went on to Caserta to rest camp and paid some more and on to Capau. Nothing doing his evening except pay day. Won a little at poker tonight. $8.00

Saturday 1 April '44

Still running around to pay the boys off. Lieutenant & I went to replacement center to pay the boys who have been transferred. Went on into Caiazzo fooling around. Drank quite a bit of Vermouth. Waited on Lieutenant till dark before he came back to jeep. Left Camp Edwards a year ago for Africa.

Sunday 2 April '44

Beautiful day. Worked on jeep this morning and have it in good shape. Took Sergeant Duncan and Sergeant Bonnette [Randall Bonnette of Port Arthur, Texas] out this evening and we went up to some town and swapped soup & matches for onions. Women are scarce but trust a GI. Rumor that 7 % of men of invasion are going home each month.

Tuesday 4 April '44

Went to other side of Capau (20 miles from camp) with Lieutenant and platoon. Taking up a mine field on the banks of Volturno laid by Germans last year. Took out 70 mines and blew them up. Italian plowing a ways off and his horses ran off and wrapped plow around tree. This evening went out to area of training and went up to a small town and drank white wine at shop where American speaking Mike is.

Wednesday 5 April '44

Went to a dispensary this morning as I am breaking out in the crotch. Dr. says insects of a sort. Had lectures on gas etc this AM. This PM. 1st platoon went back in mountains to firing range. I have a tommy gun now so shot up a lot of shells. Show tonight "Background for Danger". Letter from home telling me R.A. was accepted in army March 18.[9] Bummed a pint of rotten rum which I drank as I had blues.

Friday 7 April '44

Washed jeep this morning. This PM carried Lieutenant Beahler and Captain Bellamy [Clifton Bellamy of Fabens, Texas] & Captain Gill (Dentist) [Henry Gill of Hillsboro, Texas] to Naples and then over to Qualiano where we built steel bridge over railroad back in October. All got tite as jug at house where we knew people. Captain Gill fell off wall. Bad arm sprain.

Saturday 8 April '44

Went out to area for Infantry training and went up to see Mike our Italian friend at his wine joint. Drank lots of white wine and went back this evening. Came back by Caserta. Slept awhile this PM. Missed reveille & retreat. Carried Lieutenant to dance tonight.

Sunday 9 April '44

Easter Sunday! At the moment I am very drunk. Why? This AM I started working on jeep. Lieutenant came down and we went out to Infantry area and ended up at Mike's. Drank wine. Came back and this P.M. went up to a house back in mountain and ate. Drank wine galore.

Monday 10 April '44

Tore down and moved today. Left area at 2 PM and ended up out in the mountains. Closest town is Avellino. Nice area in wheat field. Mountains all around. Last night that party was a mess. Arnold & Griffitt [Wayne C. Griffitt of Bailey, Texas] tried to fight and Lieutenant Beahler got drunk and cussed me out. Some mess. We really put on show for Italians in that town.

Thursday 13 April '44

Drove Lieutenant with 1st platoon to a reported mine field about five miles from here near Bellizzi. One Italian farmer was killed by one awhile back. Not marked and all box mines so detector no good. Probe for them. Found one and as we left to come in a donkey set one off. Blew him into little pieces. Italian all excited. Found three more in the field where they worked. J.P., Arnold and I went up to small settlement just above us and drank some wine. 75 c a bottle! Fair

Saturday 15 April '44

Slightly inebriated (drunk) again as I have been to Salerno on pass--not much to do there but a few women. Hard to find a drink. Salerno still under about six inches of ashes from Vesuvius. Quite a mess. Had to go out to town for supper.

Sunday 16 April '44

Pretty day. Have lain in bed all day and read. Am reading "The Robe." A good book. Tonight about 9:30 had to take Lieutenant and some more up to Bellizzi as an Italian stabbed one of our boys and beat up two more. Couldn't get anything out of ones we found. Stick together.

Monday 17 April '44

Went back to the town where boys had trouble. Still no dope and can get no help from anyone. This evening I went to a creek and washed my jeep as it is to be painted. We really have no idea how long we will be here or where we will go.

Tuesday 18 April '44

Carried jeep down to Headquarters Company and finally got it painted. Looks pretty good. I have about decided we will make an invasion either on Southern France or the Balkans. That will really be rough. The Anzio beach is really a hot spot and is doing no good. Strictly a defensive action now.

Thursday 20 April '44

Had inspection in motor pool. Passed O.K. At 10 AM reported to S-1 and took Lieutenant Mueller to 58th Hosp. to see boy who was stabbed then on thru Naples and to 32nd hospital at Caserta. Got back here at 3:30 PM. Naples is more like a city now as it is getting cleaner & more cars running.

(April 21 letter to Mother)

I am not sure whether or not this will reach you before Mother's Day. In any case, it will let you know I have you in mind. I wish I could be with you just that one day and I would be willing to spend another year here. Anyhow my thoughts will be with you and I know yours will be with us boys. A few years ago, I can remember, when I wore the red nose on that occasion it really didn't seem to mean so much. Now I can see that it meant everything. I had you and didn't realize how much that meant altho now I can. I can't put into words what it does mean. But you were always on hand to help make those diversions altho you got no credit for it. Your whole life has been devoted to us boys and if we are not perfect it is not your fault. Don't feel like you have lost us, for altho we are all separated it is for only a short while. We'll need you when we get back so don't fail us.

Sunday 23 April '44

Lieutenant & I and one squad moved today about 37 miles to Sele River. Been down to Sele River all day where we were building a foot bridge out of rubber boats. Company came in about noon. Put up my pup tent.[10] Went swimming this evening. Water cold, clear and too swift to swim against. Cinders from Vesuvius are about two inches thick and blow everywhere.

Monday 24 April '44

Spent day at river where we are building & taking down footbridge. Infantry came down and practiced crossing. Some mess as river is swift and the boats are hard tokeep upright. Problem tonight from 11 PM to day light. Wind blowing hard all day. Infantry lost quite a lot of rifles etc in river as boats overturn. Down the river at another site boat up set and one Infantryman drown altho as yet his body hasn't been found.

Thursday 27 April '44

Got in at 6 AM. Sergeant Duncan & I stayed at river as guards as river was raising and we took care of boats. Started raining around 4 AM and was cold. Got up at 11:30 and packed up. Moved out at 2 PM. Raining again and cold. Got back to area in about two hours. Got bed fixed and stuff unloaded. Moving again Saturday.

Saturday 29 April '44

Got up at 5 AM and tore tents down etc and left area at 7:10. Came thru edge of Naples and on to Aversa across country and ended up a little north of Qualiano in a potato patch. A shame how the army destroys crops. About fifteen miles from Naples. Air raids started on Naples at 10 PM. Still going on.

Sunday 30 April '44

Went out to road on which we built steel bridge where platoon was sweeping road for mines as a grader reported digging up three. We swept it once before. Found no mines. Run around a bit. Ocean not far from us. Air raids all night last night. Moving in the AM about 1/2 mile as P.B.S. has to have this area.[11]

Monday 1 May '44

Moved about 400 yards across road from previous area. Took all morning to tear down and put up. This army does the damnest things. P.B.S. had other plans for that area and some one messed up in this Division. Got paid today (13.70) Owed it all and paid it. 15.00 owed to me but I got none of it.

Thursday 4 May '44

This morning I took Lieutenant Mattleman [Murray Mattleman of Philadelphia, Pennsylvania] (Headquarters Company) back to Forino, our old area by way of Naples. Got back at 4 o'clock. Naples is getting back to normal. Lots of ships in the harbor. Looks more like we are in an invasion every day. Played blackjack tonite until 12:30. Lieutenant Beahler is going to Naples for a week's vacation and I'm going along with jeep.

Monday 8 May '44

Got ready to leave for Naples this AM.[12] Left Company after dinner and got to Naples about 2 PM. Lieutenant quarters are in a hotel on bay road and mine are up on hill behind.[13] It is a large old house overlooking Bay of Naples and the view is beautiful. Has a patio with arches and roof. I am on 3rd floor. Italian people. All convenience and she does cooking. Have a cot. A beautiful set up.

Tuesday 9 May '44

Got up at 8:30. Had quite a bit to drink last night. Did a little running around, mostly on my own. Lieutenant doesn't use me much. The view over the harbor is beautiful. Old woman brought a girl up here. Fairly old and pregnant. The lady here finally ran her off. I had her in my room. Rent room below for women for $3.

Wednesday 10 May '44

Went out to 21st Hospital for Lieutenant to see a fellow. Dropped him off in town this evening. I went to Red Cross here. A beautiful place full of parade ground soldiers. Tried to locate Billy Young but failed. Lieutenant called me at 12 tonight and I picked him up. Sloppy drunk and I got him to go to bed at 3:30 AM. I got drunk too.

Thursday 11 May '44

Really felt bad today so haven't touched a drop. Picked Lieutenant up at 9 AM and dropped him in town. Laid around myself. He called me about 3 PM and I picked him up. Very drunk and had two boys with him. Had to go out to our Division area and let one boy see his brother. Silly bastards. Picked up boy in artillery. At 12 tonite carried him back. Got in around 3 AM.

Saturday 13 May '44

Didn't go out at all today except down to Hotel to get some grapefruit juice. Got tite as hell this evening and picked Lieutenant up about dark. Boy I was blowing & going. Also picked two Medical Captains and carried them to a few officer's clubs. Went to bed at 1 AM.

Sunday 14 May '44

Air raid last night at 3:30. Lady woke us up and took off downstairs to shelter. I went out on balcony to watch. Rockets launchers just behind house and they really make a racket. Beautiful sight as sky was full of tracers etc. Bombs jarred the house quite a bit. Took a sailboat ride this PM. Rode around this evening. Leaving tomorrow.

Monday 15 May '44

Went after rations for hotel. Carried Lieutenant downtown. Small air raid last night. Planes laid a few mines in harbor. Left hotel about 2 PM and started home. Stopped along for drinks and got to camp about 4:30. Lieutenant was drunk. Took Sergeant Glenn, Walker [Thomas Walker of Celeste, Texas] & Julian and went back to Naples to house where I stayed. All got polluted and I got them in around 1 AM.

Gustav Defenses Shattered; Poles Mopping Up Nazis

ALLIED HEADQUARTERS in Naples, May 17 (UP).—British and Polish columns opened a powerful, two-way attack to encircle Cassino Wednesday and by nightfall had closed the Nazis' shell-torn life line to the city to less than two miles as Franco-American forces, slashing through the last broken Gustav forts, reached the Adolf Hitler Line.

The Poles, described in front dispatches as blood-mad after being stalled for three days in the hills northwest of Cassino, resumed their attack at dawn behind a heavy barrage and battled down the far slope of the saddle connecting Mount Cassino and Mount Cairo, striking for the Via Casilina.

Overrunning strongly defended positions, they drove well into the enemy line, front reports said, as British troops in the Liri Valley to the southwest closed in on the vital road from that direction.

Dallas Morning News May 18, 1944.

Wednesday 17 May '44

Worked around motor pool this AM. Lecture this evening about malaria. We are fixing to go into action. Not sure but believe we will take to the water and hit between Fifth army front & Anzio. Be a rough go. Sand bagged my jeep. Sandbags covering the whole floor.

Thursday 18 May '44

Drove Lieutenant over to Infantry around 2 PM. This morning I made a hike with Company. Quite a rough course up & down a steep bank for 2 1/2 miles. Marched over to parade ground this evening and General Walker talked to us. Our next assignment is the beach head. 1st platoon (included me) are leaving in the morning. Go by seas of course.

8 WALKER'S MASTERPIECE

"The smell of death is everywhere and bodies too."

Anzio, a planned knife in the back of the German forces holding the Gustav Line, failed to live up to expectations. The January invasion, to this point, yielded minor results for the Italian land campaign. The 36th Division was shifted to Anzio-Nettuno beaches to participate in the major breakout attempt.[1] The Division started moving its troops, on May 18, aboard transports preparing to deliver them to the beachhead at Anzio. Even a simple task like getting troops and equipment loaded was always confusing and time consuming.

The Division was entirely on the sands of the Anzio beachhead by May 22. The unexpected attack, scheduled for May 23, would not include them. For once, they were not leading the charge, but held in reserve to be utilized when and where needed.

Major General Lucian K. Truscott Jr. was the commander of the VI Corps at Anzio. The former 3rd Division leader, in February, replaced Major General John P. Lucas who was originally in command of VI Corp. Lucas had fallen from favor with Sir Alexander when he didn't advance inland following the January landing.

Despite conflicting information on which plan of attack should be initiated, Truscott pushed aside three plans of action and orchestrated a fourth, Operation Buffalo. Operation Buffalo was a straight thrust through Cisterna and Cori to Valmontone. This plan, designed to capture strategic points along Highway 6 (the Via Casilina), would cut off the escaping Germans fleeing after the fall of the Gustav Line. Buffalo, if successful, would in effect destroy the German Tenth Army and potentially bring the Italian campaign to a quicker end.

The Allies accomplished complete surprise on the breakout attempt and the opening day attack achieved surprising success at most American-planned attack points. Some of the fiercest fighting did involve the town of Cisterna. Located only two miles from the original line of departure, Cisterna was able to hold out for two days. The Americans secured the town, which was leveled during the combat, only after fighting for it room by room and house to blood-smeared house.

At the end of May 25, Cisterna, Cori and Monte Arrestino were all in Allied hands. The 36th Division, due to the opening success of this campaign, never left reserve status. This proved surprising, since the game plan called for them to pass through the 3rd Division and head for Cori in the early phases of the breakout.

Operation Buffalo was proving to be a smashing success. Objectives were met as German resistance collapsed. The drive for Valmontone was on, thus ending the stalemate at Anzio.

May 25 took a twisted turn, stunning all involved in the good fortunes of the military aspect of the successful Operation Buffalo. One of the three plans Truscott originally discarded in favor of Buffalo was a stab thru tiny Campoleone to the junction of Highway 7 (Via Appia), near Lake Albano in the Colli Laziali

Once one of Italy's loveliest spots, the town of Cisterna was in total ruin.

(also known as the Alban Hills). Simply, it was a piercing move straight to the ultimate goal: Rome. Operation Buffalo was conceived for military objectives; now Operation Turtle was used for political ones.

What political motive would turn the northeastern movement to Valmontone into a northwestern one to Rome? None other than the obsession of Mark Clark, who wanted to be the first into the Italian capital. Clark made the decision that entering Rome first was much more important to him than destroying the retreating German Tenth Army. Military logic had disappeared, and pure ambition replaced it.

Clark's Fifth Army public relations staff was comprised of nearly fifty men. It is highly doubtful that the previous year's World Series champions, the New York Yankees, had more individual media coverage than Clark. Clark's PR staff operated under a basic premise titled the "three and one rule." Any Fifth Army news release must have Clark's name on the first page three times and on each succeeding page at least once. With all this fanfare, the decision to go to Operation Turtle was not astonishing.

Clark wanted to press forward towards Rome immediately. He knew beforehand the possible target dates of the impending D-Day invasion of France and realized his window of opportunity for front page glory was shrinking. Despite staff discussions of delaying one day to be better prepared, Clark's orders were followed. The officers in the field understood that halting an operation, reorganizing, and then proceeding in a different direction was a major military challenge. Still, the attack commenced on May 26 at 11 AM.

The 36th left their reserve status and entered a gap in the front lines north of Cisterna, created by the advance of the 34th Division to the northwest and the shift of the 1st Armored Division to reserve status for maintenance. It fit snugly between the 34th and 3rd Divisions with orders to guard this piece of real estate while keeping pressure on German forces in Velletri.

Once again, the Germans held onto defensive positions as Clark's personal offensive came to a disappointing halt.[2] Another stalemate became possible. Since entering the fray on May 27, the 143rd accomplished little in front of Velletri, the 141st had limited success to the east of the city, while the 142nd was held in reserve.

FRANK PEARCE CAPTURES GERMAN HIDING IN HOUSE

With the Fifth Army in Italy. —A few minutes after Velletri, Italy, fell three Fifth Army combat engineers captured a German in the city while they made a reconnaissance of roads. They are First Lieutenant Lee E. Bealer Jr., son of Mrs. Margaret Bealer, El Paso; Sergeant Luther S. Bruce of Telephone, and Private Frank W. Pearce, son of Mr. and Mrs. R. A. Pearce of Sulphur Springs, all of Texas.

As they walked through the shell-torn town, climbing over heaps of rubble that blocked most of the streets, they met an Italian who said a German was in his house.

The three engineers, members of the 36th "Texas" Division, followed the Italian to the straggling German, who surrendered and was turned over to the military police.

Sulphur Springs Daily News Telegram, July 10, 1944.

This set the stage for the crowning moment of the 36th Division and its outstanding commander's activity in Italy. General Walker did not want to waste any more T-patch lives on suicide style charges that already had been shown to fail. Walker, concerned at the failure to advance and fearing more losses like the Rapido River bog-down, did what few career-oriented officers do. He put his future on the line by suggesting to Truscott and Clark a different plan than they demanded.

Walker was intrigued when patrols of the 143rd, to the right of Velletri, met little enemy resistance. Upon more reconnaissance, a gap was detected in the German defenses. Walker himself flew over the area and made ground inspections before offering his plan. He then huddled with 111th Engineers' Stovall about the possibility of constructing a rough but useable road over the target area of Monte Artemisio (Hill 939) that would allow movement of tanks, artillery, and troops. Monte Artemisio was located northeast of Velletri to its rear. After reviewing the terrain, Stovall boldly said yes. This sealed the deal

Oran Stovall.

in Walker's mind—whose respect for Stovall bordered on enormous—on the feasibility of the breakthrough plan.

After several attempts to convince Truscott and Clark of the potential success of this move, they agreed. Yet they made it very clear it was Walker's responsibility totally if the plan failed. Truscott, although feeling Walker's scheme was better than his own, warned Walker over the phone, "And you had better get through".

Walker's surprising maneuver, instead of frontal pounding, located for the first time in Italy a true soft underbelly. This would not be only a great decision, but by his insistence of avoiding attacking straight into a frenzy of German fire, it did not waste the lives of numerous T-Patchers.

Each regiment moved into a job-ready position. The 142nd and 143rd, advancing through the 141st holding positions, prepared to activate Walker's calculated risk. Concealed by the darkness of May 30-31, quietly and smoothly the 142nd, under the very noses of the Germans, moved undetected up the slopes of Monte Artemisio.

The 143rd followed the 142nd while the 141st worked on the left of this movement towards Velletri, hoping to keep German attention there. Like a crouching boxer throwing punches, the 141st provided the jab to the face while the 142nd and 143rd swung a roundhouse right hook to the Germans' jaw. Walker's blow was clear and on the button.

Remarkably, the 142nd silent march wasn't noticed by the enemy until dawn. It was too late! Walker's bold move had worked. The 142nd, now faced with enemy resistance and with great bravery and spirit, managed to take control of Monte Artemisio and beat off the fierce counterattacks. The 143rd contributed by securing the east end of Artemisio. Thus, Velletri and the German defenses had been flanked with thousands of American troops embedded behind the startled defenders. The 36th had delivered a one-two knockout punch!

Pressure for building the supply road now fell on Stovall's broad shoulders and they were wide enough to bear it all. Stovall's promise that his men could construct a road over Monte Artemisio and through the Alban Hills began. The

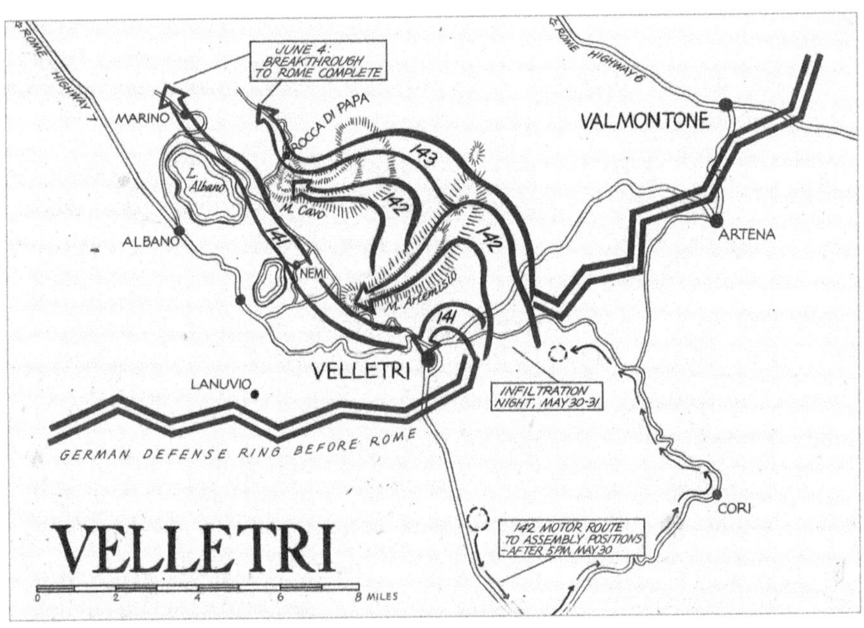

The 36th Division achieved a major breakthrough at Velletri, ending the long stalemate at Anzio and opening the road to Rome.

Plunge Over Via Casilini In Italy

Naples, June 2.—The Fifth Army captured Velletri today.

(By Associated Press)

Allied Headquarters, June 2.—Fifth Army troops have cut off Via Casilina, sealing off a main German escape route, and have broken into Velletri—already left two miles behind by an American spearhead battling on the heights in sight of Rome.

Plunging across Via Casilina, near Valmontone, the Allies slashed the main road for the Nazis falling back from the main front to the southeast.

British forces are pounding up the highway nearing Feretino, 18 miles from Valmontone, while the French forces swung toward the highway from the west.

Sulphur Springs Daily News Telegram, June 2, 1944.

major task of clearing the twenty-mile road fell on one platoon from Company A and the entire Company B, under Captain Crisman. Sniper fire never slowed the bulldozers as they edged forward through light timber, bush and enemy. With nonstop work from Company B engineers like John Parks of Spencer, Louisiana, the rugged but useable road, despite ample German harassment, poked steadily ahead. When completed, it serviced much-needed equipment for movement forward. It also guaranteed a safe supply route for the fighting soldiers battling across the Alban Hills.

On Thursday, the 141st sent all three of its battalions like a battering ram against Velletri. The 36th Engineer Combat Regiment, currently attached to the 36th Division also hit Velletri. Company C's first platoon maintained close contact with the attached ECR, reacting when needed. Despite a heavy German counterattack on the morning of June 1, the 141st entered Velletri around 5:00 and by 11:00 had established a Command Post there. Shortly after sunrise on June 2, the 36th ECR declared Velletri clear of any enemy. The old town had systematically been leveled during the ferocious fighting.

Pearce's close friend Muley Junell exhibited the normal courage of the engineers in Italy with his heroics at Velletri. Along with three other soldiers, Bert Heinlen of Benton Harbor, Michigan, Donald Curry of Madison, Wisconsin, and

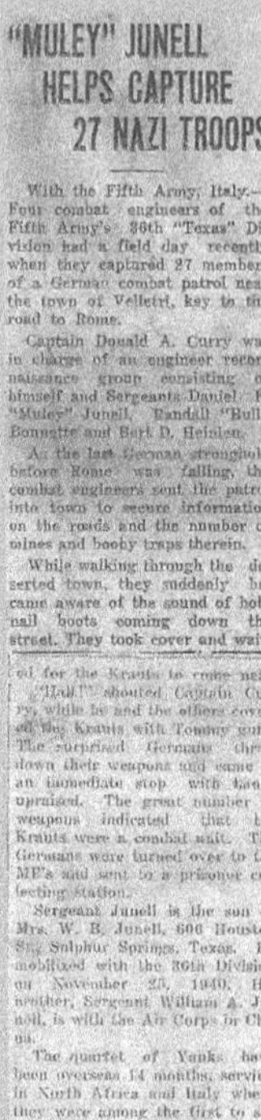

"MULEY" JUNELL HELPS CAPTURE 27 NAZI TROOPS

With the Fifth Army, Italy.—Four combat engineers of the Fifth Army's 36th "Texas" Division had a field day recently when they captured 27 members of a German combat patrol near the town of Velletri, key to the road to Rome.

Captain Donald A. Curry was in charge of an engineer reconnaissance group consisting of himself and Sergeants Daniel F. "Muley" Junell, Randall "Bull" Bonnette and Bert D. Heinlen.

As the last German stronghold before Rome was falling, the combat engineers sent the patrol into town to secure information on the roads and the number of mines and booby traps therein.

While walking through the deserted town, they suddenly became aware of the sound of hobnail boots coming down the street. They took cover and waited for the Krauts to come near.

"Halt!" shouted Captain Curry, while he and the others covered the Krauts with Tommy guns. The surprised Germans threw down their weapons and came to an immediate stop with hands upraised. The great number of weapons indicated that the Krauts were a combat unit. The Germans were turned over to the MP's and sent to a prisoner collecting station.

Sergeant Junell is the son of Mrs. W. B. Junell, 606 Houston St., Sulphur Springs, Texas. He mobilized with the 36th Division on November 25, 1940. His brother, Sergeant William A. Junell, is with the Air Corps in China.

The quartet of Yanks have been overseas 14 months, serving in North Africa and Italy where they were among the first to set foot on the Italian mainland during the invasion of Italy below Salerno.

Sulphur Springs Daily News Telegram, date Unknown.

Randall Bonnette of Port Arthur, Texas, he helped capture twenty-seven Germans trying to escape the city. Their ambush of the startled enemy, the easy capture, and information obtained, rewarded the four men with a Silver Star Medal.

Regardless of their hard-won success in Velletri, new orders on the night of June 1 were issued, and the 141st advanced with the mission of badgering and tormenting the retreating Germans. Working on the left flank of the 36th Division's movement towards Rome, they proceeded towards the cities of Nemi and Marino.

The 142nd and 143rd, taking advantage of high ground and positioning of forces, proceeded to eliminate safe escape routes for the enemy. From Monte Artemisio on June 2, both regiments, were dispatched across the heart of the Alban Hills with the 142nd flanked to the right by the 143rd.

Americans roll into Velletri.

On June 4, the 143rd took Rocca Di Papa and, in conjunction with the 142nd, secured the town of Grottaferrata without a fight. After a momentary stagger against a tank and infantry stand at Marino, the 141st blasted forward. Rome was only miles away.

Moving in support of the 141st, 1st platoon of Company C eliminated any mines slowing the route along Via dei Laghi to and through Marino. Work was conducted 4.5 miles southeast of Marino to 7 miles northeast of the town.

The 111th Engineers dodged death during the rapid advance, but several were wounded. In an ambush that eliminated two trucks of Company B on June 1, Earl P. Powers of Syracuse, New York, was gashed in the face by a bullet. The same gunfight that wounded Powers also caught Robert Findley of Paterson, New Jersey. Knocked from a truck when a machine gun bullet struck him in the hip area, Findley, much to his relief, found he was not wounded. As luck would have it, the bullet was blocked by Findley's pistol hanging at his side. Angered, Findley continued his reconnaissance mission up a mountain after eliminating one of the German snipers firing on him.

The "bend but not break" theory of the enemy had been put to rest. Not only did the German ranks bend, but their break created a flood of soldiers from both sides racing for Rome. While the Germans were looking to slip away, the Allies were speeding forward at breakneck pace. As the Nazis retreated, the 36th Division's swift movement and determination created a sinking feeling behind the concerned faces of all Germans in and around Rome.

Friday 19 May '44

Prepared to move but as usual orders were changed several times. I loaded jeep and waited. Commence to rain. At 2 PM 3 trucks & I were taken to Infantry area. Platoon didn't come. Waited a couple hours and then went into Bagnolia edge of Naples. Parked in staging area. Raining again. Sleeping in back of a truck. Don't load yet it seems.

Saturday 20 May '44

Rained all night. Got up late this AM. 1st platoon arrived around 2:30 PM. I still hadn't loaded. At 5 I drove to dock and loaded on L.C.T. It is fairly loaded with vehicles & men. Left dock at 7:45 PM. Will arrive in the morning about same time. Sleeping wherever one can find a space. I slept on jeep. Reports on progress are good.

Sunday 21 May '44

Hit Anzio about 8 AM. Nice size town and not badly torn up but ruined of course. Got off boat at 9. Bivouacked out in brush as this is a flat bushy place. [three miles east of Nettuno] Smoke pots all around our front to keep down observation. Can go five miles in any direction and hit front. Fairly quiet with some artillery & bunch of rifle fire.

Monday 22 May '44

Dug foxhole a little deeper as I expect shell fire soon. Did little else today. Rest of company arrived. In the morning the attack will start here. 3rd & 45th Divisions will start drive for a town back in mountains. First the artillery (2000 guns here alone) will lay a barrage. After they reach the town the 36th takes up there. Will be a noisy bloody battle.

Tuesday 23 May '44

Received three packages yesterday. Has been fairly quiet all day with artillery firing every once in a while. Understand the push is fairly successful. 45th and 1st Armored have cut Highway 7 but other forces are bogged down at Cisterna. We will probably go up in day or so. We have stayed under cover all day.

Wednesday 24 May '44

Air raid last night. Also 170 mm shells (Anzio Express) coming in.[3] This evening late several of us had to go up to front to move mines for artillery. Got shelled, sniped at and rough in general. Rolling country full of deep ditches full of Germans. Dead scattered, some buried, feet sticking out, theirs & ours alike. Bad smell. I got lost & got into front lines. Fighting all around us. Really a big hot battle. Got to area at 1:30. We are winning!

Thursday 25 May '44

Had to go out to same place again this morning as an artillery boy set off a mine and blew him to pieces. Mines are thick and barb wire etc. German tanks (7) knocked out in one place. Several of ours. Battles moving away. German on the run. Lots of prisoners came back at 3:30 PM. Moved out tonite at 9:13. Came up about Cisterna close to mountain. [Monte Arrestino] Cori has fallen in the mountains. 36th attacks 10 in the morning.

Friday 26 May '44

Laid around all day under cover. Germans retreating rapidly. Our area is a few miles of Cori. This evening 3 PM Mr. Pink (Hq W.O.) [Harold P. Pinck of Randolph, Wisconsin and Headquarters Warrant Officer] had to go to Anzio to get us another bull dozier (ours hit mine) [slightly injuring Welton W. Blagden of

Smith River, California] so I took him. Company moved while I was gone. Came back by Cisterna. All shot to hell and a pile of rubble & dead. Got to Company about 11 PM. Four miles from front.

Saturday 27 May '44

Air raid last night on gun positions. We are bivouacked in a deep ditch so got by O.K. Made reconnaissance this AM. Went into our front lines as far as we had. Town of Velletri under siege (shell fire). Rugged terrain. Vineyards, cane breaks, & orchards. Machine gun nest numerous but we weren't fired on. Dead Jerries everywhere. Hot weather & flies working fast. Took five gallons of vino out of cellar.

Sunday 28 May '44

We are keeping up with Infantry, so we move up a mile or so when they advance. Had air raid last night around area. Also some shells fell in. Went up close to Velletri this AM. Several of our tanks knocked. Boys still in them. Dead of course. The smell of death is everywhere and bodies too. This PM went back but was shelled and fired on by machine gun. German counter attacked. Fair battle.

Monday 29 May '44

Last night Germans attacked around 3 AM. Our artillery laid down a terrific barrage and it was repelled. This evening I went back to Highway 7 towards Velletri. Can't get closer than 1 1/2 mile as we drew fire again. Germans are resisting strongly. Not much air activity. Bodies around here are sure getting ripe.[4]

Tuesday 30 May '44

Have made a few trips up close to front (and I mean close) but as a rule I have been behind the lines. Last night the Luftwaffe (German air force) was over and caused us a little trouble. Over in force about 12 o'clock. Infantry suppose to attack in morning.

Wednesday 31 May '44

Last nite the German air force was over and bombed hell out of front lines about 4 AM. We are within a mile of Infantry, so we get the works too. Have been up close to front or I should say in the front lines several times today. Sergeant Bruce and I located a wine cellar with about 2000 gallons of white wine. Took all we could drink and finally got five gallon can full. These cellars go down about 50 feet and branch out with 500 gallon barrels set in wall.

Thursday 1 June '44

Oh but I got drunk last night. Had to go up Highway 7 to front line and put up a sign that mines are present. Made it O.K. This evening went back to 36 Engineers and stayed all evening and made another trip to wine cellar. Fighting close by. Last night planes dropped personnel bombs around us but none in this area. Front still about the same.

Friday 2 June '44

German air force kept me awake nearly all night. Bombing & strafing. This AM we took out for Velletri which fell last night. Moved mine field in road. Two vehicles hit them a few days ago. Bodies a terrible mess. Velletri a ruin. Quite large. Lieutenant B and Bruce & I (1 more guy) scouted around and captured one German. Went about three miles toward Rome but Germans stopped us. Shelled us & machine gun fire.

Saturday 3 June '44

Moved closer to front as Infantry has advanced about seven miles from Velletri. Am in a nice place and have a small room to myself. Good bed made from divan. Been up close to front where we are making fill as Germans blew huge hole in road. Plains stretch as far as I could see (hazy). Rome about twenty miles. Made a trip back to rear area tonight. Beautiful night.

Sunday 4 June '44

Pulled out early following Infantry. Germans retreating like hell. Company moving along in rear. Town of Marino held us up about four hours. In the evening I went in. People went crazy, covered us with Vino & flowers. Quite a few German prisoners taken. All worn out from fatigue. Went on thru and within three miles of Rome.

9 GOODBYE TO AN EGO AND AN ECHO

"I have never seen such a mess as yesterday and today. Everyone racing to get to Rome. Germans scattered all over country but our army by passed them and came on down the highway."

The Eternal City, with all its history and grandeur, laid spread eagle for the taking. Settled in 753 BC on the slopes of the Palatino Hills, this small village had become known as "Roma Caput Mundi" to the ancient world for hundreds of years. Here Julius Caesar was murdered, Augustus ruled, and nearby, Nero fiddled while the city burned. It held the mighty Coliseum and was highlighted by the smallest independent country in the world: the 110-acre Vatican City.

Historians still debate which American forces were first to enter Rome on June 4-5. More importantly, American forces did enter and liberate the city. For the first time in its storied history, Rome was invaded by the most benevolent and freedom delivering conqueror its classic streets had witnessed. In return, the city showered the exhausted but smiling fighting men with respect, love, flowers, and vino.

Rome was free! Since the May 11 start of Operation Diadem, the Fifth Army endured a total of 17,931 soldiers killed, wounded, or missing. Despite the heavy losses, the Italian campaign appeared to have taken a new direction. Success day by day was becoming easier for the crusading American forces.

Lieutenant General Clark and his staff drove into Rome not in a chariot but a jeep. The conqueror entered his prized conquest at 8:00 AM on June 5. Walker, who kicked in the door to Rome for Clark, continued through in his pursuit of the Germans. Walker didn't realize

Anzio Units Cleanse Former Axis Center Of Hitler Influence

ALLIED HEADQUARTERS in Naples, June 4 (AP).—Allied Fifth Army troops from the old Anzio beachhead captured historic Rome Sunday after a fierce battle through suburbs of the Eternal City.

The mop-up of the heart of Rome—the first European capital to fall to Allied troops—was completed at 9:15 p.m. (2:15 p.m., Central War Time) as an Allied force knocked out the last German rearguard unit in front of the Bank of Italy, almost within the shadow of Trajan's Column.

To the north of the city warplanes battered at fleeing German transports, wrecking or damaging at least 600 motor vehicles, as the Allied forces sought to annihilate the [illegible] Nazi divisions in Italy.

The huge air-wrecked toll of Nazi transports [illegible] congested roads above Rome indicated the enemy [illegible] no major stand in the ancient city—first European capital [illegible] be entered by Allied troops.

Opposition appeared to be tapering off.

Headquarters did not identify the first troops entering Rome.

The enemy made it a battle every foot of the way through the suburbs into Rome. The Germans hurled all they had—tanks, armor and artillery—into fierce fighting to block the Fifth Army steamroller at least until they could pull out more of their own menaced forces.

Lt. Gen. Mark W. Clark Reads Dispatches Informing Him of Rome's Capture by His Fifth Army Troops.

This break into Rome, center of Catholicism and once the seat of the ancient Roman Empire, came twenty-four days after the Allies unleashed a powerful combined offensive of the Fifth and Eighth Armies, and twelve days after Fifth Army men on the Anzio beachhead hurled forth their power drive aimed at the capital.

Lashing at the Nazi columns retreating from Rome, Allied fighter-bombers destroyed or [illegible] at least [illegible] vehicles, finding excellent targets in congested traffic above the city to Viterbo, Lake [illegible] and Lake Bolsena, headquarters said.

Other planes struck troop concentrations and gun positions.

The great roundup of prisoners continued—with more than 15,000 now taken by the Fifth Army alone. The Eighth Army has captured at least 6,000. Five of the eighteen German divisions engaged in Italy already had been virtually annihilated. Thus the Allies were well along in their avowed purpose of this offensive to crush the Nazi legions.

they had—tanks, armor and artillery—into fierce fighting to block the Fifth Army steamroller at least until they could pull out more of their own menaced forces.

Dallas Morning News, June 5, 1944.

his reward for saving Clark from a military blunder would be the loss of his combat command.

Clark, the new master of Rome, had had only a day to enjoy having his picture splattered over the newspapers of the world.[1] Operation Overlord, the Allied invasion of Normandy, began on June 6 opening another front on European soil. It also took the thunder and lightning of the Fifth Army's Rome adventure away from the front pages. In the scale of things, Clark had not gotten his "fifteen minutes of fame" despite all his efforts.

The order for the day was to go through Rome and meet in assembly areas five miles northwest of the city as quickly as possible. Only the 3rd Division would have the envious task of remaining to garrison a city starved for American attention.

Pearce, moving with the 2nd Battalion of the 141st, at 1:00 was caught in artillery fire. After crossing the Tiber River, he maneuvered past Vatican City and worked northwest. The Germans, about a mile from Rome, decided to end the party and opened on the celebrating crowd and troops. The drive across Rome did not end in a celebration. Instead, it was back to the reality that this war was far from over. Company C didn't report any fatalities from the surprise shelling, but three members of Headquarters and Service Company were wounded.

Success has its costs. The Anzio breakout, Walker's brilliant maneuver, the rush through Rome and beyond, came with a price. The expense was again the loss of numerous engineers to the enemy's reluctance to give up. From June 1, when Earl P. Powers was gashed in the face by a bullet, until Raymond F. Schick of Rochester, New York got hit on June 17, twenty-five engineers were disabled or killed.

On June 6, a rare face-to-face combat encounter caused four of these casualties. While members of Company A were on reconnaissance, an incendiary grenade was hurled into their vehicle.[2] Straughn Parker of Berlin, Maryland, Ernest Owings of Dallas, Texas, Albert Chambliss of Clovis, New Mexico, and Warren Ausland, were all burned by the flash of agonizing heat, but escaped serious injury. On June 11, German artillery continued to harass the Americans as the engineers feverously worked to clean the highways of roadblocks. Zygment Backus of Jackson, Michigan, waiting for the infantry to clear out some enemy sharpshooters on Highway Number One outside Capalbio, was killed by shell fragments. Three other members of Company A, John Lindsay of Victoria, Texas, Marvin Luckett of Santa Fe, Tennessee, and Denzol Corn of Rushville, Indiana, were wounded by the fury of this surprise barrage.

Raymond Woznicki and Clyfton N. Jones finished dismantling a foot bridge crossing stream northeast of Orbetello that Company C built earlier. On June 14, while moving the materials to a dump in the rear, both men were struck by enemy artillery shells.

On June 25, the 36th made a vigorous effort to continue driving the Germans before them. On Sunday, the 141st was released from Italian action. The following day, at 6:00 AM the 143rd was officially taken off the front. That same day the 142nd, when relieved by the 442nd Regimental Combat Team, moved back toward Rome.

The 36th Division would fight in Italy no more. There would be bloody battles to come, but none on the Italian soil they battled to liberate. Whether it was hot or cold, wet or dry, in combat or out, these soldiers accomplished their goal. At times they limped along and at others they sprinted, but the drive up "The Boot" had been successful and most of the country was free. Combat in Italy for the Division ended approximately nine miles past the city of Piombino.

Now the Division faced another unnecessary disaster. Their leader, Fred L. Walker, the man who kept the heart of the Division pumping, was relieved of command by his superior, Clark. On June 12, Walker received a letter from Clark offering him a command back in the United States. It was an order to give up command of the 36th. Walker's magnificent plan for the success at Velletri aside, he was forced out. After the war's conclusion, Clark contended that George C. Marshall, Chairman of the Joint Chiefs of Staff Committee, suggested Walker for the position. Clark said he simply took the message to Walker personally and put it on his desk. He told Walker, "I just got this, Fred. It's up to you".

Clark's letter to Walker mentioned a General McNair as the one seeking Walker's availability to be Commandant of The Infantry School at Ft. Benning, Georgia. Lesley J. McNair, Commanding General, Army Ground Forces, was responsible for the training of U.S. Army forces in the United States for combat overseas.[3] He was personally selected by Marshall to fill one of the most important leadership roles held by a stateside American officer, and he proved a natural.

The respect Marshall and other high ranked military men showered on McNair and his work were more than justified. How could Clark, as Walker suspected, have any influence with someone as powerful as McNair to request him to return to the States? Simple! McNair and Clark shared the past. Clark had been the wax in McNair's ear while serving as his Chief of Staff in the early 1940s. Clark's hard work, willingness to travel over 60,000 miles to help organize the ground forces, and leadership skills won McNair's respect. When it came time to return a favor, it was a given. It was because of this inexhaustible wave of superior military ranking that Walker finally accepted his new position. Near Naples, General Walker bid farewell to his comrades-in-arms. The 57-year-old leader never stood taller in the eyes of his men than on this day. Fatigue from the battles fought over the past ten months were put aside as the men marched smartly past their general. Respect was mutual.

As the 36th Division moved into another theater of operation, Clark remained behind with the Fifth Army in Italy. The decision to separate the 36th from Clark and his overwhelming ego brought an end to the love-hate relationship of the past year. For the veterans of the Italian campaign, the memories of the actions of Clark and Walker would transcend time. To members of the 36th in the years after the war, the mere mention of Clark's name brought forth a gusher of pent-up emotions in their vile remembrance of a man they believed had no feelings for them. The audible trembling of the same veterans, when the name Walker was uttered in their midst, was one of priceless and endless devotion. The echo of his name is summed up in *A Pictorial History of the 36th "Texas" Infantry Division* published shortly after World War II. In their final review, just before Walker returned to the States, the official book on the 36th stated, "But there was a high-priced pride in their stride, in their sharp salute, in their 'eyes right' for a leader they loved, for whom they were saying with the highest tribute they had: 'Good-bye and good luck, sir—and we are sorry.'"

Monday 5 June '44

I have never seen such a mess as yesterday and today. Everyone racing to get to Rome. Germans scattered all over country but our army by passed them and came on down the highway. We came into Rome this AM. I have never seen such a mob of people. It was so crowded with people & trucks etc. it took us four hours to cross. On north side of Rome the Germans shelled us heavily and killed three boys & wounded several (not ours). Shelling Rome while the streets were crowded with people. I thought my time had come!!

Tuesday 6 June '44

Bivouacked in edge of Rome in field. German planes were over a little. Moved out with Infantry this P.M. Slow going as thousands of tanks & vehicles moving up. Have lost contact with Germans. The road we took was a dirt one and we traveled twenty miles. German vehicles scattered all the way where our air force had knocked them out. Slept two hours and pulled out at 4 AM (7th) and moved up some.

Rome Falls! (U.S. Army)

Wednesday 7 June '44

Have slept a little today but not much. Been up to 143rd Command Post with Lieutenant as liaison. Still don't know where Germans are. There has been a lot of vehicles passing for two days now bumper to bumper. Radio says invasion started yesterday. Are we glad! Moved up some more. Planes look for us at night and bomb & strafe. One went down last nite.

Thursday 8 June '44

Got up at 12 last nite and traveled till 5. Ended up close to sea as we came northwest. German planes over all night but failed to locate us. Our own planes bomb & strafe us as we travel so far & fast. Went out this PM on road recon. Germans are about ten miles from here and we are shelling them. Probably a small force. Rolling country.

Friday 9 June '44

Got a good nights sleep. Moved twice today. Cutting inland again. Are bivouacked out of town of Tarquinia which was held by Germans yesterday. Only a holding force as Germans are still retreating. Believe they are quitting Italy. Company worked on bypass till midnight. Few mine fields around and quite a few bridges blown.

Saturday 10 June '44

Did a little running around this morning. A powder plant close by. Lots of mines etc there. Picked up four German mine detectors. This evening we moved up to Montalto 110 kilometers from Rome (70 miles). Bridge blown there so we made a recon on bypass. Dust was really thick as lots of traffic. Got in about 9:30.

Sunday 11 June '44

Moved out early and advanced about 10 miles farther up highway 1. Still going up coast. Tyrrhenian Sea can be seen. Am up with our front. Artillery shelling Germans and they are shelling us. We are by a big house owned by a Fascist and he left with Germans. I found fifteen bottles of Peroni beer. Weak but good taste. Germans tried to flank us but artillery stopped it.

Monday 12 June '44

Had chicken & squash for supper. Was quite a few at this place but all gone now. Owner was Fascist, so we don't care. Other Italians getting them too. Stayed at Battalion Headquarters today as Captain is acting S 3 and I drove him. Have to go out tonight as we are up to a river and all bridges blown [Albegna River]. Nights are literally freezing but days hot.

Tuesday 13 June '44

Got in at 8 AM. One of the biggest messes I've ever seen. We got to river before dark and could have finished in 2 hours but Headquarters and Service Company sent bridge to wrong place and we didn't find it till 4 AM. It was at A Company and we couldn't find A Company! Could see Germans blowing bridges on other side but nothing we could do. The so & so's. Seeing our work created before our eyes.[4]

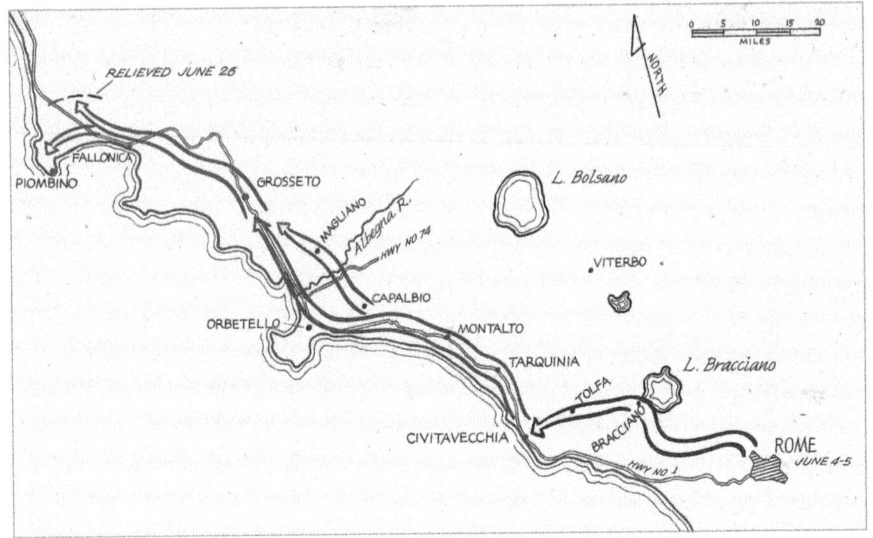

After the fall of Rome, the 36th Division advanced up the west coast of Italy for the next several days until receiving a new assignment.

Wednesday 14 June '44

Today I have been up front at 143rd Command Post with Lieutenant Woznicki as liaison officer. [Raymond Woznicki of Conshohocken, Pennsylvania] He was hit by piece of shrapnel, so I now have Lieutenant Kilby. The Germans are fighting hard around this river. All prisoners I have seen are Mongolian or Russians.[5] I don't know just where they are from. The Infantry makes a push tonight. I'll be up all night.

Thursday 15 June '44

Was up all night and running back & forth. Ran off in shell hole once and boy was a jolt. Also ran into ditch and turned jeep up on side. Black night and of course no lights can be used. Troops broke thru and today has been another race up Highway 1.[6] We went back and moved Company up. Am now up close to Grosseto. Flat rolling country with irrigation ditches.

Bridgehead established over the Albegna River.

Friday 16 June '44

Went up to river [Ombrone River] to check on building bypass as all bridges are being blown as the Germans retreat. They shelled us out so came back. Have run around quite a bit this AM. This PM I have slept a little. Plane dropped two bombs just a little ways (200 yards) from us last night. No one hurt but shrapnel sure flew.

Saturday 17 June '44

Out last night till 1 AM. Did nothing this AM except wash my clothes. This evening Arnold & I took off in jeep and had a good time. People very friendly and we ate and drank plenty and they played their phonograph and we danced with the girls. I came back and ended up by telling Lieutenant Beahler to get himself a new driver.

Sunday 18 June '44

Slept on sidewalk at 143 Command Post in Grosseto and it rained so I got wet. Turned jeep over to new driver when I got back to Company. I am fed up with these damn officers who do nothing but run around. Keep a guy out all the time and treat him as if he was a moron. Am back in 3rd squad. Squads don't have too much to do. Black balled again.

Wednesday 21 June '44

Moved north of Grosseto about five miles.[7] Can see our artillery hitting hill across valley. Germans seem to make a stand wherever possible. Then moved on up about seven miles. Bridges all blown so had to wind around. Saw tank traps on highway. Holes dug ten feet deep & twenty feet long and ninety feet wide (approximate) and then surfaced over by thin pavement. Looks very natural. Very little for us to do as Infantry is at a standstill.

Friday 23 June '44

Have done nothing at all today but lay around. Infantry didn't advance so we have no work. At present, we are sixty miles from Leghorn. No big advances made and there are lots of Engineers in this sector, so we do very little. Drank a little vino today. Moved up about five miles late this evening. There are fourteen German graves just behind this house which was used as aid station for day or so. Had hair all clipped off.

Saturday 24 June '44

M.E. 210 came skimming over low early this morning heading for home.[8] Went right on thru as no one seemed to recognize it till to late and very few awake. Played cards a little and lost of course. This evening we went forward about 10 miles and have been taking up a big mine field. Got shelled but no harm. Rumored 6 divisions moving down on us from north.

New haircut.

Sunday 25 June '44

Spent night at mine field. I was sick all night & today. Did nothing at all but lay around. Some jeeps pulled into field below us and one blew up. Driver not hurt, two more boys in it and one was blown about forty feet and one about twenty. One was practically dead & other had leg mangled. Really our companies' fault on the Lieutenant.

Monday 26 June '44

Moved up late yesterday evening and then back about twenty miles. Today have done nothing. We are now relieved. Going back close to Rome tomorrow. Played cards (hearts) all evening and of course I lost. The town we were up to on the front was Follonica a seaport. Guess *we are* finished in Italy.

Tuesday 27 June '44

Nothing doing this AM. Played cards till noon. This evening at 4 we pulled out for Rome. Traffic heavy all the way. Traveled 130 miles. The last fifteen or twenty miles we used lights! It has been ages since we did that. Got to bivouac at about midnight. About nine miles from Rome.

Wednesday 28 June '44

This morning as usual nothing to do. All that are not on some Company duty could go to Rome this PM. So I went. It is not to be compared with Naples. It is clean and no kids worrying you to eat or such. Very little to drink and hard to find a woman. A beautiful city filled with beautiful girls. Oh the poor love starved soldier.

Thursday 29 June '44

Got paid this morning.[9] I owed more than I drew but can manage. Passes to Rome again so I went. Arnold and me. I was wrong about very little to drink as there is plenty. Bars open from 11 to 1 and 5 to 7. Been all over. Went back to apartment of a certain girl and shot the bull some more. Have a date tomorrow at same place. Promised to bring food.

Friday 30 June '44

I can't understand this. More passes to Rome & I still have no duty. Also Beahler & Kilby (Lieutenants) and Captain Petree are not with us anymore. Have Lieutenant Mueller (good guy) as company commander.[10] Went thru St. Peter's Cathedral. Beautiful beyond description. Then Arnold and I went back to apartment and did O.K. Leaving for Salerno the 2nd.

Saturday 1 July '44

Last day for passes so into Rome I went. Saw all I could and went to a stage show in Italian. Boy there were some cute girls. I'm ready to leave now as I've seen all I want of Rome. Leaving in the morning. Went to show tonight here in area but machine kept breaking so wasn't too good.

Sunday 2 July '44

Left area at 10:15 AM and drove till 11:00 PM. Not too much traffic. About 250 trip down to below Salerno. Not far from where we landed Sept 9. Out in open wheat field and it is hot as hell with no shade at all. Hear we will be here a month.

Thursday 6 July '44

Same today as day before yesterday. Reveille, calisthenics, close order drill, rifle inspection this morning. Cleaned up our equipment as tomorrow we parade for General. After supper we had to go and practice just how we will do it. Our officers don't know a thing about drilling.

Fred L. Walker bids farewell.

Friday 7 July '44

This morning at 10 we paraded before General Walker who is leaving us & going to States. The rest of the day I did nothing. It is really hot now. Doesn't get dark until about 10 PM. Went to show last night at 143 Infantry about a mile walk. Stood guard for another boy.

Sunday 9 July '44

Moved this morning between Battipaglia and Salerno. Will start taking training. A good irrigation ditch close by and cool clear running water. Helped dig pit. This evening had to fall out in O. Ds. for Colonel to present medals to some of our company. Loaded explosives after supper. Benedict got French books from home, so he and I are studying French for our entry into France, if that is where we go. Going to next camp tomorrow.

Company A's Homer Figler of Rochester, New York, instructs the infantry concerning the various land mines they would face in France.

Monday 10 July '44

Left camp at 8 AM. Got to next camp about 9. Couldn't get in till 4 PM so we went to service club and stayed. At 4 we came back. Couldn't get in till 6. Such a mess. No rations for us until tomorrow. Stayed at Red Cross club till 9. Had 36th Division band. Went to show tonight. All set now. This is really a neat camp with nowhere to go. It is located on a hill along where we made invasion. No towns very close and all are off limits. Have a fair Red Cross. Pretty good food.

Friday 14 July '44

Have done nothing today except calisthenics this morning. Am now a member of a Duck squad. A Duck is an amphibious vehicle.[11] This squad has to do demolition on beaches during an invasion. May be a rough job! One job is as good as any other. On guard from 9:30 to 12:30 PM. Got back in time to take typhus shot and test our gas mask. Got new masks for invasion. A lighter model and more comfortable.

10 LE TOUR DE FRANCE

"They cut us to pieces and infiltrated all thru us with tanks & Infantry. They used mortars, rifle grenades & artillery. The assault force had machine pistols & machine guns"

The 36th Division, for the third time in little over a year, was called on to enter a new arena of combat. With the battles in Italy seemingly less important since the taking of Rome, and the frustratingly slow push of the Normandy landing force across France, new pressure on the overextended Germans was needed to hasten the ending of the war. A second front in France was predicted to stretch and test the tensile strength of the Nazis' line of defense. Operation Dragoon, the planned invasion of Southern France between Cannes and Toulon, had sat on the backburner of Allied agenda for over a year.[1] When approved for action, Allied commanders felt they had to establish a beachhead quickly and in the ensuing days capture the ports of Toulon and Marseille. The final task was a drive inland to connect with the Third Army, moving in from the Normandy invasion.

The actual plan for the invasion of Southern France became a reality on June 24. Allied forces, such as the 36th Division, were removed from the Italian theater and added to the strike force of the Seventh Army. The commander of Seventh Army was American Major General Alexander M. Patch, whose leadership qualities were evident earlier in the Pacific battle at Guadalcanal. VI Corps, under Truscott, with three U.S. divisions in the 36th, 3rd, and 45th, made up the measure of the Seventh's French coast landing. The new man in charge of the 36th Division was John E. Dahlquist of St. Paul, Minnesota. A military officer since 1917, he previously was the commanding general for the 70th Division.

John E. Dahlquist.

On August 15, 1944, Operation Dragoon became the first daylight beach landing for the 36th. Carbon copying the invasion of Salerno, the same companies of the 111th Engineers supported the same 36th Division infantry units. To the mild amazement of all, the enemy didn't give them a Salerno style welcome. The soldiers, landing east of the cities of St. Raphael and Frejus, met only scattered resistance.

Where were the opposing forces? Much of the German forces were busy slugging it out with the Allies in the broadening theater of Western France. Others, on the disintegrating Russian front, were trying to contain a revenge-filled foe. At 8:00 AM, the men started wading ashore on the various colored beachheads. Again, like Salerno, arranged left to right on the beach, they were Red, Green, Yellow and Blue. The Yellow beach landings were scuttled since German gunners had an excellent crossfire advantage in the U-shaped landing area.

The 2nd and 3rd Battalion of the 141st put ashore on Green Beach and were able to get four waves on the beaches before facing concentrated German fire. In short time they cleared Drammont and Cape Drammont, which surrounded their landing zone. While the 2nd Battalion worked north through Agay before encountering strong resistance, the 3rd seized the high ground in front of Green beach. Company A's 2nd and 3rd platoons got into action on Green Beach at noon and remained in support of the infantry. They were joined at 8 PM by 1st

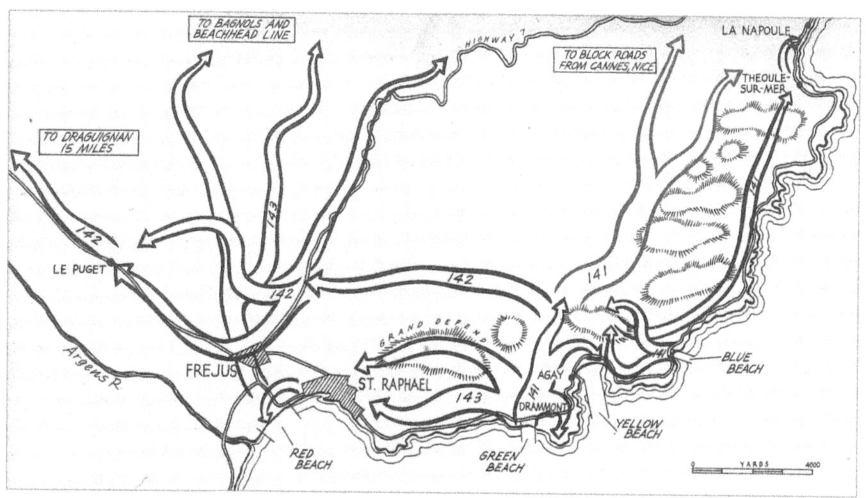

The 36th Division played a vital part in Operation Dragoon, the invasion of southern France.

platoon of Company A. The 143rd plus Company C followed the 141st onto Green Beach. After the successful landing, it began to drive west with an objective of St. Raphael.

Blue Beach, for 1st Battalion of the 141st, was tougher. German anti-tank guns fired on the men as they moved in to unload. Still, they quickly overcame the resistance and captured more than twelve hundred prisoners.

The 142nd plus all of Company B planned to go in on Red Beach, west of St. Raphael near Frejus. Due to a heavy German presence, and with Green Beach clear, the 142nd, using an alternate plan, was directed to Green around 3:30 PM. Without opposition, they moved north and then west to attack Frejus from the rear.

Thus, the rocky shale shore of Green Beach, except for a single Battalion, was the jumping off spot for the entire Division. In an area 2 1/2 football fields wide and a long pass from an average quarterback deep, over twenty thousand men dispersed.

The 36th Division would have plenty of company to keep the Germans busy as the other two invading American Divisions landed sucessfully. The 3rd Division sloshed ashore on southern beaches of the St. Tropez peninsula as the 45th Division hit France in the middle of the VI Corps zone, near the town of Sainte-Maxime.

Green Beach. (Another Wave: Aarons, YANK)

Action all night and into the morning of August 16 resulted in both Frejus and St. Raphael coming into American hands. After taking St. Raphael, the 143rd moved to clear Red Beach from behind the German defense. Meanwhile the 141st pushed through the Riviera cutting off avenues of escape at Cannes near La Napoule.

Success came quickly for the Allied forces. With the consolidating of the entire VI Corps front, Truscott refused to let his forces stall. Unlike the hesitation of Lucas at Anzio the past January, he ordered a push inland, never letting the Germans regain any semblance of balance.

The Engineer Battalion survived the first day of the invasion with only six casualties. Of the six listed, just one was serious enough to be transported to a hospital. Artillery took down Charles Simpson of Flint, Michigan (both hands), David Wray of Bessemer City, North Carolina (hand) and Murray Mattleman (hip).

The other three injuries were the result of an abnormal type of warfare. Erwin Knuth of Milwaukee, Wisconsin, received cuts to his left arm after getting caught in a barbed wire entanglement, Stephen Sinchak broke his right instep

Beachheads Secured, Extended by Yanks French and British

ROME, Aug. 15 (AP).—Thousands of Allied troops, mainly Americans and French, swarmed onto the south coast of France on a broad front between Marseille and Nice Tuesday, seized and extended firm beachheads against inconsequential German opposition, and drove northward with the avowed intention of joining the Allies in northwestern France.

An Allied communique at 10:40 p.m. said American and French troops before dawn took the Sentinel Islands of Port Cros and Levant, ten miles off the coast, and seized Cap Negre, on the mainland due north of the islands and twenty-eight miles east of Toulon.

Other specific locations were not given, the beaches being placed merely in the 125-mile strip of coast between Marseille and Nice.

The Germans said the focal point of the Allied invasion was at St. Raphael, thirty miles northeast up the coast from Cap Negre, and also said there were landings west of Toulon and at Bormes, twenty-five miles east of that one-time naval base.

American airmen who flew over the beaches late in the day said there was no sign of any concerted enemy opposition and that American vehicles were running all over the countryside.

Dallas Morning News, August 16, 1944.

Aubrey Jeter.

while seeking protection during an air raid and James Cave of Tyler, Texas, near an explosion, received a head shot from a rock.

On the morning of the August 16, Richard W. Conrad of Philadelphia, Pennsylvania, and Aubrey Jeter were shot and seriously wounded by machine gunfire. They were checking an enemy roadblock on Highway 98, 1 1/2 miles west of Boulouris when fired upon. The following day, despite medical attention, Conrad died. He became the first, and far from the last, 111th Engineer to lose his life in France.

Pearce, due to complications, didn't get on beach until the second day of the invasion. His introduction to France was in the Sainte-Maxime area. Driving cautiously off LST 994, he found himself in the 45th Division invasion site south of the 36th Division. He and companion Newton Foote of Port Arthur, Texas couldn't immediately catch up with their division because of a bridge blown over the Argens River.

General Fredrick Butler, pushed forward from Draguignan chasing the retreating Germans. The force included 2nd Battalion of the 143rd plus 2nd platoon of Company C. Butler's mission was to get behind the German lines of withdrawal, stop their retreat and take the town of Grenoble. With reinforcements from the rest of the 36th, their goal was to destroy the German 19th Army.

Two days later, in a change of plans, Butler was ordered to Montelimar, a small town on the east bank of the Rhone River. His orders were to make a defensive stand at that point and block the German retreat north. There he was to hold until the 36th, scattered but now moving in his direction, could add reinforcements.

Butler, following Truscott's directions, turned his troops west into the Montelimar area. The Rhone Valley narrowed here and the high ground to the northeast was a perfect position to dominate the Germans route to safety. Truscott felt this was the spot to slow the German retreat and keep a close rein on any vain effort by reinforcements coming out of the north to aid them. Meanwhile, another force consisting in part of the remainder of the 143rd, followed Task Force Butler to Sisteron before charging ahead and seizing the town of Gap and threatening German control of Grenoble.

With this rapid advance, fuel became critical. Butler's expedition continued, in part, with captured German fuel. Gasoline liberated from dumps at Draguignan, Le Muy and Digne, burned in the American engines and propelled American vehicles forward as they entered, on August 22, the Montelimar region. On the same day, Grenoble, over two hundred miles from the coast, fell to elements of the 143rd.

Even with the success of the two task forces, most of the Division, on foot and in truck shuttles, was still working forward. Because of the whirlwind movement, the 36th was scattered over hundreds of miles of French territory, but in high gear to catch up.

The battle around Montelimar commenced on the twenty-third when the recently arrived 141st moved on the city from the north.[2] Without supporting shell fire, because of the artillery's low and "be conserved" status, the 141st was stopped just short of the town. Fighting then progressed into a full-fledged small arms engagement.

Although the 141st was forced to withdraw, the fight didn't slow. The battle placed the 36th Division against Major General Wend von Wietersheim, commander of the 11th Panzer Division, and patchwork infantry divisions of the Nineteenth Army under General Friedrich Wiese.

One ominous spot threatening the Germans was a core of American controlled hill masses to the north and northeast of Montelimar overlooking Highway 7. Fleeing Germans, desperately seeking to escape up the Rhone Valley, tried to open a gap in the American lines. Highway 7, through Montelimar, was the Germans escape north and they fought to secure it. The German infantry, on the 23rd, cleared the route north by driving the Americans blocking their path away from the highway.

Wiese, on August 25, ordered Wietersheim to clear the Americans from the entire area around Montelimar. It was showdown time for the two sides. Fortunately, the entire 36th was close to Montelimar by Thursday and hurriedly moved its men to the battle line. Realizing the Germans posed a significant threat to the 36th advance, the division shifted to the defensive.

The 142nd moved swiftly from Gap and Guillestre while the 143rd was transported down from Grenoble to add its veterans to the battle. General Dahlquist decided to have his forces secure positions along the Rubion River (streambed) since the area could be protected by artillery from the hills behind the river. Division forces were organized along the river with the 141st on the west, the 142nd to the east, and the center, near the town of Bonlieu, defended by the combat engineers and headquarters' personnel. The thinly defended front for the 36th, facing the threat of a German onslaught, contained little depth while stretching vaguely here and there well over twenty-five miles.

The Bonlieu front, where Pearce's gun was added, featured a combined company of two platoons from Company A, one platoon from Company C, with a third platoon from Headquarters and Service Company. Their defensible line, originally planned as a spot for the 143rd to man, stretched thirty-five hundred yards along the Rubion River with the defender's field of fire obstructed by a low hilly terrace south of the river. Reading like a book left to right, the yardage was defended by 1st platoon of Company C holding the town of Bonlieu with Company A's 1st and 2nd platoons to the west of Bonlieu butting up to the 3rd Battalion of the 141st. The Headquarters and Service Company remained in reserve.

This group, defending the middle of the streambed, gave the eerie sensation of appearing to be extremely similar to those at the La Cosa creek stand in Italy.

If a man could pull a trigger and shoot in the general vicinity of the enemy, then he moved up and joined the altercation. Wietersheim launched five different attacks, all along this front, to drive the Americans back. German armor achieved success at spots along the Rubion and Drome Rivers, surrounding some American positions.

At 4 PM on August 25, Germans troops from the 198th Division were reported to have infiltrated 1st platoon of Company C's positions in Bonlieu. The enemy, supported by tanks, overran the platoon, and destroyed it as a fighting unit. This breakthrough put other defenders in jeopardy. Two retreats followed with the next line of defense three hundred yards behind the town. This line lasted forty-five minutes before crumbling in the face of the German attack. Three hundred more yards fell to the attackers as the third new line of defense was organized. It was held until units from the 143rd and 142nd arrived to shore up the position. This stopped the American retreat, but the Germans had blunted the enemy ardor for pursuit.

The tenacity of the conflict at Bonlieu cost the 111th: seven men were killed, three were wounded, and twenty-five men went missing. 1st platoon of Company C reported no casualties, while Company A was pounded hard with five killed and twenty-one missing. Giving their lives defending the Bonlieu front were Charles P. Kemeny of Detroit, Michigan, Volney B. Simpson, Jr. of Eldon, Missouri, Ephraim F. Watson of Greenville, North Carolina, Joseph A. Calvari of Corona, Long Island, New York, and Louis F. Rullo of Newark, New Jersey. Also lost in action from Headquarters were George B. Butt of Fullerton, Maryland, and Norval E. Sparks of Fellows, California. Wounded, but not among the captured, were Terry Rimes of Blakely, Georgia, Frank Szczesny of Chicago, Illinois, and Malcolm Cox of Annapolis, Maryland.

On August 26, with the Americans bloodied and stalled, Wiese ordered von Wietersheim to bring the 11th Panzer Division back to Lyon. For the next three days, the Germans kept up their attacks against the 36th in the Rubion and Drome River areas to keep the Americans occupied, thus allowing the Germans to retreat.

American artillery, still in position to accurately fire on the retreating Germans, wreaked devastation. Mile after mile of Highway 7, bumper to bumper with traffic, came under fire. Because of the encounter near Montelimar, the Germans

Montelimar slaughter.

had 11,000 casualties in the battle and their 19th Army was shattered. Amid the carnage were twenty-one hundred destroyed vehicles, thousands of dead horses used in aiding the retreat, and enough artillery pieces to equip two divisions.

Once the Germans cleared out, the 36th linked up with the northern moving 3rd Division, ending any threat of a major German counterattack. The enemy now back peddled north to avoid total defeat and capture. Sixteen days into the invasion, Truscott's Seventh Army, while sustaining over twenty-seven hundred killed, wounded or missing in the fighting, captured fifty-seven thousand prisoners.

Moving eighty miles in three days, the 36th entered Lyon, a city known for its silk manufacturing as well as its historical use of the guillotine during the French Revolution. While fighting in the city continued, primarily between the Maquis seeking the necks of the Germans, the 111th Engineers came in to evaluate the situation concerning which bridges still spanned the Rhone River. To their dismay, every bridge had been blown. Still there was a bright side. As the Engineers motored in to check the bridges, they were embraced by jubilant

French citizens who showered them with gifts, drinks, and kisses. The French had shown spirit, with no loss of courage, during the enemy occupation. With renewed energy from the French welcome, the Americans exploded forward, hoping to put an end to German resistance.

A battle for Lyon never materialized as the Germans, running a gauntlet set up by the French at every street corner, withdrew from the city. The fast Allied pace continued beyond Lyon, slowed only by several hold-at-all-costs German rear guard units. A German stand near Besançon at the Doubs River, fell apart and Allies pressed on.

Yet will and determination cannot feed fuel to thirsty tanks. With each mile, German resistance became a mere nuisance, while timely arrival of needed supplies and fuel became a necessity. Logistics of getting gasoline from the beaches of the south to the battlefields in the north proved insurmountable.

Luckily, the 143rd captured a fuel dump, in the Besançon area, containing over seven hundred thousand liters of 80-90 octane gasoline. This windfall convinced the Americans that they would have the juice to press on to Germany. Fighting northward, the 143rd, never having time for a snooze, met the enemy at little known spots like Oiselay-et-Grachaux, and then at Fretigney, brushing aside small rear guards. The German retreat turned to rout.

The 143rd, with Pearce in tow, eventually pulled up short on the morning of September 11 by taking the high ground overlooking the town of Vesoul. Here, the Germans decided to turn and fight to keep the Americans out of The Fatherland. Two Battalions of the 141st stormed into Vesoul, overcame fierce German resistance, and after nine hours took the formerly beautiful town. The 142nd and 143rd pursued the enemy past Vesoul until the Germans were cleared out of the way.

One September 16, the 143rd entered their next major stop, Luxeuil, at 1:00 AM to find the city empty of German troops although heavy fighting continued for the 142nd east and then north of the city. The German retreat was coming to an end, and with their back to their precious Fatherland, the fighting now became more than desperate. It became vicious. The VI Corps countered by changing the direction of its attack and drove straight across the Vosges Mountains toward Germany. The 36th Division, without rest from its month-long dash through France, was to ford the Moselle River.

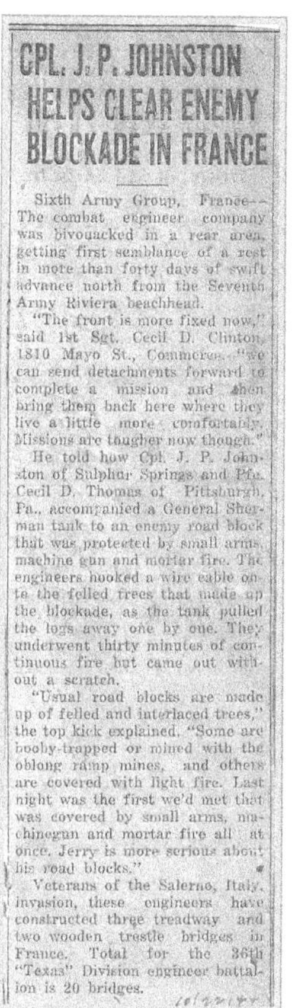

CPL. J. P. JOHNSTON HELPS CLEAR ENEMY BLOCKADE IN FRANCE

Sixth Army Group, France—The combat engineer company was bivouacked in a rear area, getting first semblance of a rest in more than forty days of swift advance north from the Seventh Army Riviera beachhead.

"The front is more fixed now," said 1st Sgt. Cecil D. Clinton, 1810 Mayo St., Commerce. "We can send detachments forward to complete a mission and then bring them back here where they live a little more comfortably. Missions are tougher now though."

He told how Cpl. J. P. Johnston of Sulphur Springs and Pfc. Cecil D. Thomas of Pittsburgh, Pa., accompanied a General Sherman tank to an enemy road block that was protected by small arms, machine gun and mortar fire. The engineers hooked a wire cable onto the felled trees that made up the blockade, as the tank pulled the logs away one by one. They underwent thirty minutes of continuous fire but came out without a scratch.

"Usual road blocks are made up of felled and interlaced trees," the top kick explained. "Some are booby-trapped or mined with the oblong ramp mines, and others are covered with light fire. Last night was the first we'd met that was covered by small arms, machinegun and mortar fire all at once. Jerry is more serious about his road blocks."

Veterans of the Salerno, Italy, invasion, these engineers have constructed three treadway and two wooden trestle bridges in France. Total for the 36th "Texas" Division engineer battalion is 20 bridges.

10/22/44

Sulphur Springs Daily News Telegram, October 22, 1944.

On September 20, on a moonless night filled with light drizzle and fog, the 141st crossed the Moselle River at a spot scarcely as wide as a baseball infield. The crossing was quiet, and they remained unopposed. Rugged terrain and trees seemingly on top of other trees allowed enemy snipers and mortar teams to harass and slow the offensive gesture. The 143rd moved up to help, and using the same firm riverbed crossing as the 141st, they struggled up the steeper far bank of the Moselle and maneuvered north to Eloyes which it took three days of close combat to capture.

A battle for Remiremont wasn't any easier as the 142nd faced determined Nazis who refused to fall back. The 142nd, under heavy bombardment, slipped gradually into the town. As if in slow motion it went yard by yard, house by house, and street by street, but by the night of September 23, Remiremont was in American hands.

The Engineers took a few causalities capturing Remiremont. German machine pistols at very close range cut down two Company B engineers as they cleared a road block a couple of miles southwest of town. On September 22, an enemy patrol opened on the exposed men, downing Paul Lupia of Ridgewood, New York (shoulder), and Alex Kuntz of Cleveland, Ohio (ear).

In a separate encounter the next day, a truck from Company B ran over a mine west of Remiremont. The ensuing tornado of shrapnel struck Lee Lassiter of Sunset, Texas, Dee Winn of Bowie, Texas, Arthur Rose Jr. of Clarkson, Michigan, and Domenic Caldereone of Ardmore, Pennsylvania. Carl McCluggage of Lawrenceburg, Tennessee, also along on the ride, suffered bruised ribs from the explosion and a jammed neck as he was ejected from the vehicle and landed helmet first in a nearby potato field.

Near the last of September, the 142nd overran Tendon as the 141st captured, on the right-hand side of the bridgehead, the town of St. Ame. The 143rd, beating off counterattacks and withstanding heavy artillery fire to the left of the front, took the town of Docelles. A new foe, the severe weather, was also becoming an issue helping the Germans to slow down American progress.

The Moselle River bridgehead was secure with the Americans controlling over twenty-five square miles across the river. Combat action in France now took a 180° turn. What had become a familiar stride for the 36th—cutting quickly here, bouncing there, and accelerating at remarkable speeds like a jackrabbit—slowed to the crawling pace more fitting of a terrapin.

Sunday 16 July '44 [3]

This morning we went down to beach and had a lecture on waterproofing charges of C-2 explosive.[4] This evening we blew several obstructions out in the water such as we might run across in invasion. Tomorrow early we go on a L.S.T.[5] for invasion practice.

Wednesday 19 July '44

Spent night on L.S.T. and slept on steel deck. Just anchored offshore. Rolled all night and felt a little sick. Came off at 6 AM and at 8 came into Company. Did nothing else the rest of day. Still don't know if we will get ducks yet. Got four bottles (12 oz.) of beer today. 10 c a bottle. Second in fifteen months.

Saturday 22 July '44

Had the evening off. Ice cream for dinner. Went to show tonight. Pretty good. We are moving back to Qualiano tomorrow. That is where we were the last time before going to Anzio. Probably go by boat to Leghorn. The invasion training was all a blind, so it seems to make Germany think we're coming.

Sunday 23 July '44

No reveille today or anything to do at all. Laid around all morning and took a bath this evening. Show tonight "Guadalcanal Diary."[6] It was a good laugh as it was not very closely related to war but just a bravo picture for the public. Things are not that way. If they are we can lick Japs ourselves.

Tuesday 25 July '44

Came thru Naples etc last night and got to area at 2 AM. Rough road and quite a drive. About 75 miles. Have done little today. Put up tent and of course the usual details of pits, etc. Walked over to show about 1/2 mile. Not too good.

Wednesday 26 July '44

Hike this AM. After breakfast I made sick call with my foot. Went to C Company 111th Medical. From there to 111th clearing station from there to 638 clearing station. Stayed there 6 hours before getting out. Went to Naples to 103rd Hospital. They gave me one metatarsal support. Got back to company by hitchhiking. 10 hours to get that! If a man was bad sick he would die before getting anywhere.

Saturday 29 July '44

Loaded our trucks today. They go on boat in few days. I am now a member of a demolition crew on a ¾ ton. We will be first Engineers ashore and probably have a rough time. More of a suicide squad. Maybe we won't hit it rough. On guard tonight from 12 to 3. Saw a show.

Friday 4 August '44

Close order drill this AM. Also a rifle inspection. Went to beach this afternoon and fired our rifles. Still killing time it seems. Played cards rest of evening. So hot and dusty around here. Practice invasion to be held soon (Monday on) but I don't think I have to go. Will be glad when we get the real thing over. This routine is demoralizing.

Monday 7 August '44

Going to load on ship. I am with one of the trucks as assistant driver. Packed my bag and took down tent and got ready to leave with truck. Left area at 1 o'clock and went over to assembly area, about 1/2 mile from here. Staying here until 2:30 tomorrow evening. The usual way of the army. I go back to Company for meals.

Tuesday 8 August '44

Went back to Company this morning and stayed till noon. Played cards all morning. This evening we finally left and came into staging area known as Dallas. In the edge of Naples about where we were before loading to go to Anzio. We load probably on the 10th! Fully believe France is our destination and I don't like it.

Wednesday 9 August '44

Stayed in this area all morning and most of evening. Terribly hot and no shade. Left here about 4 PM. In a big hurry and came about 1/2 mile to Texas area where we are now sitting. Might load tonight they say. We load on L.S.T. 994 and are 31st vehicle off. No place to sleep as ground is oiled and damn little to eat!

Thursday 10 August '44

Still in this hot hell hole. No water close and living on "C" rations. We still have not loaded but probably will sometimes tonight. The dope I got today is that we will hit France along where Italy & France join about the 16th. Don't expect too much resistance for several days. 141st takes one flank 142nd the other and 143rd the center. Biggest operation yet.

Friday 11 August '44

Loaded on boat at 10 last night. Didn't leave dock until this morning and then we moved out into harbor just opposite Vesuvius. Got a bunk but it is sure hot down below.[7] The rest of the Company is on some other boat.

Saturday 12 August '44

Pulled out at 3:30 PM and are proceeding up coast of Italy. The rumors are we hit Tuesday morning. There are 75 gun emplacements to be knocked out. Which our Air Corp will do before we go in. There are several hundred ships in this group and will be joined by more.[8] Guess I've seen my last of Italy.

Sunday 13 August '44

As near as I can tell we are going north, northwest. No sign of land but quite a long convoy can be dimly seen in our rear. We are heading this as far as I can tell. As yet we have been told nothing. Foote and I have no orders and no one with us so guess we'll do as we see fit.

Monday 14 August '44

Passed Corsica this AM. All is explained. We hit (36th) beach close to where France & Italy join. 45th on our left & 3rd hits close to Toulon. Navy & Air Corp start blasting at daylight and first wave hits at 8 AM. As for where I will get off I don't know. First daylight invasion we have ever pulled.

Tuesday 15 August 44

Got up before dawn at 6 AM. Navy opened up on beaches. At 6:30 the bombers came in. No German planes showed up all day. This boat is manned by green horns and kids and don't know what to do so we have cruised around all day and nearly had a bad collision about dark. One German plane over at dark. Very quiet.[9]

Wednesday 16 August '44

After going into shore and backing out a few times we finally landed at 1:00 PM in 45th Division area and found we couldn't get to 36th Division area as bridge over River is gone. We have a French house where old lady speaks English and after having given her various items we are fairly well fixed for night.

Thursday 17 August '44

Waited all day before bridges finished and finally got to Company just before dark about fifteen miles inland. Gliders all over this area where troops landed.[10] Most them torn up but very few men hurt. Trees and poles German set up cut wings etc. off in landing. Beautiful country and nice people. We are still advancing.[11]

Friday 18 August '44

As we are doing nothing I will add a few details. I saw one L.S.T.[12] hit by bomb & burn with quite a few causalities. We had two men shot. Sergeant Jeter of Greenville [Aubrey Jeter] shot twice and a boy from 3rd platoon. Both will make it. We are bivouacked by a beautiful house with nice flower garden with gravel walks etc. German planes over about dark. Bombers.

Saturday 19 August '44

Did nothing this AM. On guard last night 2 to 4 AM. Moved about three miles today to another house. German Headquarters. One dead German Colonel here. People took all wine etc. and hid it and officers won't let us take a thing but they have quarters inside. I took a bottle anyhow. Everything quiet. Partisans roaming everywhere. Leaving August 18, a specially created armored Task Force.[13]

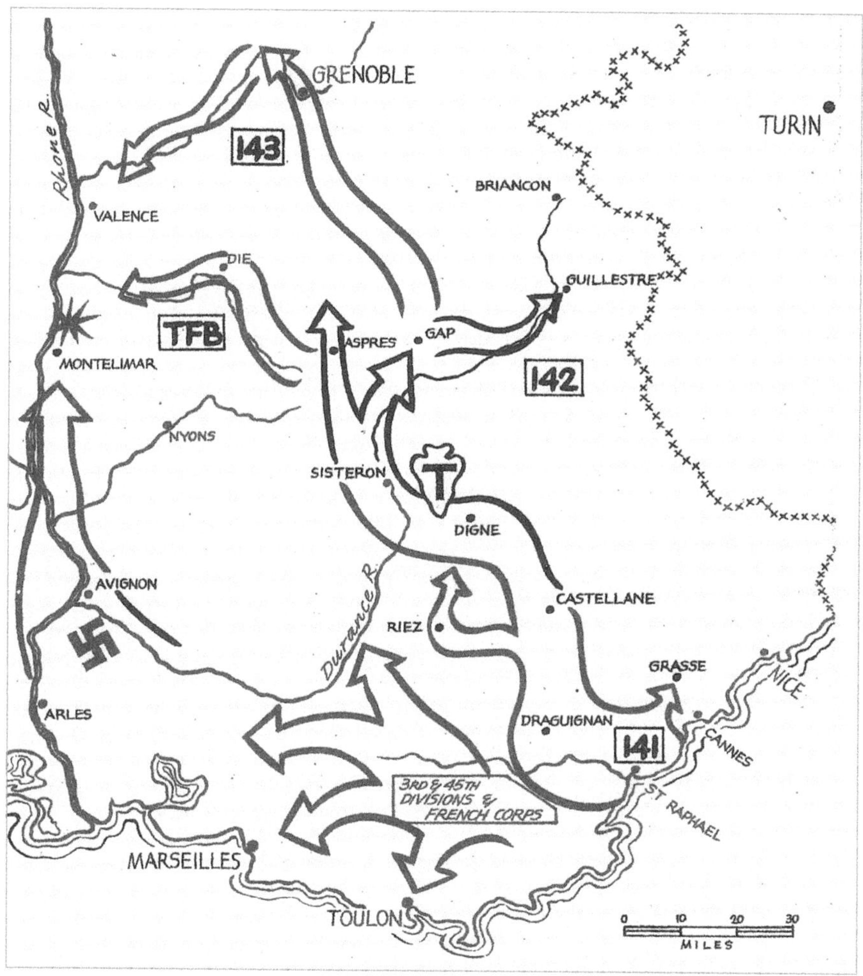

Allied forces, aided by French partisans, cleared the region between the Rhone River and the Italian border of enemy forces and opened the road north into the heart of France.

Sunday 20 August '44

Started moving north and came about eighty miles. Thru mountains on narrow roads. A few German vehicles scattered along a few miles inland. We came thru a few towns and on the Verdon river we stopped to fix railroad bridge for traffic as all others are blown by partisans to stop Germans. Close to Sisteron.[14]

Monday 21 August '44

Tooled around all day while Lieutenant tried to figure out how to do job. Do a little and tear it up. Will listen to no one. So we putter around all day and at night we start and work till 12:30 and still do very little good. Heavy traffic moving up all day. French Indo Chinese troops stationed here.

Tuesday 22 August '44

Finished flooring bridge about dark. Two days & nights for a job we could have done in five hours. It is the Army! People very nice and happy to see us. [at Sisteron] They said the Germans shot three before leaving. All work in an aluminum plant by river. They have plenty of vegetables but little else. Had a good shower today (bath).

Wednesday 23 August '44

We were gotten up at 2:30 AM and drove till 8 AM and stopped after contacting Company and then drove some more and are now close to Rhone river by Marsanne.[15] We are at least hundred miles inland. The 11th Panzer Division is opposing us on the river. We are now Infantry reserves. On guard tonight.

Thursday 24 August '44

About 11 o'clock last night while on guard the Germans shelled this area. Hit mighty close and we had to scatter. Then they shelled about day. We had no holes handy so sure were pretty bad scared. We are merely waiting for anything. No work. Am going up to Frenchman home late this evening. Trade chocolate for eggs.

Friday 25 August '44 to Monday 28 August '44

It has been four days since I had a chance to write in this so will have to sum it up as I can.

Yesterday evening the Corporal came to house & got us and we went to the front to plug up a hole. 1st platoon of "C" Company, part of "A" Company & Headquarters Company. Got set up by 3 AM in a very bad spot. No field of fire. At about 2:30 PM the Germans hit us with everything they had. About two Divisions of them being pushed in at us and the only way out was thru us. They cut us to pieces and infiltrated all thru us with tanks & Infantry. They used mortars, rifle grenades & artillery. The assault force had machine pistols & machine guns. Our Lieutenant (Woznicki) ran off immediately and we were left with no command or contact.

About 7 PM (Friday) fourteen others & I attempted to get out as we were practically surrounded on all sides and could not fight on account of woods etc. We retreated up a road to left flank leaving our machine gun.[16] We ran a gauntlet of 20 mm cannon fire & machine gun fire etc. How we got thru can never be said.[17] We finally contacted the 142nd Infantry and fought with them for a night & day. And pulled out on the night of Saturday after being under constant mortar and artillery fire all the time. The name of the little town we were around was Von Lou. [Bonlieu]

Tuesday 29 August '44

We were just behind the lines ready to go in again Sunday night in case they broke thru but 3rd Division came up on left flank & relieved pressure, so we came back to bivouac area last night. Latest count is 42 missing. Our Company lost none. Lucky us. Spending tonight in Crest. Sleeping in basement of building.

Wednesday 30 August '44

Left Crest about 8 AM and are following the 141st Infantry as reserves. The Germans came into Romans-sur-Isere and burned it & killed 500 French partisans, so they say. Our Infantry attacked this morning and we are pushing on. We (Engineers) are going into Romans tonight as it has fallen. Our planes giving them & us a fit. Can't be helped.

Jarrel Julian.

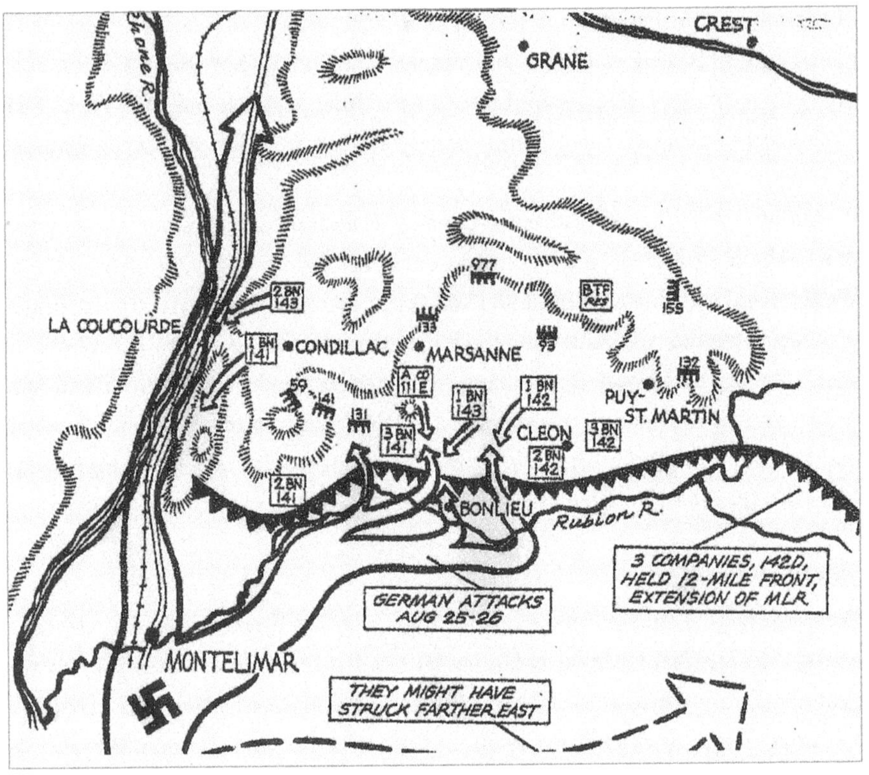

Even though retreating, the German forces continued to be deadly and could inflict serious damage to the pursuing American forces.

Thursday 31 August '44

Rained last night quite a bit. Nothing stirring. The town of Romans was shot up quite a lot with small arms. Quite a few buildings burned. Also lots of cars. Moved on about twenty miles and bivouacked by a blown out bridge. Built bypass fairly quick.

Friday 1 September '44

Moved out early this morning. Moved about fifty miles. I'd say we're within fifteen miles of Lyons. Gun fire can be heard plainly. Stopped in Beaurepaire several hours and people all very nice and handed over wine. The roads are full of partisans (Marquis). They all help us even in work.

Saturday 2 September '44

Rained hard all day. We advanced along road to Lyons and was in sight of it once. Out in front of our troops and didn't know it. Nearly got fired on. Am now in some little town about 8 miles from Lyons. Spending night in a building. Moved lots of roadblocks made by piling wagons, cars etc up. Also some mines.

Sunday 3 September '44

Beautiful day. At about 3 PM we went into Lyons. The streets were jammed by people waving, cheering, shaking hands and kissing us. Girls climbed all over truck. Got three glasses of beer!! All 23 bridges over Rhone (center of Lyon) blown. Railroad bridge least damaged so we are removing tracks in order to make road.

Monday 4 September '44

Worked all night at bridge.[18] 344th Engineers relieved us today. At 12 O'clock we left Lyons amid cheers etc. Came north about seventy miles by round about way. Right on point so had to stop several times to let Infantry pass us. We are somewhere a little north of Macon. Last little town had a rose arbor with welcome sign over street.

Tuesday 5 September '44

Passed thru Bourg-en-Bresse yesterday which is not far from Switzerland. Pulled out early this AM and stopped to fix a bridge over a tank ditch the partisans dug. People came out with eggs, fruit, hot milk, bread etc and even helped us work. We traveled on up close to Sens-sur-Seille and bivouacked. We are preparing for a long drive. Sens is not the one 3rd Army took.

Wednesday 6 September '44

Have driven about 25 miles today. Don't know exactly where we are. Bivouacked about noon. This PM we went down to a stream and washed our clothes and bathed. I have never been so filthy. As soon as Division is motorized we are going 200 miles and close a trap at Belfort on 200,000 Germans in Southwestern France. Join up with Third army. Maybe really rough.

Soldiers of the 36th Division received a hero welcome in French towns like Bourg, *top photo*, and Gap, *bottom photo*.

Thursday 7 September '44

Suppose to pull out at 7:30 AM but didn't. Started raining about 6 AM and poured till noon. Of course I got soaked. Just sat in truck all morning and it was a cramped place. Built fire and dried out. Got spark in my eye and it gave me a fit the rest of the day.[19]

Friday 8 September '44

Got up at 3 AM and pulled out. At 7:30 we reached Besancon. We were right on point and at the outer edge we drew machine pistol fire, so everything halted. Last Germans cleared this town at 6 AM so the people said. Ten Divisions-nine Infantry & one panzer. Battle going on all day at edge of town. People walk around as if nothing is happening. Germans making a stand.

Saturday 9 September '44

Stayed in a house last night on a bed. Sleep fairly good. Did nothing today. Have rheumatism or something in my back. Must be getting old. They say the Germans are digging in twelve miles from here. We are 75 miles from Germany now.

Sunday 10 September '44

Slept in same place. Got up early to pull out but our truck was gone hauling lumber. We finally pulled out around 3 PM and went 12 miles. Ate supper and are fixing to pull out again with 143rd Infantry task force which is advancing on a town fifteen miles from here.

Monday 11 September '44

Moved up all night. Fighting on all sides. Convoy move hundred yards & stop for thirty minutes. About 8 this morning we pulled off road and ate. Gun fire all around. Stayed in this place all day. One of our planes knocked out one of our own trucks this AM. Hell of a mix up. Picked up two Germans in civilian clothes. One a Lieutenant.[20]

Tuesday 12 September '44

Moved about four miles into a little town for the night to be handy in case Infantry needed us. I was on guard. Artillery roaring overhead and some planes flying low. Don't know who's but nothing dropped. Moved back to other bivouac today to be with Company. Kitchen has just arrived.

Wednesday 13 September '44

Late yesterday we pulled out to be part of a task force moving up but only went a short way and pulled off in field and spent night. This AM we pulled out and stopped again in heavy woods. We don't know what goes on but we are always a short way from gun fire. Now in some little town in schoolhouse. Raining.

Thursday 14 September '44

Left town early and were following a task force. Same thing. Move a little set an hour. 20 mm fired on us once from quite some distance. Bivouacked on side of hill. Two platoons of Jerries spotted just across valley. Battle raging from about 6:30 on into night. On guard tonight. Rained all day. Five dead Jerries on road here.

Friday 15 September '44

Same old go. Move up a little & set awhile. Finally stopped in a field. Quite a battle going on in valley below us. We catch small pockets of Germans and Infantry clears them up. About 11 tonight had to get up to move and didn't. 2nd and 3rd platoon walking up with Infantry. We are now about 25 miles north of Vesoul.

Saturday 16 September '44

Got up at 3 AM and moved up close to a small town of St. Maria to build a bridge.[21] Very foggy & dark and Infantry had only a short while before passed here. Had a battle at bridge. Three boys lying on road. Machine gun got them. Rained all PM after going back to be traffic guard on bridge. I am now in a building in Luxeuil. 60 miles north of Besancon.

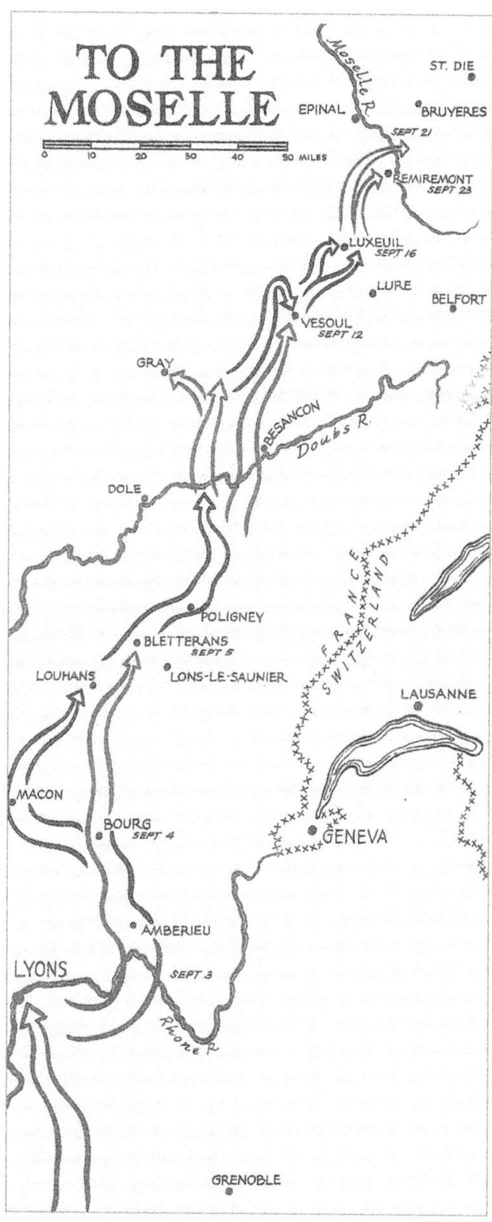

German resistance collapsed in the south of France and the Allied Forces linked up on the Moselle River.

Sunday 17 September '44

Laid around all day. Had hot cakes for breakfast. First cooking the cooks have done since Italy. Rained all day. We are out on edge of town and in buildings. I have my bed in hay loft which is always built on house. People don't seem to mind too much as some sleep in house. Front is not too far away.

Monday 18 September '44

Expected to move last night but now we are told we will be here several days for a rest. Had a rifle inspection this evening. All put in 40c each and cook bought steak so had steak supper. Things are really high over here. Time was set back 1 hour yesterday. Rumored we go to U.S. Oct 6!!

Tuesday 19 September '44

Nothing to do today so have played cards etc. all day. It is rumored that all men who made Salerno invasion will be sent home next month. Boy that's too good to believe. The other day I saw the people clip three women's head for consorting with Germans, put red streaks on scalp, swastika on cheek and haul around in cart.

Wednesday 20 September '44

Did nothing this AM. This evening we went to Headquarters Company and loaded four trucks with assault boats & also went to 36th Engineers & got some more. Then carried them to A Company up close to Moselle River. Company moved up there while we were gone. Infantry will cross river tonight. We came back to same old area as our stuff was here. Spending night. Cooked in house on stove.

Disgraced women of France.

Thursday 21 September '44

Got up early and loaded truck and moved to other area. Infantry crossed river in places with no opposition. Did nothing after getting to area. Tonight I went back to Luxeuil with truck to pick up bridge equipment. Got in about 1 o'clock. Have heard one of the men wounded on the landing died. Name of Conrad. Jeters sent back to States by plane and is in Florida.

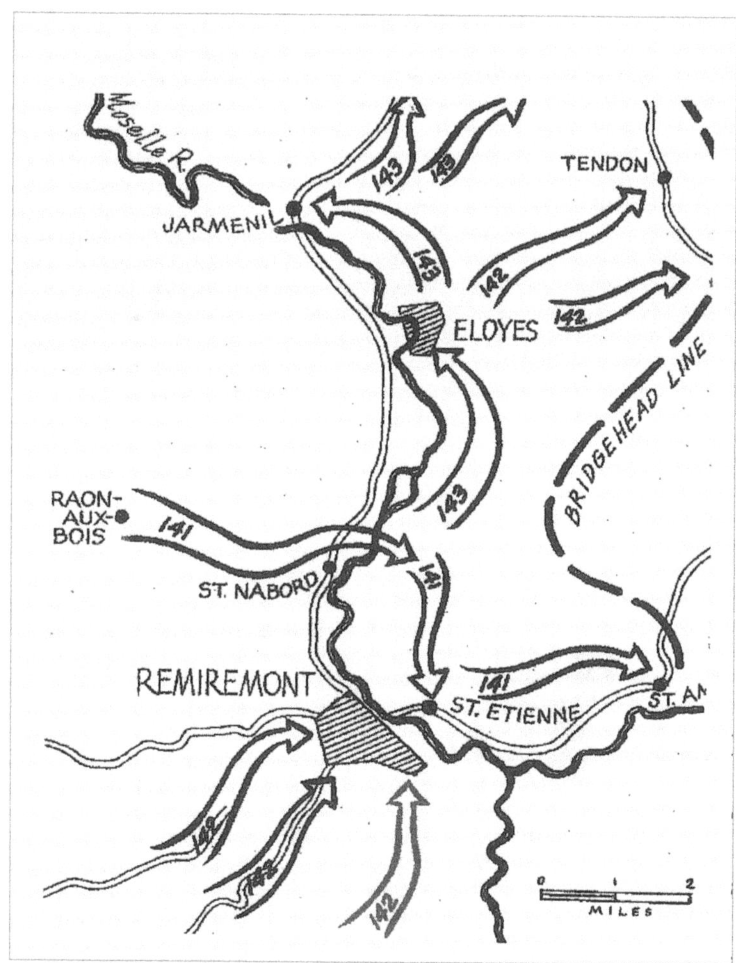

The 36th Division crossed the Moselle River at Remiremont against still opposition before pressing into the Vosges Mountains.

The Moselle Bridehead crossing.

Friday 22 September '44

Did nothing this morning. Pretty day. This evening we went to gravel pit and started the old routine of loading trucks. Worked till dark and came in for supper and went back but as usual about 10 o'clock orders changed so we came back in.

Saturday 23 September '44

Bright and early we went back to pit and started working. Raining hard all day. Later we moved down close to river and got gravel off of railroad track. Sure a mess, raining all time and we all were wet. Got relieved about 10 o'clock PM and came back to area.

Sunday 24 September '44

Truck in shop so we did nothing this morning. After dinner we loaded up equipment and took out. Still raining. Came on up nearly to front and are bivouacked in a card board factory. Quite a lot of shells falling around here. We must be getting close to Germany.

Monday 25 September '44

Had to get up at 1 last night and go out to guard a bridge [Moselle] so Germans wouldn't slip up and blow it. I went out as out post with Brodbeck. Very dark and disagreeable. Feet nearly froze. Few shells hit close. Relieved at 7 this AM. Slept all day. On guard tonight-8 to 12.

Tuesday 26 September '44

Rained all night and raining off & on today. Haven't seen sun in several days. Did nothing this AM. This evening had to go up a ways and blow some mines. Late this evening went out on mine sweeping detail.[22] We went up past Infantry out post to a road block but Germans were there so we withdrew.

Wednesday 27 September '44

Have done nothing today. That deal last night is what gets a guy's goat. Told us we wouldn't need rifles and then we go past our lines 500 yards and run into some Jerries but luckily they didn't hear us so we got out O.K. Shells falling all around this factory last night. Big stuff & air burst. We are about ten miles north of Remiremont.

Thursday 28 September '44

Put up a shower this morning behind factory as a good stream runs by here. Have done nothing this evening. Some big shells hit all around the building this afternoon. Getting colder every night. Didn't rain today. Very foggy and cold tonight.

Friday 29 September '44

Went up to a large woods and started making a road thru it on old trail. An immense woods and of course we don't know what is in it as our Infantry is going thru tonight. Spread gravel till dark and then went and picked up our stuff and moved up to town of Charmois. Small place.

Saturday 30 September '44

At 9:30 last night had to go back to woods. Got there and as usual no one knew the score. We stood around till 1 o'clock freezing and then started walking thru woods. Got lost and contacted German out post but got out O.K. Finally found Lieutenant and walked behind jeep till 4 AM and then we all were lost. Got back after daylight. Worked some today. Damn mess.

Sunday 1 October '44

Worked till 2 PM on road in woods in rain. Came in and moved to Docelles a small town. Am in a hose weaving shop on 2nd floor. Start eating in kitchen tomorrow. Have to get up at 5:30 in order to eat. Few planes over this AM.

11 UNCARING METAL

"Germans threw in 3 mortar shells & 3rd one hit on road about 10 ft. from me."

The Vosges are a range of mountains in France running along the west side of the Rhine Valley in a north/northeast direction for approximately 150 miles. In these supposedly impenetrable mountains, the Germans stopped and turned to fight in a last-ditch effort to stall the Allies. Their cause might seem hopeless to many, but the Germans still possessed the ability to deal the iron fist of death to those trying to enter their country. On what would become an almost forgotten front of the war, they did just that.

With no rest since the invasion, the bruised and pierced 36th, just like their vehicles, existed on fumes. The old men in the division had witnessed it all. Now, near the end of this war, they would once again see death; and like in Italy, a slow advance through cold, wet, miserable weather against well-defended positions.

Elaborate German roadblocks mixing mines, entire trees entangled together, and artillery coverage produced untimely stops. These were not makeshift obstructions left by a fleeing enemy, but well-designed anti-vehicle exclosures.

Just one example of these was located one-and-a-half miles southeast of Tendon. Self- propelled guns,[1] furiously defending an abatis roadblock[2] several hundred yards in length, created an eleven day hold up. From late September until mid-October these guns stopped double digit attempts to push the obstacles to the side of the road. The guns' bright orange flashes delayed the engineer's work progress plus eliminated a tank sent to guard them. Adding to the wreckage at the abatis were two disabled tank dozers.[3] The first ignited a mine hidden among the interlocked trees and a second was hit by the shell of a self-propelled gun. Luckily, only two engineers, Benjamin Fennell of Decatur, Texas, and Richard Halley of Indianapolis, Indiana, were scarred during all of this.

Company B's 2nd platoon, after multiple attempts, finally succeeded on October 11 in removing the remaining blockage. The price? Two more men, Samuel Howard Jr. of Pawtucket, Rhode Island, and George Altschul of New York, New York, got as their reward for hard work, a dose of German shrapnel.

The American offensive attack began on October 15 to capture the town of Bruyeres. Laval, a small town outside Bruyeres, fell to the 143rd on the first day and Champ de Luc capitulated to the same force the next. Bruyeres, on October 18, was captured in a dual attack by the 143rd and the 442nd, a Japanese-American

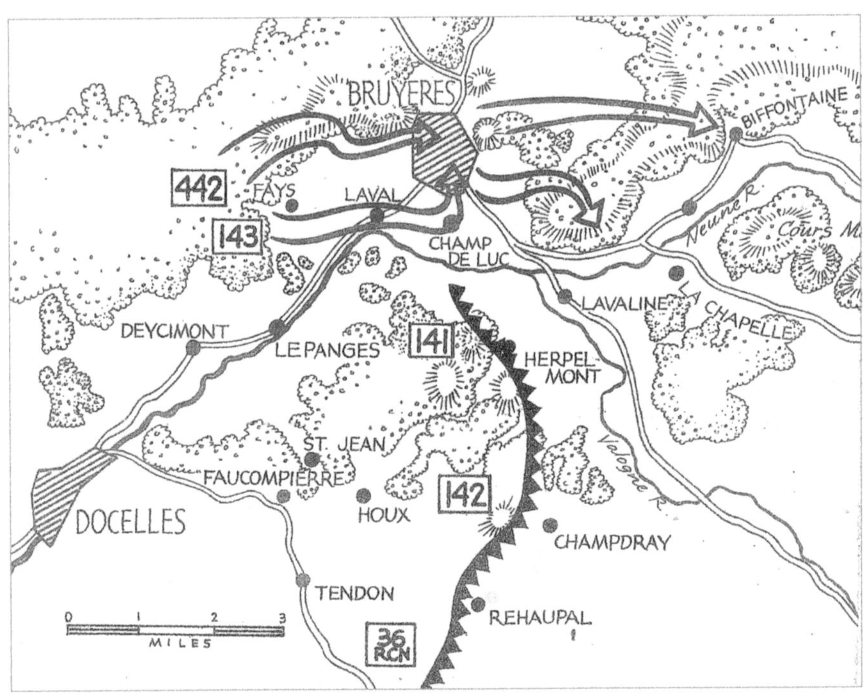

The advance through the valleys and ridges of the Vosges Mountains was a deadly grind in increasingly bad weather.

regiment, which recently joined the 36th. The town, now just a pile of scattered roof tiles, bricks, and rocks, was secured but under the threat of German artillery fire.

1st Platoon of Company B, on October 19, was left numb with shock from a hard blow when four men were killed and five wounded in a minefield explosion about a half mile east of Bruyeres. While part of the platoon cleared out a minefield, containing German R-M-43 mines,[4] the rest moved to secure the area. Turned back by a hail of machine gun fire, they were forced to return to the crew working the minefield. Nearing the minefield, someone detonated a mine that resulted in various others discharging.

On this barren spot of earth, James E. Dyer of Lafayette, Tennessee, and George M. MacLaine were instantly obliterated by the detonation. Although being helped by medical teams, James P. Maher of Elizabeth, New Jersey, and Thomas Cooney added their names to the death toll.

The havoc caused by the butchering blast also hurt Milton Fondberg of Detroit, Michigan, Leonard Halpern from Queens, New York, Martin Nunberg of Brooklyn, New York, Oliver Bowland of McDonald, Kansas, and Gerald Bullis of Niagara Falls, New York.

Not only did the Germans have plenty of artillery, but their variety of weapons and craft for killing and maiming kept the engineers nimble on their feet. In a seventy-two-hour period, the Germans violently added notches for Fritz Johanson of New York, New York (small arms fire), Thomas Corwin of Utica, New York (artillery), Frank Santacroce of Sag Harbor, New York (artillery), Thomas Baker of Victoria, Texas (artillery) and Clinton Hall of Raeford, North Carolina (S-mine) among those savagely injured by war.

One mile north of Biffontaine, on October 24, several not-so-agile men of Company A were riddled by a blast. Millard Earman of Falls Church, Virginia, David Johnston of Olivet, Michigan, and Lester Shaw of Springfield, Ohio, all

Left: Harry Oesterlen. *Right*: Arthur Truman.

received head wounds from an enemy volley. Albert Chambliss of Clovis, New Mexico, suffered a concussion caused by the pointblank firing of enemy tanks.

On a beleaguered October 30, Company B suffered again, in another mine explosion, as Harry U. Oesterlen of Philadelphia, Pennsylvania, and Arthur Truman were killed in action. Truman, stepping on a S mine in a field south of Laval, ignited the mine that devoured Oesterlen and injured both Joseph Dlugos of Bath, Pennsylvania, and Robert Findlay. France was becoming deadlier each day for the hard-working engineers.

Allied officers did not want to give the enemy time to prepare well-fortified positions in the easily defendable mountains. Reconnaissance parties, looking to keep continued pressure on the Germans, scattered across the forest of the Vosges, searching for the easiest path the infantry could use to attack.

With an objective of taking the high ground overlooking La Houssiere, 1st Battalion of the 141st, on October 24, started its move into the mountain forest by following a cart track as deep as possible. The rarely-used passage then changed

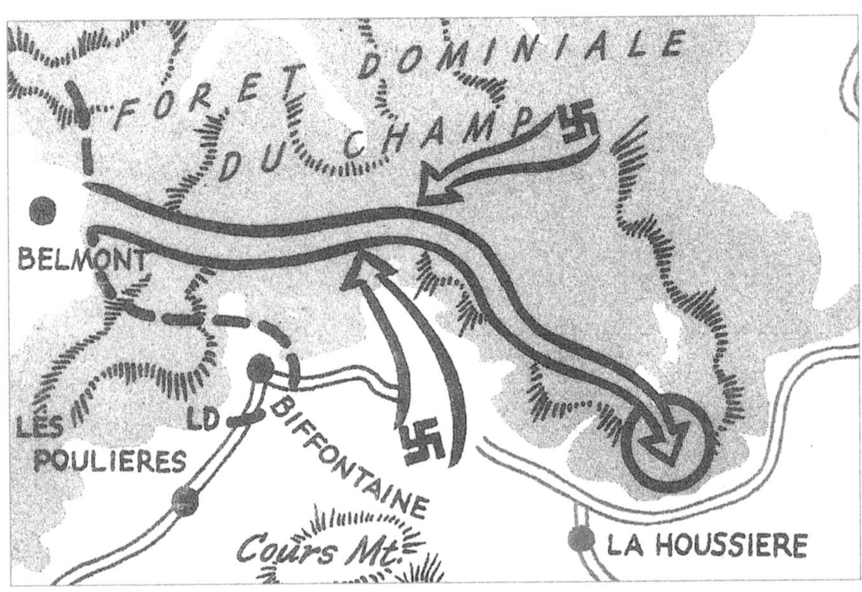

The fighting around Bruyeres and the rescue of the "lost battalion" of the 36th Division became the stuff of legends.

direction away from their objective, forcing the battalion to continue on a smaller trail. The path, only a few feet wide, twisted like an excited snake through the heavily wooded forest, further slowing the advance.

As the Americans struggled on, the Germans, despite a lack of mobility in the overgrown forest, launched a massive counterattack. The unexpected force of the blow split the 141st, with several companies from the 1st Battalion being surrounded. Repeated attempts by the rest of the 141st to break through and free the desperate soldiers failed. For the next week, with very limited supplies, the trapped men, known as the "Lost Battalion", were under constant fire and bombardment.

The Lost Battalion, fighting off certain extermination from exposure, heavy bombardment by Nazi artillery, and brutal infantry attacks, held on for seven days with little food, water, or ammunition. On October 30, the 442nd broke through on Hill 679 and rescued 211 surviving soldiers.

Rescue of the Lost Battalion was due in large part to the building of a mountain road, plus over 125 miles of existing roads maintained by the 111th Engineers. The 111th, with the 232nd Engineers Combat Company attached, spent their time

A section of the road the Engineers built to save the "Lost Battalion." (Petrie)

constructing a seven-and-a-half-mile mountain road through the dense forest of the Vosges Mountains. The road wound from the valley onto the mountain located northeast of Belmont-sur-Buttant. As the engineers continued to improve the new soggy, disintegrating road, it became frighteningly clear that the ground was unstable for walking across, much less driving over. Still the work went on.

Rain, teaming up with the tank traffic, made life hell for the shovel digging, rock carrying, wood laying engineers. As quickly as a spot was repaired, it was destroyed by troop and tank movement over it. What didn't drop from sight was forced up between ruts from the tanks and damaged smaller vehicles traveling over it. At exasperating times, it seemed the road was as deep in mud as it was wide.

When the Lost Battalion was rescued, the engineers' much traveled mountain road was under heavy use by four infantry regiments, three companies of tanks, and numerous other personnel. Under miserable weather conditions and constant handicap of German fire, the mission was accomplished. Much like the road over Monte Artemisio in Italy, the engineers showed true grit, proving nothing was impossible for them.

The 142nd, on November 5, continued the 36th offensive slowly steering their way down and through the heavily wooded Les-Rouges-Eaux Valley. Within the week, the Germans gave up the villages of La Houssiere, Vienville and Corcieux.

All the surrounding woods, heavily covered with mines and booby traps, continued to maim individuals and slow the troops' progress. 1st Platoon of Company C, working at Biffontaine around 2 o'clock in the afternoon, suffered multiple injures when Joseph Nines of Philadelphia, Pennsylvania, stepped on an S mine sending a mixture of big and little pieces of devilish metal into those around him. In addition to Nines, Bryson Hayden of Tyler, Texas, Lind Salmela of Menahga, Minnesota, Andrew Cromarty of Sedro Woolley, Washington, Eugene E. McDonald, Gilmer Ellis and medic Marvin Braune of Gonzales, Texas, were caught in the explosion.

Patrols from the 143rd, on the morning of the twentieth, traversed the Meurthe River at St. Leonard and Anould to test German resistance. When the troops learned it was not heavily defended, a new plan for the 36th was developed. Once the 143rd established a firm bridgehead on the far side of the Meurthe, the entire Division was ordered to veer and attack the St. Marie Pass.

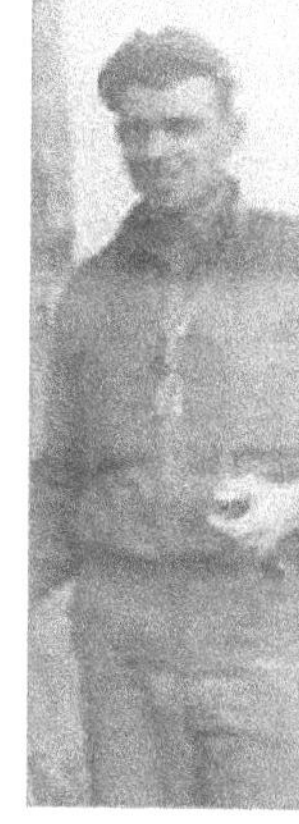

Left: Kenneth Hand. *Middle*: D. B. Mainord. *Right*: Joe Warren.

There was never any hesitation by the Germans when a target came into range. Since there was no time for allowing cautious probing forward by the 36th, the savagery inflicted on the soldiers rarely tapered off.

In three separate incidents, the red stained soil indicated Company C's undesirable situation. D. B. Mainord, while slashing a pick into the ground of a presumably clear area, struck a S mine whose fury abruptly sent ball bearing into his right leg and into the chest, head, groin and legs of Joe D. Warren of Celeste, Texas, seriously injuring each. Kenneth Brodbeck of Ottawa Lake, Michigan, was torn apart while removing an R-M-43 mine close to Anould, with Steve Sinchak wounded in the same explosion. Near Le Souche, another of the deplorable, yet seemingly limitless hidden Schu mines detonated resulting in the serious leg injury to Kenneth Hand.

Clearly there were still cliques of Germans holding out on both sides of the river. One such group rained jagged chunks of metal down on Pearce as he and the engineers cleared mines from the streets and buildings of a burned out Anould. The flicker of a machine gun's bullets reinforced just how close the pockets of enemy were.

The mortar fire and subsequent stream of flesh-tearing steel put three men out of action. Anthony Vesce of Bronx, New York, Robert J. Sleator, and Pearce were each abused by the fierceness of the exploding shells. Their first stop was

Anthony Vesce.

the nearest battalion aid station. Here wounded men received morphine, had their wounds dusted with sulfa powder and dressed in sulfa-saturated bandages. Plasma, due to loss of blood, was critical, and tetanus shots were given to reinforce previous shots. Doctors at the aid station then made a decision on the ultimate destination of the injured soldiers—a field hospital or a clearing station.

Field hospitals, most operating in stretcher carrying distance of the division aid stations, were prepared to house forty-five to sixty severely wounded patients. These hospitals were designed to accommodate soldiers with life threatening wounds such as massive hemorrhages, multiple fractures, amputations or need of immediate transfusions.

The next step for a less injured soldier deemed well enough to travel was the evacuation hospital where surgeons, working in shifts of twelve to sixteen hours, waited. After a quick examination, indicating Pearce could handle transport, he was sent to a clearing station and on to the evacuation hospital. Seven hours after being bit by the German mortars, Pearce was at the evacuation hospital in Epinal. Here more plasma was administered, and penicillin was injected to prevent infection. After doing what was medically feasible over the course of a couple of days, Pearce was sent to the rear. His new home would be the 21st General Hospital in Mirecourt.

On November 21, disdaining a river swelled by rain, the 143rd attacked. All three of its battalions, mastering the waters of the Meurthe, started from St. Leonard or near the small town of Anould and began the job of amassing as much ground as possible. The excellence of the Division was clear to all, as they shoved onward against a foe suddenly realizing the tenseness of the situation. Throwing more forces into the battle, the Germans hoped to halt the American juggernaut.

On the twenty-second, the 141st sent two battalions across the river to clean up opposition on the right flank of the 143rd. While the 143rd remained on the attack, the 141st secured the flank and maintained contact with the First French Army on their right.

Also, on the on the twenty-third, the 1st Battalion of the 142nd plus Company B's 1st platoon (which had been held in reserve) started forward over a road that wormed through the mountains and in several places narrowed to postage stamp size. The Germans made a stand at Haute Mandray to stop the Americans, but this was one encroachment not to be halted. Haute Mandray fell, and over the next two days the 1st Battalion took LaCroix-Aux-Mine and Wisembach, the last town below the seemingly impregnable St. Marie Pass. That same night the rest of the 142nd moved up to Ban de Laveline.

The St. Marie Pass, at over twenty-five hundred feet altitude, was a gateway from the heights of the Vosges Mountains to the flat, fertile Rhine river valley. On the cold, foggy morning of November 25, Company L from the 3rd Battalion of the 142nd moved up towards the pass jabbing slowly forward. Their mission was to engage Germans positions, indicating a full participation of the Battalion, and occupy enemy attention.

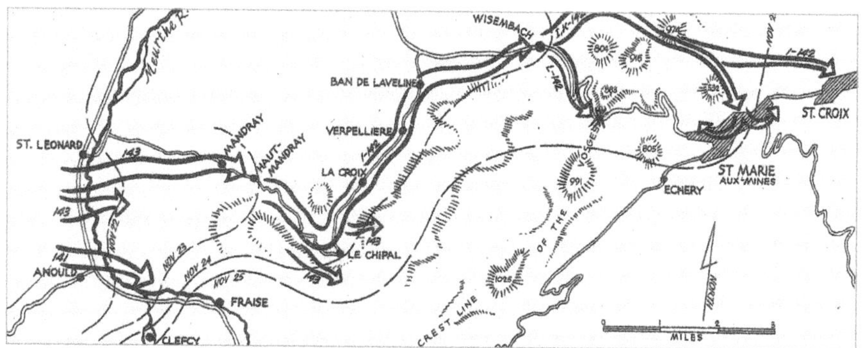

The push up the valleys of the Vosges Mountains continued to take a toll on the 36th Division.

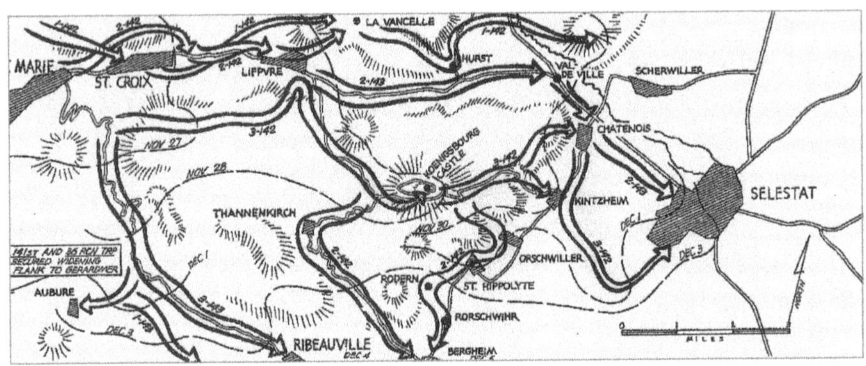

The important city of Selestat was key to the Alsatian Plains and the Germans fought hard to keep it. Pearce became an early casualty during the advance toward this objective.

While this was taking place, the rest of the 3rd Battalion circled two miles northeast of Company L hoping to surprise and penetrate German fortifications near the town of St. Marie aux Mines. After four hours of working through the wooded area, the Battalion got behind the German lines. While they may have toiled up the mountain with all the grace of an overweight offensive tackle, the descent into St. Marie aux Mines was as swift and smooth as a halfback. The Krauts were stunned when the Americans roared into the backside of the town. St. Marie aux Mines and its startled defenders were decisively overrun and taken out of the war by late afternoon.

The unexpected fall of St. Marie aux Mines and the daring resolution of the forces slowly moving straight up to the pass demoralized the Germans. Company L, aided by heavy artillery fire, took the pass and early on the twenty-sixth opened it to traffic. It was a headliner. The toughest assignment, control of the St. Marie Pass, was victorious and 3rd Battalion did it.

Over the next few days, the 142nd achieved much more. In two days of fighting, they took St. Croix and then liberated Liepvre. Despite fierce combat and heavy German shelling, the engineers would suffer only one loss of life in November. After the sunrise following Pearce's bandaged removal from Anould, Company A was tumbled when Walter L. Baker of Newaygo, Michigan, during a mine sweep between Anould and Clefoy, stepped on a Schu mine and lost his leg.

Amid the same chaos, Lawrence Turner of Howell, Michigan, to a much lesser extent, was also hit. Schu mines, sending a terror-stricken feeling through the engineers of 2nd platoon of Company A, claimed another man. On November 23, George W. Smith of Petersham, Massachusetts, lost his right foot when setting off one of these ungodly hounds of Hades.

Even the Commanding Officer of the 111th Engineers was wounded. After a reconnaissance mission with Company B, Oran Stovall returned to the command post near Ban de Laveline to decipher the acquired information. A German shell found its mark crashing into the building containing Stovall, 142nd S-2 Clifford J. Clyburn of Big Spring, Texas, and Stovall's jeep driver, Rolland A. Allen of Groves, Texas. Stovall and Allen were injured in the attack that killed Clyburn.

Company C was afflicted with only two casualties. Clarence Smith, Jr. of Willis, Michigan, and Luther Matlock were both struck on November 27. An explosion of the feared Schu mine injured Matlock while Smith was subjected to shrapnel from an exploding shell.

By November 30, with the 143rd taking Val de Ville at the mouth of the pass, the 36th Division achieved their goal of moving through the Vosges Mountains and into the Alsace plains. In the north, American forces took Strasbourg, while in the south the French cleared the Belfort Gap.

Disaster blurred the air for Company B, as November turned into December, when an enemy round crushed a truck carrying troops. After a mine sweep, the men were moving to a new location when Satan swept in. The breath was punched out of the soldiers as Ernest Vanier of Cohoes, New York, was instantly killed. Wounded men, in the shattered remains of the inoperable vehicle, were Edwin W. Newmann of Caloma, Michigan, Thomas Frost of Baltimore, Maryland, Kenneth Engelhardt of Hastings, Nebraska, and Joseph Friday of Tyler, Pennsylvania.

On December 2, the 3rd Battalion of the 142nd was called on to help clear the city of Selestat. By the end of the next day, with support from the 2nd Battalion of the 143rd, the city was secured, and the 3rd Battalion assumed defense of it.

Working along another typical, booby-trapped mountain road, this one wiggling over eight miles southeast of St. Marie aux Mines into the lowlands, the 3rd Battalion of the 143rd, with Pearce's Company C of the 111th as an assessor, elbowed on. In a bitter but successful assault, they fought for and took Ribeauville on December 4. The same day the Division was shifted to the command of the 2nd French Army Corps (for less than two weeks) and assigned with clearing out a pocket of resistance near the city of Colmar. With the 36th obviously overstretched in defending the territory it had captured, and travel hampered by the Alsace plains becoming a swamp due to rains, the Germans struck back.

A frantic, last-ditch attack by the Germans on December 12 engaged the 36th. Heavy artillery fire and then an all-out attack along the lightly secured 36th front commenced. For two days the fighting was heavy in places like Selestat and Riquewihr, but with seemingly superhuman qualities exhibited by the Division, the attacks in the Colmar Pocket were beaten back and ended.

On the evening of December 13, Companies A and B were plunged into the front lines as infantry filler near Riquewihr. Amidst chilling winter winds, Company A's luck quickly turned sour. Clinging to a frontline spot one mile south of Riquewihr, at 1:00 AM, some of the company were overrun in the German attacks. 1st platoon of Company A was completely surrounded. 2nd and 3rd platoons of Company A withdrew several hundred yards and created a new defensible perimeter. Holding out until noon, the punch-drunk engineers were relieved by elements of the infantry. 1st platoon had suffered drastically. Arthur Hertel of Detroit, Michigan, Ernest Boddye of Beloit, Kansas, David LaLicata of Corona, New York, Francis Berchem of St. Paul, Minnesota, Nis Nielsen of Harlon, Iowa, Floyd Lewis of Sandwich, Massachusetts, and Franklin M. Philpott of Huntington, West Virginia, had all fallen prey to the dense Nazi wall of fire and been killed.

Sergeant Hertel, a squad leader in Company A, received the Silver Star Medal for his gallantry. Refusing to withdraw before the enemy assault, he inflicted heavy casualties on the Germans as they slowly overran his position. His bravery allowed other members of Company A to retreat to a new defense line. Hertel was killed in close-range fighting, but his courage saved many lives.

Twenty-five members of the engineers were listed as MIA. Many of the MIA in the melee were captured and sent as Prisoners of War to Stalag 17 in Austria. Almost immediately, 3rd platoon of Company B was rushed from reserve into position to replace an outpost between Company B and Company A. Before gaining a better defensive grip, four men stationed at one of the forward outposts were added to the growing list of captured men.

1st platoon of Company B, although not coming nose to nose with any direct attack, received smoldering artillery fire from the Germans. Gerald Bullis was killed, Joseph D. Brown of Lakewood, Ohio, seriously hit, and George Pengressi wounded.

After 133 constant days of front-line action, on December 25, the 36th officially closed its stay. They enjoyed five days in Strasbourg serving as security for the city and defending, without incident, positions along the Rhine River. After this major change in living conditions, compared to the mountain fighting, they were moved fifty miles from the front to a training area near Sarrebourg. Here, far away from the mines[5] and booby traps, the men settled in for a much-needed rest. When they did return to combat, they would spend the next four months pushing north-northeast through France and Germany never once crossing to the ever-present east side of the Rhine River. The west side had trials of its own.

The recapturing of France had not proven easy. The closer to home the Germans were shoved, the more they stiffened. Pearce's Company C took it on the chin the entire month. December 6 started the month in a horrible way. Earnest W. Wickham of Palmyra, Tennessee, was mistakenly shot and killed by an American infantry security team as he checked a roadblock created by the

Thomas Gautier, Jr.

Germans. On the same day, Ralph R. Thompson of Salem, Virginia, was mortally wounded by inadvertently setting off a booby trap.

A tragic loss was a former officer of Company C, Captain Thomas Brown Gautier, Jr., who was now a member of Headquarters serving as the Battalion's intelligence officer. On December 7, while on reconnaissance for a possible bridge site near the town of Chatenois, the twenty-three-year-old stepped on an S mine. Two days later he died.[6]

Oran Stovall, in a letter after the war, described the terrible events of December 7, 1944. "I have often thought of that day; we needed to make a flight over the Rhine valley to look at some roads and this road was to be checked. I told Tommy of the two jobs and asked which he wanted. He took the "walk" because he hated to fly. So I flew the mission without mishap & learned of his fate upon my return to the battalion. We can never know, but I would have felt even worse about the affair if I had ordered him to do the "thing" he did not want to do and had been killed."

Gautier was a hero many times over. During the invasion of Southern France, a L. S. T. carrying ammunition was bombed and destroyed by a lone German aircraft. As a fire raged and ammunition on the L. S. T. exploded, Gautier sprinted into the slowly lapping waves and swam towards an eerie Fourth of July scene. For

Philip DiCarlo.

several hours following Gautier's single-minded effort to help others, members of the engineers helped save over ninety men from the burning wreckage.

With camp established in Ribeauville, on December 18 enemy artillery struck home. A shell exploded into the side of a building the Company C had bivouacked in. Two boys, Earl E. Watson of Monmouth, Oregon, and Philip DiCarlo of West Worick, Rhode Island, were lost to the violence sustained in the 8:00 AM shelling. The unfortunate 210 mm shell taking the lives of DiCarlo and Watson also wounded Albert Coker of Emory, Texas, and Arnold Glenn.

The joy of the non-stalemated movement across France, the feeling experienced by seeing the freed French people, and the hopes of an end to the conflict perished near to the entrance to Germany. 1944 ended with more doubts than it began.

Monday 2 October '44

Got up at 5:30. Same old mess of dry eggs etc. Immediately went up to front. Spent day in house with old people. Quite a bit of shelling. Did nothing all day but sit. Our Lieutenant Cathcart[7] carries us everywhere he goes. Tonight we swept road and built bridge and got in about 10 PM. Have to get up at 5:30.

Wednesday 4 October '44

Have done nothing today as Junior (Lieutenant Cathcart) finally woke up to the fact there was no need for us all to go up & sat around. Rumors are we will be relieved the 6th or 9th. I'm tired of seeing waste & dead people. Our artillery are rationed on shells on account of transportation. Twelve a day.

Friday 6 October '44

Quite a bit of noise echoing up valley last night. Small arms and artillery.[8] Had to go out to where we built bridge last night and two boys & I stayed all night. House close by so we stayed in cellar as lots of Germans shells hitting area. Relieved this AM and have done nothing today. Rumors we are going to Normandy front and around Paris and old men going home. Ho-hum!

Saturday 7 October '44

Yesterday there was the heaviest artillery barrage I have ever heard. Germans were preparing to attack and our artillery broke it up. This AM I worked up to front on roads draining water off. Pretty day. Our Infantry is shot to hell and are doing good to hold. Lots of men killed every day.

Sunday 8 October '44

On guard last night from 2 to 4 AM. Artillery still blasting. Today was back to front and it is really rough. Germans are using tanks and firing direct and have lots of machine guns, etc. We are only holding and damn lucky to be doing that. This war isn't over yet!

Monday 9 October '44

All I've done is go up to 1st Battalion Headquarters with Junior who had bright idea of stringing tracing tape down into woods to Company Command Posts so they can find the way at night. Of course it would also assist the Germans so they wouldn't let him do it. Such going ons! I don't like this fighting in the dense woods. I am lucky and know it. No mail yet!

Thursday 12 October '44

Spread gravel today on supply road up front. Didn't need it but we have to do something. Two Jerry planes over about noon but ack ack kept them high. The only man in the Company who has never been on front line & had snap job went home yesterday on furlough.[9] Really helps one's moral.

Saturday 14 October '44

Moved this morning after chow. Came down a different highway to town of Deycimont. Are bivouacked in another hay loft. All French buildings have one. Living quarters, cow stables and hay barn. All well built. Went to see Medicos & got a dose. Really keeps me trotting.

Monday 16 October '44

Went on thru woods and swept for mines on other side. The road led to Laval (area) and Bruyeres. Bruyeres was being shelled and fighting going on. Germans shelled us as we were out in open. [Company C's Joseph Corazza of Freeland, Pennsylvania, hit in right thigh] Tonight went back and swept on up close to town. Very scary as no troops out front of us. Rained like everything.

Tuesday 17 October '44

Have done nothing today but take it easy. Weather is getting bad. A misty rain nearly all time. More hash for meals. Our food is terrible and can get no mail. My morale is sure getting low. Seems like we are being kicked around. Longest we have ever been on line with no relief & none in sight. (while on reconnaissance near Belmont, mortar fire wounded Eugene V. McDonald)

Thursday 19 October '44

Last night Junior carried us up to Laval so we could go in Bruyeres and clean out mines but infantry didn't want us so we came back. This morning we went into town. It is fairly well wrecked and some buildings burning. Not all ours. We swept on into town and Germans shelled the town and small arms broke out. Quite a spot.

Friday 20 October '44

Finally got out of Bruyeres yesterday. I saw one shell hit in the midst of about twenty infantry boys and not a one went down but I'm sure some had wounds.[10] The fighting was for high ground on outer edge.[11] People ease out of doors and run to next. Planes over us all night, but no harm to us. Rested today.

Sunday 22 October '44

Hot cakes for breakfast. Weather still heavy. Moved this morning to Laval just a short ways from Bruyeres. Bivouacked in a paper factory, a three story affair of concrete. A few shells landing around but this place is good protection except for windows. Got a bath yesterday and a change of clothes (used). First bath in over a month. Also got a haircut. Women barbers. Got radiogram[12] & letter from home night before last (19th).

Tuesday 24 October '44

Loaded gravel this morning and went with truck. Carried it up on mountain behind Bruyeres. Very heavily wooded and road narrow & steep. Quite a few dead Jerries around. We have it as far as the top. Unloaded and got out just as Jerry started shelling. Heavy barrage for 1 1/2 hour. Bad stuff as shells explode in tree tops. Shells hitting all around factory tonight. Gave me a headache.

Wednesday 25 October '44[13]

Shells jarred us all night. This morning loaded more gravel and had to run a artillery barrage to get there. Shells hit on both side of road as we flew past. Started back and the Germans were shelling Bruyeres and when we got to Laval, also there. Company was moving as shells were hitting our buildings. Moved to Fays, a small place out from Laval. Germans have plenty of artillery now.

Thursday 26 October '44

Went to Docelles last night and loaded some paving blocks. This morning we started back to mountain. Had to bypass Laval fast as Germans were shelling it. Went back on top of mountain and worked on road all day. Germans threw heavy barrage in all day. Also counter attacked several times and the damnest small arms battle took place. Bullets zing around us but we kept working. Didn't have gun anyhow.

Friday 27 October '44

Back to same job. Heavy fog all day and visibility there was zero. Very quiet all day although an attack was planned to try and get to a Battalion that has been cutoff for several days. We have put truck after truck load of rock on road but still bad as lots of traffic. Wounded coming out and replacements going in. Got mail from home tonight.

Saturday 28 October '44

Same job. Still can't tell we've done much good as mud works to top. Quite a lot of fighting just below us and again bullets clipped limbs over our heads. Germans firing big ack ack at observation plane just over our heads. Quite a lot of wounded brought out, some in bad shape and road being rough makes it worse. Pretty night—cold.

Sunday 29 October '44

A heavy frost this morning and ice. Went back to same job. Looks as if we will be working there all winter unless the fronts move up. German artillery cut a big pine down across road just a few minutes before we arrived so we cut it out to let traffic by. A hot battle raging all day with our P 47 planes[14] giving support. Quite a few prisoners taken.

Monday 30 October '44

Cold again this morning. Back up on mountain to work on road. It is getting away from us so we are corduroying it with trees and also No 1 planks (3 x 4) which we are getting at Laval. Putting gravel on top. Guess we made 300 yards today. Slow but good. Late this evening the Germans began to shell us so we quit as it was getting dark. Quiet day.

Tuesday 31 October '44

Worked half day on road then came in & got pay. Suppose to go take bath but Corporal Ellis & I got off truck and went to Docelles and drank wine all evening. Got in about 8:30. A quart of wine cost $3.60. Money doesn't go very far over here. Cost me $11.50. First I've had in a long time.

Wednesday 1 November '44

Another day working on road. We are nearly thru. Our planes have really been strafing today. What a racket. The 1st Battalion was relieved from the trap yesterday.[15] Only had twenty odd causalities. Tonight Sinchak & I had to report to Lieutenant on account of not taking a bath yesterday. The Lieutenant was going to make Sinchak & I walk the road up there for punishment but Captain refused to let him. These 2nd Lieutenants thinks they are the stuff. He is very insulting and a guy has to take it. On the bad side again.

Saturday 4 November '44

Back up to mountain. Went in two miles further where 1st Battalion 141 was cut off. Hell of a mess, trees shot to pieces and dead Jerries scattered around. Worked a while as road is in terrible shape. Came in early and left one squad to work. Understand we will only be relieved for few days and go in again.

Sunday 5 November '44

Our squad didn't go out at all today. Was I surprised. The sky stays leaden now but still no snow. Weather fairly cold. Our chow is terrible. Not the food but how prepared. I sometimes wonder how a guy keeps going on such stuff.

Monday 6 November '44

A hectic day. First I missed going with squad so went on another truck. We fell thru a bridge & had hard time getting out. After dinner we went a way back into woods to work. About fifteen of us in a bunch and I stepped across road and one of the boys stepped on a "S" mine (bouncing type). It jumped & exploded. Eight of our men & one Japanese Staff Sergeant wounded, two seriously. Private Nines had about forty slugs in left leg and left shoulder. Japanese leg nearly torn off. Corporal Jones, Corporal Ellis, Private Cromarty, McDonald in our squad and our medics all hit. My luck still good. These woods are death in person.

Wednesday 8 November '44

Got up at 5 AM and went up on mountain [about three miles north of La Houssiere] before breakfast to remove a roadblock of trees across road. Suppose to be thru and back for breakfast. Same road but about two miles deeper in. There were three roadblocks of huge trees. Still raining in valley but snowing up there. I really froze especially my feet. Got back about 12 o'clock and then I didn't get any dinner as they threw it away while I was warming up. These Lieutenants have no idea of what work is as they have never cut timber. Such a life.

J.P. Johnson, right, at a German made roadblock.

Thursday 9 November '44

No work today. Snowing all morning. Mountains turning white as snow sticks on evergreen trees. Drew new boots today. More of an overshoe with feet pads in bottom and heavy socks. Went out after dark to 143rd area (15 miles) to put up foot bridge over swift stream. [Vologne River near Jussarupt] Very dark and had hard time seeing until it snowed. Got in a 12.

Friday 10 November '44

Didn't get up till 10:30. Have done nothing today. Snowing again. Not sticking to ground much. Sloppy. My feet really stayed warm last night. We had heck of a time as we had to cut lumber & two trees in dark and get two men across stream. Six Infantry boys on other side all that was between us & Jerry. Jerry patrol reported at bridge fifteen minutes after we left.

Wayne C. Griffitt.

Sunday 12 November '44

Still snowing off & on. Ground white this morning. I didn't go out today but most of squad did. Laid around & read. Sergeant Griffitt & some men ran face to face with Jerry patrol last night while sweeping for mines. All got away. That's the kind of cooperation the Infantry Command Post gives us. All clear & our patrols out. Bologna![16]

Monday 13 November '44

My birthday (29th). At 10 AM had to go out on mines sweeping detail over to 143rd Infantry area around Jussarupt. Quite a ways. Missed dinner as I didn't get back till 3:30 PM. Had a "K" ration (canned pork loaf)[17] which I hate. Snowing today. Was five inches deep up there. Front very quiet so my job was uneventful. Very few men did I see.

Thursday 16 November '44

Started out today to move a roadblock but as usual everything messed up. Tank dozier had dead battery etc so finally three men went with our D 7 bull dozier and the rest of us stayed in. Our food is bad and skimpy. Mail has slacked up. We move tomorrow into tents. Don't know where yet.

Friday 17 November '44

Moving day. Clear last night and today. Ground froze. Packed things up and pulled out about 9:30. What a mess we have, big bed rolls, stoves and junk. Moved on up about seven miles. Don't know just where but are out in woods in pyramidal tents.[18] Built myself a bed up off muddy ground. Guns all around us and shells can be heard very close.

Saturday 18 November '44[19]

A pretty day. Our planes went out in number and I could hear them diving and strafing just over the mountain. Got a larger stove pipe so now our stove doesn't smoke us out. I am fed up with this kind of life. No amusement, whiskey, women or a damn thing but soldiers & damn officers.

(November 18 letter to Iona)

I am afraid this letter will prove to be a failure as I have nothing to write about. So, the object of it is just to let you know I am O.K. and doing fine. Once again we are back in tents as the housing problem is acute around here, but the weather has been pretty for a few days and we are all fixed as if it does change we won't suffer. Personally I had just as soon be in these big tents as in a house as we can get things more to our liking. It is surprising how tite one can make these tents and of course we have a stove and plenty of wood around.

As yet I haven't received any packages but should before long. There's no need for me to try and make you believe I am perfectly satisfied. I would give plenty to be able to come home. It gets me worse when we are idle. I suppose if I were home I would be restless and want to be somewhere else. I still miss so many small conveniences. Haven't seen a show in over three months.

Sunday 19 November '44

Pretty day. Had beer today from Bruyeres. Very weak. I drank a gallon and didn't feel a thing. Keeps a guy running out to the trees. Sergeant Mainord & Warren both wounded by S mine. Mainord badly. Places are thick with them and the little wooden shoe mine. Luck get you by.

Monday 20 November '44

Today has been one of bad luck. Corporal Brodbeck was killed by a mine and Lieutenant Hand had a foot blown off. I was out till midnight. Went out with Infantry platoon and moved about fifty shoe mines[20] & six S mines & two ramp mines. I have never seen so many in one place. Platoon went in & left me so had quite a time contacting Company for transportation

Tuesday_21 November '44

On this day I was in the town of Anould and blew up some mines. The town was burned so there was no cover. Germans threw in three mortar shells & third one hit on road about ten feet from me. Knocked me down and two pieces hit me in right calf of leg, two in upper right arm and three pieces in left back. I was numb all over but managed to get up and they threw some more at me. I crawled in a burnt house and St. Matlock [Luther Matlock of Ravenna, Texas] went for aid. In about an hour ambulance came and picked me and Tony Vesce (also hit) up. We were supposed to have that town but as usual we were misinformed & Jerry was on hill behind town. They fired at us with machine guns but buildings protected us. I was carried to 143rd Aid Station then back to clearing Station in Bruyeres and then to 95th Evacuation Hospital in Epinal. I was hit about 1 PM and at 8 PM I arrived in operating room. They used penatal injection and I came to the next morning about 4 AM. Took penicillin shots every three hours for two days and as no complications set up they stopped them. On the 23rd I was carried to 21st General Hospital in Mirecourt about twenty miles from Epinal.

Luther Matlock.

PVT. FRANK PEARCE WOUNDED IN ACTION IN FRENCH SECTOR

Mr. and Mrs. R. A. Pearce, Texas St., received a telegram from the War Department Monday, advising them that their son, Pvt. Frank Pearce, U. S. Engineers, had been wounded in action in France on Nov. 20.

Pvt. Pearce, with the famous 36th Division, has been overseas twenty months, and has been in combat service sixteen months, serving in the North African, Sicilian, and Italian campaigns before being transferred to France where he participated in the first invasion there.

Sulphur Springs Daily News Telegram, date unknown.

Wednesday 22 November 44-Thursday 21 December 44

[In the Mirecourt General 21st Hospital-no diary entry.]

(November 22 letter to Family)

I hope this reaches you before any telegrams do from the War Department. You see I managed to be in the wrong place at the right time and as a result I am in a hospital. A mortar shell got me while working on some mines on the front. I was hit in the lower right leg, right arm and twice in the back and few minor places.

I am not seriously hurt but can't get around for several weeks. So don't worry as now you know I am out of any danger for quite some time. Really I am not seriously hurt so please believe me.

(November 25 letter to Mother)

I'm sure you are anxiously awaiting a letter from me so here it is. I am getting along fine and getting a needed rest. I had forgotten how a bed felt with a mattress and sheets. I assure you it feels fine although I have a little trouble getting in a comfortable position.

As you know today is my fourth anniversary in the army. For fourteen months of combat I think I am lucky to be put out of action only once. I did want to go

111th Engineers removing a roadblock on the drive for the Rhine Valley.

into Germany but guess I won't get to do so with my Division. I hope this is over before I get out of here. And again I want to be with the boys when they go to Berlin. I can stand some more if I have too.

(December 3 letter to Mother)

I hope you don't jump to any dire conclusions because you hear from me at intervals. I just can't get enough ambition to write. I have no idea when I will receive any mail as the Company is probably a long ways off. Maybe not till I get back. So I find little to write about.

I am getting along fine now and should be up and around in a couple of weeks, maybe. After checking up on myself I find I only had five holes in me. But all are doing nicely and I feel much better each day. I still have all the pieces in me as they were too deep to be removed so guess I'll bring em home as souvenirs.

(December 14 letter to Mother)

I hope you have no doubts about my injuries. I have told you the truth and hope you believe it to be so. I am practically all healed but can not walk much yet. It will take a little time before the muscle in my leg limbers up enough to walk naturally. I manage to make short trips on my toes. I may have a slight limp but really don't believe I will have much of one. The bigger trouble is just the fact that

I have too much time on my hands. I average a book or two a day but it has been so long since I was in some place where there was no activity that I hardly know what to do with myself. It was a needed rest for the first two weeks but now that I feel so much better I am restless. I don't crave to go back but I do miss being with all the boys. I don't know whether or not I will be sent back to the company but hope to be. I could do better somewhere else probably but I like old "C" company even if I have had some bad breaks there. J.P., Arnold & Muley were still O.K. They envy me laying back here so snug but everything has its bad points.

I suppose this will be another dull Christmas for you all. At least I'll have a little better one than last year. I remember last year we were beginning to butt our heads against the outer defenses of Cassino and living and eating mud. We've come far in the past year and I wonder how we could have had any morale at all after seeing how much we had to overcome and still it goes on. It's a good thing we can't see into the future or it would seem hopeless.

Naturally I wish for your sake I could be there for Christmas. As for me I seem to have lost all feeling of time and for material things. I make no efforts to cultivate a close friend as it doesn't pay and in that way there is no deep hurt. I merely try to be liked and like all the boys to a point where one can depend on each other. Even then it hurts but not too much. Sounds brutal but I find it to be the easiest way to stand it and not go nutty or something.

I suppose this won't reach you until after Christmas but hope it does before. I'm sorry there is no way I can make it a happier time for you. Surely R.A. and family will be there as usual so have a good time with Sarah [born in 1935] and Robert [born in 1943] and don't put a damper on things worrying about Marvin and me. You can be sure I'll be thinking of you all and of course I know it will be the same with you. I feel sure I'll be home by next Christmas and all the past will be forgotten. So, take good care of yourself and I'll do the same.

Friday 22 December '44

On this day I managed to walk to registers office & drew clothes and was put on train for Paris. After fooling around all day we pulled out at about 9 PM. Nice compartments but 7 men in each. No way to relax or sleep. Traveled all night and moved very slow.

Saturday 23 December '44

Traveled all day and went thru Chateau Thierry and other World War I places of interest and arrived in Paris about 8 PM. Got off train and took bus to 108th General, the largest in Europe. Twelve floors. I was on tenth floor. Nice toilets and even a bath tub. Really a nice place. They were going to send us to England but I was too near well so stayed on at 108th. Six pieces of shrapnel still in me. Could get nothing done for my foot but being off it has helped a lot.

Monday 25 December '44

Spent Xmas here in 108th General. Weather is cold. I can see Eiffel tower well from here. Red Cross gave us a sack with a piece of candy, gum, & 1 pack of cigarettes. Can't get out as Paris is off limits. Germans spies in G. I. clothes in Paris so all G. I's are picked up.

(December 31 letter to Mother)

Well, in a few hours the New Year will be in. The past one no doubt must have its good points but to me it has been only another year of this war in the past. If I could have seen what was in store for me and all the others this time last year I'm afraid it would have been a gloomy year to look forward to. This upcoming year of course will be very much like the past one except I believe the war will be over here in Europe. That is at least the one I am interested in. I hardly look for anything resembling peace for the next few years in Europe. To me it appears the only reason some of the countries wish to be free of Germany is so they can start scraping among themselves. The political groups work themselves into such a frenzy there is no way to settle it except by ridding themselves of any opponents.

Now my opinion is: let em fight it out as long as it is merely a civil war and offers no threat to us and gets me back to the good old U.S. I used to feel sorry for the people over here but now I don't. It is all their fault whatever happened or will happen. Each one seems to want all for their own personal gain and let the rest starve. All this big talk about a lasting peace is all bunk unless we smash any sign of military power before it gets started.

Then there is another side to the thing. If we attempt the above then it is possible we will have to step on the one big powers toes [Russia] who in my opinion is going to practically do as she pleases with Europe. If ever a permanent peace can be had in Europe it is impossible for me to see how it can be arranged. An impossibility. We haven't even got unity in our own hemisphere.

It's plain to see the countries who did fall in line are only tolerating it for the material gains they can get from us. All I can see is trouble from now on but I personally will have no part in it but the next generation will really have a headache trying to figure it out.

As for me I am about as well as I'll ever be. I am getting very restless just hanging around and intend to go back to duty as soon as possible. I have hopes of going back to the company but will have to go thru the replacement depots so can't say just where I'll end up.

Guess I'll be a little gun shy for a while but that is to be expected. I'll soon get over it. My main objective right now is to get back to the same outfit. Here's hoping all is well with you all. I hope you haven't worried too much about me. I'll let you know where I end up.

12 BROKEN HEARTS

"Quite a few old men have been killed while I was gone."

The joy of the New Year, along with the slacking of combat, was not a feeling lost to the needling winter winds as at the start of 1944. Despite a tough finish to the year, the dawning of 1945 was full of potential. The adaptation of the American fighting man and his weaponry into a productive war machine had brought them this far. In the minds of the GIs, more tapping of American potential should help bring a close to the war in the months ahead.[1]

Still, when an animal is backed into a corner with no way out, its foe experiences the best last ounce of fight it has left. It wasn't the chill of the winter wind that smacked the guys back into reality, but a German offensive charge, code named Nordwind, in the yawning moments of the New Year, that did the trick. German forces south of Bitche streaked blatantly into American positions with solid results. Nicknamed the "New Year's Eve Offense" by the Americans, the attack was sudden and threatening.

Back in the States, it was "Bowl Day". As teams battled back and forth on the safe gridirons at home, the 36th was routed out of its rest period. While eighteen-year-old Oklahoma A&M star Bob Fenimore, backed by several discharged World War II veterans, passed and ran the Cowboys past TCU 34-0 in the Cotton Bowl, many similar young men, tracking through the deep snow, moved forward to face a deadlier group than the TCU Horned Frogs. Their New Year's celebration wouldn't be holding a hot date but dodging smoldering bullets.

First to battle was the 141st plus Company A, which moved 40 miles to the Bitche front to help close an exposed gap. By January 2, the entire 141st was in contact with the Germans. The rest of the Division was delayed due to lack of transportation.

On Wednesday, the 142nd plus Company B and 143rd with Company C braved a heavy snowstorm and extremely cold conditions to move to Montbronn. They were placed as reserves for the 141st and eventually alternated days at the front with them. The addition of the 36th had salvaged the situation in the Bitche vicinity. By the sixth, Operation Nordwind attacks were ceasing and their menace ending.

On January 13, the 142nd and Company B moved to the battle line near Saarbrucken, west of Bitche, and were pleased to find a serene front with little confrontation. They would remain here until the 18th of January.

The lettered companies spent the first weeks of the New Year salting, sanding, and graveling ice covered roads to improve transportation. From a defensive standpoint, they laid seventeen mine fields, prepared for demolition of bridges, and had guard duty at various roadblocks. The ground was so frozen and covered with snow, help was given to the infantry and artillery in setting explosives to dig fox holes and artillery installations. January became a month of a defensive

Engineers constructed barbed-wire barriers for secondary defense.

mentality. Earlier in the month, the Germans seized a bridgehead on the Rhine River ten miles north of Strasbourg. The newly acquired ground, near Gambsheim, was reinforced and soon became a legitimate threat to Strasbourg.

While the 141st remained in Montbronn, the 143rd aided by Company C moved to reinforce other Americans in what was becoming known as the Gambsheim Pocket. The German presence was severe enough that a decision was made to motor the 142nd with Company B eighty miles to Haguenau to join in the attempt to end the Nazi intrusion.

A vibrating defeat, during the second week in January, suffered by an inexperienced 12th Armored Division near Herrlisheim, sent shock waves bouncing off the startled American commanders. On the night of the twentieth, all American forces retreated and prepared new defensive lines from Bischwiller to Weyersheim.

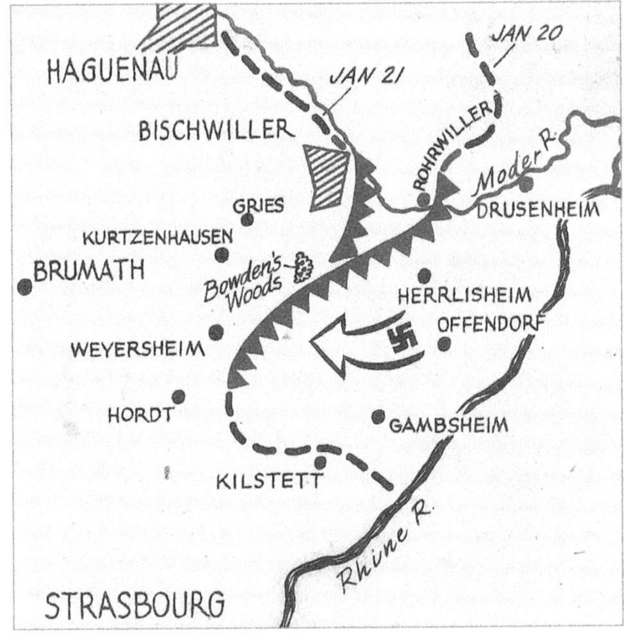

The German Operation Nordwind was designed to help ease pressure on the failing Ardennes Offensive farther north. American units were roughly handled in Alsace, but recovered quickly.

Jack Cleek.

The retreat took the enemy by surprise, and little torment was dealt to interfere with the regrouping. With all the flabbergasting enemy successes, thoughts of genuine concern faced the men. Then the 2nd Battalion of the 143rd produced a shining moment. Near Kurtzenhausen, in a wooded setting, contact between the two sides was made and hand to hand fighting developed.

Battling eyeball to eyeball throughout the snowy afternoon, 2nd Battalion in a spectacular counterattack killed or captured two hundred fifty of the enemy. After this morale booster, the enemy made little progress in the Bischwiller-Weyersheim line defended by the 36th.

Accidents regretfully do happen. When dealing with the amount of explosives the engineers handled, things can and do go wrong. It wasn't a case of a German strike and it couldn't be attributed to friendly fire, but in the early morning of January 21st eight Americans lost their lives in a few seconds' time. Company C had placed over six hundred mines in a minefield a quarter of mile south of Bischwiller, when something went terribly wrong. For an unknown reason over one hundred fifty British Mark 5 anti-tank mines suddenly ignited. The resulting shock wave dramatically downed 16 engineers.

When the explosions subsided and the area was secured, the count against Company C was eight men killed: John R. Simons of Scotland, Texas, Chester A.

Huebner of St. Louis, Missouri, Albin A. MacHeese of Girardville, Pennsylvania, Roy A. Pfleger of Easton, Pennsylvania, Frederick V. Hibbard of Oil City, Pennsylvania, Joseph J. Bliss of Philadelphia, Pennsylvania, Joseph A. Ford of Roxbury, Massachusetts, and Isadore Keller of Brooklyn, New York. Echoing across the blast darkened snow littered with bodies, moans of pain led searchers to the eight survivors: Louie J. V'Dovick of Grand Haven, Michigan, Stephen Somal of Hastings, New York, Jack F. Cleek of Kansas City, Missouri, John J. Giordano of Philadelphia, Pennsylvania, Robert T. Hall of Henderson, North Carolina, Boguslavis Kayota of Brooklyn, New York, Carlton R. Cowan of Wichita Falls, Texas, and Thomas W. Walker.

Less than two weeks after the tragic circumstances of January 21, Company C was again ripped apart. Incredible but sadly true, a second accident in January happened, this time at the Battalion dump near Bilwisheim. A mine detector crew of six, operating out of a three-quarter ton weapons carrier, swept for mines and recovered several. In unbelievably cold weather, the men found several irremovable fuses frozen tight in the mines. A decision was made, and the crew loaded them up anyway and brought them back to the dump. As fate would have it, they picked up two men thumbing a ride, who had been to the showers in Brumath. Pearce, also at the showers, decided to take a different truck since this one was overcrowded. After arriving at the dump around 3 PM, in the truck driven by Wellington Gilbert of West Chester, Pennsylvania, somehow the mines exploded.

The six man mine detector crew and the two unlucky bathers were all instantly killed. There were no survivors. The losses included Lawrence D. Fye of Sperry, Iowa, Lawrence E. Saline of Superior, Wisconsin, Winfred Weems of Dallas, Texas, Herbert Loree of Otisville, Michigan, John Meese of Philadelphis,

Left: Bobbie Sleator. *Middle*: Richard "Terry" Nims. *Right*: Winfred Weems.

Ohio, Richard "Terry" Nims, Bobbie Sleator and Gilbert. Thirty-one days into 1945, Company C had lost more men to tragic accidents than had been lost in combat the preceding two grim years.

John Benedict, in his personal diary of the war around him, wrote on January 31, "They were all good boys and six of them had come a long ways. The other two (Fye and Saline) were fairly new to us. We didn't know them too well. But it was hell to die by your own mine's boys, I know. If there were any way I could help you, I would. But I can hope the Lord will take care of your weary souls. May you rest in peace. So long Sleator and Lorrie, you did your best, that's all a man can do".

One of the killed, Herbert Loree, appeared to his fellow engineers as an indestructible force. Since being drafted in February of 1942, a towering six-foot four-inch, 185 pound Loree's firm determination and will to exceed impressed all. Consistency was his trademark. A truck driver with a grammar school education, he earned his doctorate for heroism in combat.

Loree received a Bronze Star for gallantry in action with his heroics between January 29 and February 2, 1944, plus an Oak Leaf Cluster to the Bronze Star later that February. A Silver Star Medal was added November 6, 1944, for courageous action in France, and an Oak Leaf Cluster to the Silver Star Medal on January 30, 1945, the day before the accident.

Herbert Loree.

If this wasn't enough, for extraordinary heroism in action, on October 17, 1944, he was awarded the Distinguished Service Cross. The award read:

> "For extraordinary heroism in action. On 17 October 1944, near Fay's France, enemy troops, having converted a roadside house into a strong hold, halted the advance of friendly infantry driving on Bruyeres. Private First Class Loree volunteered to move forward along a road and clear a roadblock of anti-tank mines to permit tanks to move into position favorable for firing into the house. Although the roadway was under direct enemy observation, he crawled cautiously forward, halting in a ditch from time to time to seek shelter from rifle and machine pistol fire. Reaching the block he worked calmly, detecting and removing six anti-tank mines. After he was certain the block was passable, he returned to the lead tank.
>
> The tank commander informed him that, in order to move the tanks into suitable firing position, it would be necessary to proceed beyond a second block which was two hundred yards in advance of the block he had just cleared. Fully aware of the hazards of this mission Private First Class Loree again volunteered; set out along the same route and, after being halted several times by hostile fire, reached the second block.
>
> Dependent wholly upon his own resources and without covering fire from friendly troops, he detected, and removed by hand, ten anti-tank mines, working coolly despite this knowledge that any one of them might be booby-trapped and detonate immediately. Returning a second time, he reported that the roadway was clear. Private First Class Loree's heroic actions enabled the tanks to go forward. With this stronghold wrested from the enemy, the infantry troops were able to advance to positions from which they successfully attacked the town of Bruyeres, France".

His overwhelming popularity was confirmed when he was bestowed an honor in July. After the conclusion of the war in Europe, the lettered companies moved to the Bottingern, Germany area. Here they selected a bivouac site at a former German Officers' Candidate School called Altes Lager. At the main entrance to the camp an overhead sign was placed that changed the name of this facility to "Camp Herbert A. Loree". Despite broken hearts, memories of good friends never die.

This post in occupied Germany memorialized the much-loved and highly decorated engineer killed in an accident in early 1945.

Ironically, on this same date when these heroes were killed, the only American soldier to lose his life for desertion was also executed. Private Edward Slovik, near a town the 36th fought so hard to take, St. Marie aux Mines, was shot by a firing squad consisting of members of his own 28th Division. Clearly a coward, his name would be remembered years after the war in Hollywood movies, while true warriors like Loree, Sleator, and others faded into history.

Meanwhile the New Year's Eve/Gambsheim attacks fizzled to a halt as the last major German offensive attempt of the war gained little ground with much loss of life. When January came to an end, the Germans had lost almost twenty-three thousand irreplaceable men. Seventh Army losses totaled approximately fourteen thousand men. Several thousand of the American wounded were to another set of enemies, trench foot and frostbite.

The 142nd, on January 31, initiated an Allied thrust by moving across the Moder River to occupy the town of Oberhoffen. It was several days of give and take, including withstanding a powerful German counterattack, before they could capture the city.

On February 2, a new offensive, with troops from each of the three combat units, started. Several unseasonably warm days added more troubles for the GIs, as melted snow created miles and miles of freezing flood lands. 1st Battalion of the 143rd plus a platoon from Company C, wading through the cold, skin

Oberhoffen cleared of the enemy.

piercing, waist deep water, took Rohrwiller and then held firm against attacks. A Battalion from the 143rd and the 141st squeezed Herrlisheim from the north and south, but here the Germans deflected a clean American sweep of the operation. With great determination, they beat back both American battalions without relinquishing the small town.

Even with some success in inhibiting the American attack, the Germans feared being surrounded by more American troops rushing headlong into battle. A couple of days later they pulled back, giving up Herrlisheim and Offendorf without a fight. The Gambsheim Pocket had been cleared. Incredibility, to the relief of the combatants, an eerie silence engulfed the battle lines for the remainder of February.

Joseph Pohl.

An American tank destroyer leads an armored column through the German town of Rohrwiller northeast of Strasbourg and southeast of Hageunau.

A distant sound and sudden boom ended the life of many an engineer. In the early afternoon of the eighth, while laying mines for defensive positions near Oberhoffen, a Nazi mortar barrage caught Company B and Joseph H. Pohl of Portland, Michigan, in the open. The result was another American losing his life in the waning months of the war.

Wednesday 3 January '45

Left Hospital today. Rode across Paris & caught train to 9th Replacement Depot at Fontainebleau forty miles out of Paris. 3rd class cars but not bad. Weather cold.

(January 10 letter to Iona)

It is hard for me to write since I am unable to receive any mail. I hope you all are all right. I have been out of the hospital for a week now and am O.K. None of my wounds bother me. I do have a bad cold which is the first in a long time. But being indoors so long must be the cause. I guess I lost my resistance to colds while taking it easy in a good warm place. By the time I get back to action I should be used to the weather. Everything is fine with me and I'm hoping it is with you.

Monday 15 January '45

Loaded on box cars (40 & 8)[2] this afternoon. Snow pretty heavy. Traveled all night and very uncomfortable and cold. Built fire and burned hole in floor.

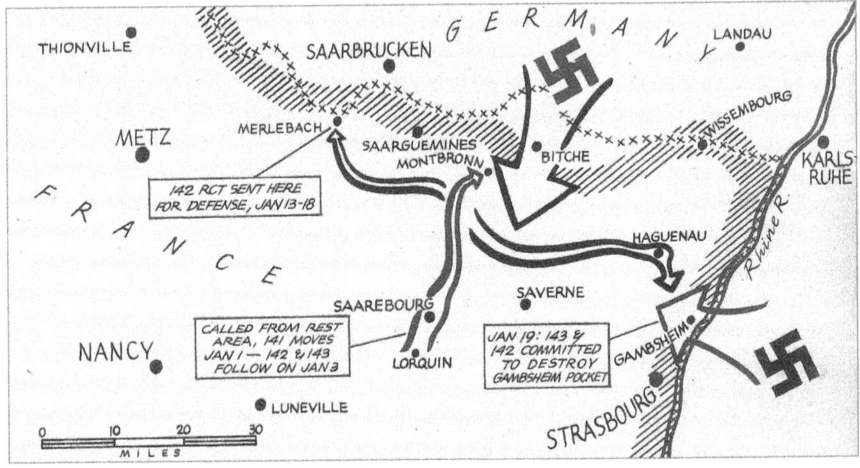

The Germans defended the frontiers of the Fatherland with tenacity.

Tuesday 16 January '45

Traveled all day and after dark got to Neufchateau. Unloaded at 14th R.D. Moved in stables of old French garrison. Nearly froze before morning.

Wednesday 17 January '45

Was still at 14th today and my eyes are nearly out as we built open fires in the building and smoke is terrible. Got some hay for bed tonight.

Thursday 18 January '45

Left 14th in evening by truck and traveled fifty miles to 2nd Depot at Epinal. Sure cold. Put us in textile mill and still no fire. These depots are overcrowded and miserable.

Sunday 21 January '45

Left depot on trucks so crowded no one could move. Traveled about 65 miles to Sarrebourg to Army Depot. Our truck froze up so had to switch. Nice place here.

Monday 22 January '45

Did nothing while in this depot as most of guys in charge are old combat men. Ran into Corporal Ellis just as we left 2nd depot so we go back together.

Tuesday 23 January '45

Left Sarrebourg today and made over to 36th post office. Caught a mail truck out to company. Quite a few old men have been killed while I was gone. 200 mines blew up & killed about eight guys two nights ago.

Wednesday 24 January '45

Went out into woods by building we are in and shot a deer. Some good eating. Drove jeep with mines up to front. Germans attacked and ran us off. Made me pretty jumpy as shrapnel was sure flying.

Thursday 25 January '45

Back up with more mines tonight.[3] No trouble. Frozen German bodies scattered all over. Snow deep. We are laying mines & wire. Defensive positions.

Friday 26 January '45

Did nothing today or tonight. Sergeant Glenn was hit while I was gone. Squad full of new men. Still snowing and really cold.

Saturday 27 January '45

Moved up into town of Dorlisheim and are in houses. People don't seem to mind too much. All talk German.

(January 27 letter to Iona)

I'm sure you are wondering what has been going on with me. At last I have gotten back to the company. I was darn glad to get back as these depots are a rough deal and very crowded and transportation was an ordeal. I've been packed in box cars and trucks to a degree that would make a sardine blush. It was very uncomfortable as the weather is cold. If I never see snow again it will suit me fine. It is a rough go now and I think getting worse. Snow is getting quite deep. It's not as bad as it could be as we are able to get into houses. Seems the people share their houses with good grace. I'm having to get use to people who speak German so suspect all.

The country is different from what it was when I left. Better I'd say. The first thing I did was take a little hunting trip in the wood by where we were and believe it or not brought in fresh meat, a deer or I should say an overgrown jack rabbit as they are small, standing about three feet high but move like lightning. Sure good eating but have no wild taste.

My first contact with enemy shells etc. made me a little jumpy but will get back in the groove. First night they really put on a good show for me but I didn't enjoy it too well as those slugs singing around had me jumping.

I didn't get to go out any while I was in Paris as it was off limits. I could see all I wanted to from the hospital as I was on the tenth floor and could see the Eiffel Tower quite plainly. Too I rode thru when I left so am satisfied about the whole thing. Things are at an unheard off price there[4] so I wouldn't have liked it at all.

Tuesday 30 January '45

Went up to town of Brumath and worked on rubber boats for a river crossing. Cold & snowing. Don't know what we are to do.

(January 30 letter to Iona)

Everything is O.K. with me, in fact I find I am in pretty good shape. Being off my feet has helped my bad foot a lot. The main trouble around here is the snow. It is very cold but it doesn't seem to hurt me except my feet. When we are not working, we have a pretty good set up as we always have a house to go in to sleep. These people sure watch every little thing and raise the dickens when we appropriate a stove pipe etc. But we tell them "C'est La Vie" and they go away talking to themselves and come back later and have it all over again.

While I was in the hospital I accumulated a little cash so am sending 100 bucks back as I don't need it at the present. If I were to go out to have a little fun a hundred wouldn't last one day. A small drink of schnapps or cognac cost all the way form 40 c to 80 c. I don't intend to give them my money as I figure can have a lot more fun on it when I get back home. So, stick it in the bank and if I need any money I'll write for it. I hope everything is alright with you all. I've heard from Marvin and he's O.K. Things are looking a little brighter, but I don't want to get too sure of any of it. Never can tell.

Wednesday 31 January '45

Worked on mines. Eight men killed. Truck hit stack of our mines and exploded. Weems, Loree, Sleator, Meese, Nims, Gilbert, & two others. Bodies ripped apart and scattered 75 yards. I started to ride that truck!! About a hundred mines exploded. Someone must have carelessly left a live mine laying by stack and ¾ ton truck hit it. Blew nearly all the windows out of this town and jarred tile of lots of roofs. Six were old men. Very hard to identify them. Can't find two at all.

Thursday 1 February '45

I was made acting Corporal today in first squad.[5] This evening we moved to Bischwiller. 143rd suppose to attack. Quite a hot spot as shells hit quite frequently. Good room to live.

Friday 2 February '45

Didn't go out last night as 142nd couldn't take objective so 143rd was called off. They attacked tonight at 7:30. I had to go up & wade canal waist deep in ice & water to measure bridge at 11 tonight. Small arms & artillery thick. Snow thawing fast & water rising in low spots.

Saturday 3 February '45

Went out at daylight up to town of Rohrwiller, which Infantry attacked, to remove trees on road. Big battle going. We moved it with rifle bullets whizzing. A. A. T. gun fired direct across road with tracer. They put two thru church steeple. What a noise. My nerves are on edge.

Sunday 4 February '45

Last night shells rained in this town. Some hit out in street here. My nerves are strained to the breaking point. No place to go for cover and these houses won't stand much. Out this PM blowing up mines we had fused. Too dangerous to defuse. Blew windows out & tile of roofs.

Monday 5 February '45

Worked all day putting wire around mine field. Shelling off far enough away. Lots of dead Germans. Water over everything as all snow melted. Raining today. I got soaked.

(February 5 letter to Mother)

I'm sure you are wondering how I am making out. Physically I am O.K. now. But I can see a little difference in my reactions since being back. I don't mean I am all shot or a nervous wreck but a little more jumpy. But I find I am getting better use to it each day. I don't need to tell you how tiresome this gets or how I wish I could come home. That feeling is mutual with every person over here. Naturally we are watching the Russian advance with real interest and have hopes of this thing coming to an end soon. Hope you are feeling lots better. Keep yourself going and don't weaken.

Tuesday 6 February '45

Went into Herrlisheim and swept roads for mines. Town just taken. I counted 28 of our tanks knocked out (12th armored) American & German dead all around. Town a total wreck. Still snipers there. Young was killed by mine last night. Hit it with jeep. [Russell T. Young of Atlanta, Georgia died in an explosion of an anti-tank mine northeast of Rohrwiller that also destroyed the vehicle he was driving]

Wednesday 7 February '45

Moved back to town we were in the other day. Roads are giving away as water is bad. We worked all day and until 9 PM building plank road.[6] Raining off & on. Everyone worn out. Hard work.

Thursday 8 February '45

Loaded lumber in yard at Bischwiller all day. Other squads laying. Bombers over today and Jerries put up ack ack. Sun shone today. No snow left. Weather moderate.

Saturday 10 February '45

Back to lumber yard. Today we had civilian workers.[7] I had 27 loading lumber. Hard workers. Just as we were quitting a shell hit fairly close & shrapnel & tile flew all around. No one hurt but all scattered like quails.

Part of the thousands of yards of planking the engineers repaired muddy roads with.

(February 10 letter to Iona)

There is no need for you to be so worried about how I am getting along. I have been doing some real hard work lately and am standing up to it like a young buck would. One would think by your letters that I am a physical wreck. So please don't think I am all shot to pieces.

Also I know how much you would like for me to come home but you have a few wrong ideas about things. There are hundreds of guys who have done more and been thru more than me and who are still here. So, don't feel that I am being mistreated or subjected to mistreatments of any kind. It's impossible for us all to come home and the ones that do are very lucky. I realize how you feel but don't be selfish about it. My turn may come some day.

At the present I am suffering in comfort. I have a nice place to sleep and a good bed with springs and feather pillows etc to sleep on. The only trouble is I don't get to stay in it as long as I would like.

The weather is not uncomfortable at all. The snow has all melted and it feels like spring. It makes things hard on us with so much water around. The point is I can sleep at night without fear of being blown out of bed. I can face the stuff in the day knowing I can get a little decent rest.

It has been a long and hard row to make and I wonder how we have come as far as we have. But at last I am able to see the objective we have fought so for, Germany itself. On a clear day I have looked across into the darn place. But you know the old saying, a dog fights hardest in its own front yard.

I hope by now Papa is a lot better and Mother is still keeping up and about. I'm sorry if I gave the impression that I was in bad shape. I've never been better, honest! So get those thoughts out of your head.

Sunday 11 February '45

Back to Bischwiller and worked on road all day. Am in charge of squad as Sergeant is in next camp. P 47s really strafing and bombing just a short ways over. Road going to pieces. Had other platoons working with Infantry.

Monday 12 February '45

Am now a Corporal! Same job today. Raining. Heavy shell barrage 500 yards from us. Germans really throwing it in. Our food has been terrible for a week. Short on bread and no sugar except for breakfast. Hard work & short rations.

Tuesday 13 February '45

More road work. Get one place fixed and another goes. Our planes strafing & bombing just to our left. Lines can't be over 1000 yards away. Can't understand why the Jerries don't shell us off job.

(February 14 letter to Iona)

Today has been a beautiful one. Clear and warm. Seems good to feel the sun again. It will take a lot more like this to dry things up. The best part is I have had the day off so got a shower and cleaned up. At the moment the old lady is making up my bed. I sure hate to have to leave it as it is the best one I've slept on since leaving home. The old lady seems to be a little off and is always running in to see if we are burning the place up. Comes in and dusts things off and talks all the while. Of course I understand nothing she says but an occasional "ya" seems to satisfy her. She has a boy in the German army but hasn't heard from him in over four months. When she told us this she started crying. I feel sorry for her but what could I say? I see I will have to remake my bed as she has wadded the bottom blankets up and spread the top one over them. I suppose she has good intentions.

I received your Feb 5th letter in seven days. I'm sure by the way you write my mail is not doing that well. I suppose Mrs. Glenn was all upset about Arnold. At least she should be happy to know he is pretty well off back in a hospital. That is one thing a person can be thankful for, that it is merely a case of being wounded. Muley and J.P. are O.K. if their folks should ask.

Well, due to circumstances beyond my control I am now a corporal. For how long I wouldn't say but guess I'm capable of doing the job, at least I'm doing my best. I'm not too happy about it as it puts some responsibility on me and over here there are times when I'd rather not have it. So, I'll do what I think is best and hope for the best.

Thursday 15 February '45

Moved back to Bischwiller today. Got same place we stayed in last time. A little quieter now. Weather is nice. Still muddy & lots of water.

Saturday 17 February '45

Tonite we laid 1300 mines. Infantry carrying for us. They really cussed. Worked till 2 AM. Going towards German lines. Got so close to lines we were under flares continually. Small arms & artillery etc heavy. Few shells jarred us up. A Company had 1000 mines to blow up. No one hurt.

Sunday 18 February '45

Same work. Tonight we put out 1000 mines. As yet we have had no trouble with patrols. We have Infantry as a guard but they are no good. More scared than I am.

Monday 19 February '45

Same job. Tonight we finished the English mines & started on Americans.[8] Put two in hole as one doesn't blow a tank track. Infantry really quit us on carrying so we had a mess on hand. Came in about 12.

Tuesday 20 February '45

Turned down trip to Brussels yesterday. Trying to get to go to England some time. Finished mine field about 8 tonight. Met where A Company left off. Raining tonight. This squad I have isn't worth a damn. Old men about all gone and new men are guys TOed out of other outfits.[9]

(February 20 letter to Mother)

It seem odd that I should just now be getting letters that were written so long ago but I am. Yesterday I received quite a few dated from October on up which have been following me all over France. In the group was your letter written on my birthday. You have no idea how I appreciated it. I was very glad to get the picture of you and thought you looked so well and natural. The flowers and all were beautiful. I can't see why you aren't better satisfied with such a beautiful place. It appears to me to be such a nice place.[10]

Now don't get all excited about what I am about to write but I have hopes of getting over to see Marvin. You see we are allowed a man to go there about every three weeks and also one each week to Paris and Brussels. Yesterday I was selected to go to Brussels but I talked to the Lieutenant and told him I had rather take my chances on getting to go see Marvin. So I didn't go. I may never get to go but I feel like he will do his best to give me an even chance. You remember Sergeant Griffitt the Sergeant who came home with me from Florida. Well he is there now [England] but I didn't get to talk to him before he left. Anyhow I hope to be able to go within the next few months. Of course I would have liked to have seen Brussels but knew it would help us all if the other deal comes thru.

I hope you are feeling a lot better by now. Heck, sixty-four is not so old. You should be good for lots of years yet. Don't give up just yet. It's all too near over for you to give up now. Carry on like you used to and before long it will seem like just a dream.

Friday 23 February '45

French have relieved us in this sector. Left Bischwiller this AM and moved to Haguenau. Large place. I immediately went to front and stayed in house. Suppose to blow up a building if Germans take it. 3000 pounds in it. Situation doesn't look to good as we have one side of canal & Jerries have other.

Saturday 24 February '45

About 10 PM last night Jerries shelled heavily and then attack. I had no contact with no one as really had a bad time. Heavy fighting & bullets thick. About 12, a seven man patrol broke thru and Infantry contacted them around my house. What a battle. Killed squad leader so the rest surrendered.

Sunday 25 February '45

Yesterday evening Sergeant Duncan came up & got me. I am selected to go to England, so I spent last night back at Supply. Was I glad to get out of that strain and not spend another night. Rode to Saverne & took auto car (rail) to Luneville. Caught train for Paris.

13 ENGLAND

"Breakfast is really good. French egg & ham. Pub opens at 11:30 so we drank ale till 1 and had lunch. Then walk around or sleep till pub opens at 7."

Frank arrived for the unannounced reunion with his brother Marvin, who was serving with the 14th Combat Bombardment Wing, 491st Bomb Group, 854th Squadron, in North Pickenham near Kings Lynn, England. Name any emotion that can fathom what brothers, who haven't seen each other for over two years, feel when they first meet eye to eye. One walks into a barracks in a faraway country and looks at the second, who is staring down boringly at some paperwork. The second, after hearing a familiar voice, glances up and tries to focus on an unbelievable, unexpected, but joyful surprise. The smiles, the wild hugs, and a room warmed by a rebinding of brothers' hearts follow.

Then it was blow out time! The boys from a black dirt section of East Texas, bringing along Wallace Lawhon of Greenville, Texas, were let loose in Cambridge on a two-day pass. Frank, who hadn't seen civilization, law and order like this since loading on a boat in New York two years before, enjoyed every passing minute of it. Pub after pub, downed beer on top of downed beer, and conversation upon conversation transpired.

After days of celebration, it was time to return to France and the war. Frank and Marvin wouldn't dare admit it until years later, but tears did stream down each man's cheeks. When each was suddenly alone after the emotional reunion, hearts sank, a surge of melancholy struck as an unexplainable wave of helplessness flooded their brains, and both were left with only memories of this special experience.

Monday 26 February '45

Traveled all night and got into Paris about 7:30 AM. Good car (day car). Spent today in Paris. Things are sky high. Went to G. I. theatre and listened to Glenn Miller Band.[1] Left Paris at 8:20 tonight.

Tuesday 27 February '45

Traveled all night and got to Le Havre at 5:30 today (AM). At 7:30 caught trucks out about fifteen miles to processing center. Drew new clothes & got a bath & cot. Even got a blouse & all campaign ribbons.[2]

Wednesday 28 February '45

Spent night at center. Needed the sleep. Everything about set. Loaded on trucks at 6 PM and went to Le Havre. Got on ship S.S. Explorer at 10 PM. Don't pull out until tomorrow night. Dock area is a total ruin & several blocks around.

Thursday 1 March '45

Boat pulled out in harbor & set all day. I am working in butcher shop. Get good eats there. Went up and went to bed about 6:30. When I awoke we were under way. Raining.

Friday 2 March '45

Anchored off South Hampton when I got up. About 10 AM we docked. Got our passes stamped, caught train to London & switched to another station & caught train to Norwich. Got to Norwich around 8 PM. Spent night at Red Cross.

Saturday 3 March '45

Caught 10:25 train to Holme-Hale. Met boy from Marvin's base so he brought me down. Got here around noon. Walked in on Marvin. Was he surprised. Went over to Pub tonight. English beer not much. Staying at base.

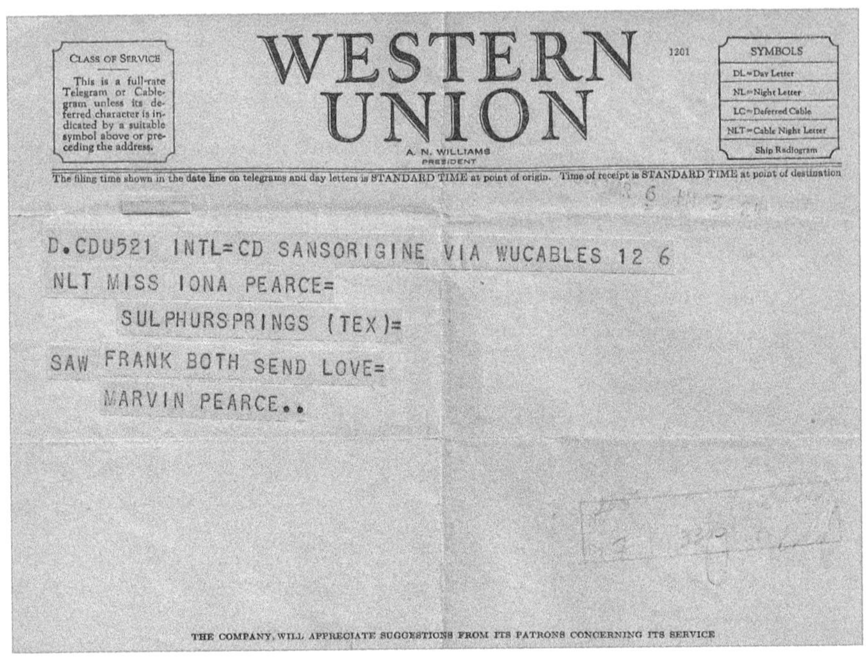

CLASS OF SERVICE
This is a full-rate Telegram or Cablegram unless its deferred character is indicated by a suitable symbol above or preceding the address.

WESTERN UNION

A. N. WILLIAMS
PRESIDENT

1201

SYMBOLS
DL=Day Letter
NL=Night Letter
LC=Deferred Cable
NLT=Cable Night Letter
Ship Radiogram

The filing time shown in the date line on telegrams and day letters is STANDARD TIME at point of origin. Time of receipt is STANDARD TIME at point of destination

D.CDU521 INTL=CD SANSORIGINE VIA WUCABLES 12 6
NLT MISS IONA PEARCE=
SULPHURSPRINGS (TEX)=
SAW FRANK BOTH SEND LOVE=
MARVIN PEARCE..

THE COMPANY WILL APPRECIATE SUGGESTIONS FROM ITS PATRONS CONCERNING ITS SERVICE

A cryptic telegram from Marvin Pearce to the folks back home that he had seen his brother and that all was well.

Sunday 4 March '45

Went over to strip and Marvin arranged a plane ride for me. Went up in B 24 and was up three hours. Pretty country from air. Flew to coast & around by Cambridge etc. Really enjoyed it. Raining this evening.

Monday 5 March '45

Marvin, Wallace Lawhon, & I caught train at Brandon to Cambridge as they got two day pass. Got a room there & hit the pubs. Just having a good easy time. Pretty weather for picture taking.

Tuesday 6 March '45

Breakfast is really good. French egg & ham. Pub opens at 11:30 so we drank ale till 1 and had lunch. Then walk around or sleep till pub opens at 7. Got a few drinks of scotch.

Left: Near Kings Lynn, England the brothers met for the first time in over two years. *Right*: Pearce and his brother Marvin enjoying life at a pub in Cambridge, England.

Wednesday 7 March '45

Had good breakfast at hotel and we caught train back to Brandon. Got to base about noon. Went to show. Pretty weather. Really enjoyed myself. Hotel cost us $14.

Thursday 8 March '45

Fooled around base. Boys at supply gave me a lot of good warm clothes & gloves. Got a bag full. Went into Swaffham to pub. Had a nice time.

Friday 9 March '45

Got stuff ready to leave. Marvin gave me a couple of good watches & a pair of glasses. [binoculars] Left at 6. Hated to leave and Marvin hated to see me go. Caught bus at Swaffham to Norwich. Got to Red Cross about 9 PM.

Saturday 10 March '45

Left Norwich on 8:45 AM train arrived in London 11:55. Caught taxi over to Red Cross club where we have to assemble. Had to be at Waterloo Station at 2 PM so fooled around. Got to South Hampton at 11:10 PM. Spent night there.

Sunday 11 March '45

At 6:30 A.M. gathered in groups and got on same boat at 10 AM. Pulled out tonight for Le Havre. On K. P. tonight at 12. Pealed potatoes till 4 and went to bed.

Monday 12 March '45

Docked at Le Havre this morning. Got off at 7 PM and made to processing area. Billeted in hotel. Cold tonight. Same procedure as coming.

Tuesday 13 March '45

Turned in blouse.[3] Changed money. This PM I caught a ride to Le Havre and looked up Pee Wee. [Thomas E. Carnes of Sulphur Springs, Texas, and U.S. Army] Was he surprised. Spent the night with him. He's got a good go.

Wednesday 14 March '45

Left Le Havre early and had a hard time getting back to Etretat. Walked about seven miles. Left here by train at 4:30 PM and went a short ways & then waited three hours on a siding.

Thursday 15 March '45

Train crawled along all night and about 9 AM we pulled into Paris. Seventeen hours and made around 100 miles. Really tires one out. Major gives us two days here. B Company boy & I managed for a room as quarters furnished are lousy.

(March 15 letter to Mother)

I'm sure you were very surprised when you received the telegram from Marvin. The whole thing came up quite suddenly, so I just walked in on him. In case you wonder how one finds anyone over here it is quite simple if one goes to some Red Cross Center or R.T.O. office. I was five days going over. It is a hard trip as transportation over here is not the best. To say he was surprised is putting it mild. We spent a couple of days in Cambridge. Good ale and good food sure makes a difference. I sure hated to leave all that as that is the first place I've been where I could walk in a café and order. Of course I had to take a plane ride and stayed up three hours. Enjoyed myself very much. All the boys were really good to me.

After getting back to France I went to Le Havre and visited Thomas Carnes over night. He was as surprised as Marvin was. He really has a good job. He looks about the same. It was a short visit but I enjoyed it.

Right now I am in Paris knocking around. Can't get things like in England. I sure want to send you and Iona something from here but the prices are unheard of and I know nothing about perfumes so would get gypped on that.

I'm sure you'll understand why you haven't been hearing from me as I am traveling around so much I haven't taken time to write. By the time I get back to the Company I will have had a three week vacation. I hope I have a stack of mail when I get back. The news is encouraging but there is still a long ways to go. I feel like I should be home within the next six months. I hope.

Friday 16 March '45

Fooled around in Paris. Bought perfume for Iona. Made several shows & drank cokes at Red Cross. Caught train at 9:30 PM. Another slow one.

(March 16 letter to Iona)

With the recommendation of the Red Cross I went to a place and bought you some perfume. Now being as I don't know the slightest thing about such stuff I wash my hands of any incidents which may occur if you use it. The one that says "Fluer de Tobac" (tobacco flower) is supposed to be for dark headed persons. I bought two kinds of smells so if one is repulsive you can drown it out with the other and if you should mix them who knows what you are liable to smell like. I kind of had an idea you would like something from Paris, so I did my best. You should be proud of me. I could have nearly bought a bottle of cognac for the same money which smells better to me anyhow.

You know I thought I had just about seen everything but today I saw a woman with light purple hair! Peroxide (ultra ultra) blondes and weird red heads. It seems the predominating style now in hair dress is to pile it all into a mound of 8 inches or more on the front of the head. Hats the same way. Skirts fairly short in some cases. I came to the conclusion the reason some women don't smile is because their paint job might crack. Not being a beautician I can't name the shades but one in particular I noticed is the oriental shade of tan. All very interesting to an old dog face who ain't seen nothing but dirty gals who live in cellars to keep living. I am practically beaten blue getting around the streets and subways with such crowds going all directions. I guess I've nearly been run down dozens of times by autos and trucks and bicycles and high fast stepping gals. Worst than Saturday on the old home square.

I intended to ask a Wac to select some exotic smelling stuff but I wasn't dressed correctly to approach one as my pants are not highly creased and I have no blouse bedecked with stripes and ribbons as I had to turn it in at the processing center after I came back from England. The only one I saw with whom I might have had a chance was extremely cross eyed and I couldn't seem to get in her line of vision. But all in all I have had enough of city life and am ready to go back to where there are not so many people.

As a favor to me I want your honest opinion on the stuff when it arrives and don't tell me a fib. It won't hurt my feeling any and I want to know if I got gypped out of twelve bucks. (I managed to ease the price in kind of unconcerned like didn't I?)

The guy there put some on my hand for a sniffing test and it's been about five hours and I still haven't gotten it off. I hope it goes away before I get to the company or I'll have a lot of explaining to do which no one will believe. Just a warning how persistent it seems to be.

Really tho I have had a marvelous time the past three weeks even if it has been tiresome and boresome traveling. Seems I'm quite a traveled person now, Rome, Paris, London and a few other smaller dumps. Guess I'll have to see Brussels next and then Berlin or at least were it use to be, I hope.

As I said regardless of the consequences my intentions were good. Maybe the fortune teller was right and it will overcome some old codger to the point of proposing to you. P.S. Keep it hidden from Mother as Papa is too old to be left alone!

Saturday 17 March '45

Train fooled around all night on sidings etc. Arrived in Nancy at 3:30 PM. 150 miles in eighteen hours. Spending night here. Nice city and a good place to eat with a waitress. Free beer at night really a good set up. Rest camp here.

Sunday 18 March '45

Left Nancy at 11 AM. Met Lieutenant Cathcart at Station. Arrived in Saverre at 3 PM. Trucks picked us up after six. Got to Brumath & spent night as Company is on advance & no contact. Reports are that we are advancing good.

14 FOOTPRINTS ON THE THIRD REICH

"We really caught hell from mortars, shells and those terrifying screaming meenies. The mountains were full of pill boxes & trenches & how they were ever taken beats me except they were short of men. We lost more men than Germans."

With the Germans' Fatherland so near, it was time to start the final push to end the war and go home. On March 15, the 36th began the attempt to cross the Moder River. For this movement, the death-dealing firepower of the entire Division was on the job. The main task fell to the 143rd with Company C, who started at Pfaffenhoffen where a small bridgehead over the Moder already existed. Attacking at one in the morning, without artillery preparation, they captured Bitschoffen, cleared the western edge of the Haguenau woods, took Mietesheim and then occupied the far bank of the Zintel River. Company C's only statistic in the action was the slight wounding of Leo E. Howell of Canton, Ohio, by an enemy shell. 142nd with Company B, also in the AM, moved on Mertzwiller and by the sixteenth the city by the Zintel River was secured. The 141st along with Company A overran the city of Haguenau on the first day and established a point at the edge of the Haguenau woods.

The attack to clean the Germans out of this section of France had begun well. Haguenau was free of the enemy and the quest of crossing the three rivers was nearly accomplished. The Moder and Zintel had been breached, with the Sauer soon to follow.

The first mission for the Division was completed when the 143rd took Griesbach on the sixteenth and established a bridgehead over the Sauer River by taking Gunstett on the seventeenth. On the same day, the 141st loped past the Sauer River and took Surbourg, opening the way to the ultimate capture of Soultz.

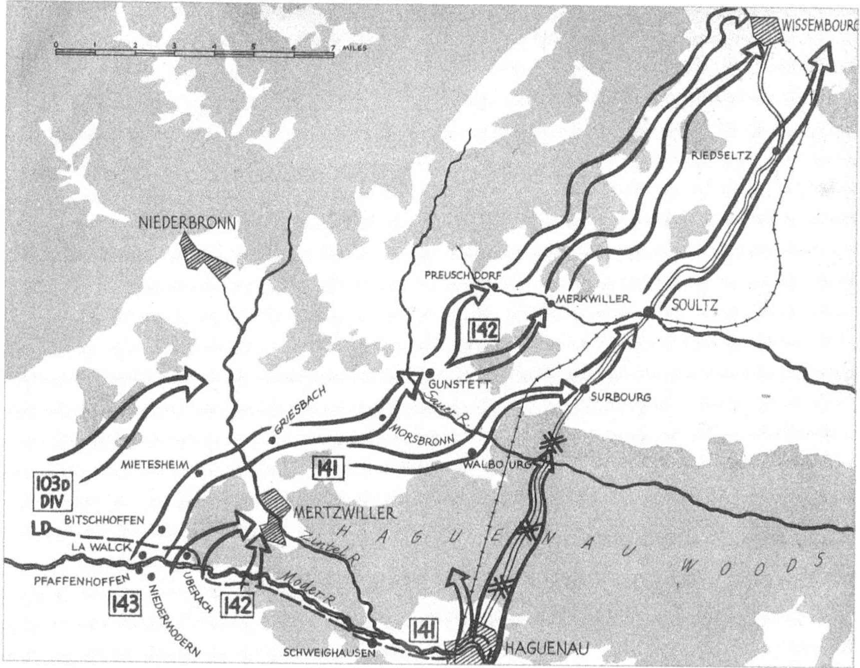

The 36th Division drove steadily toward the German border but ran into determined resistance.

Two days later, elements of the 36th Division enjoyed a timely arrival into Germany. At 11:00 AM, 2nd Battalion of the 141st, crossing northeast of the French town of Wissembourg, became the first unit of the Division to touch soil on which the Thousand Year Reich was built. All three of the 141st Battalions were able to tread on precious German sod during the day but couldn't push past the enemy lines.

Also on the nineteenth, the 1st Battalion of the 142nd, with the sun high overhead, took the last major French town in German hands when the enemy simply evaporated and let Wissembourg fall. Later that day, Company C arrived for mine sweeping duties in Wissembourg.

Two miles from Wissembourg a heavy fortification, known as the Siegfried Line or Westwall, faced the Allies as they entered Germany. The most heavily fortified positions were along the 36th sector of the front. Continuing forward, the 1st Battalion of the 142nd, despite shelling, took Ober-Otterbach and by nightfall all of 142nd was at the German main line of defense. The 142nd attempted extending its advantage but found the fortifications too plentiful and concentrated. Due to murderous fire, a token force was left facing the Siegfried Line, and the rest were withdrawn to support the Division's potential move into the hills on the west side of Ober-Otterbach. There was a slight dent in the Siegfried Line as 2nd Battalion of the 142nd knocked out the pillboxes of Ebnung Hill west of Ober-Otterbach, and then held off repeated enemy assaults to reoccupy them.

The hard education in Italy, utilizing mass Civil War type charges that once pulverized the youth of the Blue and Gray, had been a lesson well learned. So the lives of the 141st and 142nd were not dashed against the dragon's teeth pyramidal obstacles, concrete machine gun filled pill boxes, or steel reinforced fortifications. Instead, the call was a hard march wearing out boot soles, but not costing living souls, and it worked to perfection.

The plan was to work almost parallel to the Siegfried Line up a steep mountain trail and hopefully surprise the Germans defending the Grassberg heights. With only a first quarter moon showing dimly in the March 19 sky, 3rd Battalion of the 142nd with 1st platoon of Company B started an exhausting twelve hour climb to

German pillboxes were hidden in the dense forest on Grassberg height across this wide gully.

a position overlooking the Grassberg height. The Nazi installations here were not as extensive, and the major obstacle up the one-way trail was 1st platoon's time consuming removal of roadblocks, fallen trees, and mines.

Despite the harsh climb, the 3rd Battalion succeeded in taking the height by late afternoon. The advance stopped here for the time being due to lack of ammunition, obvious leg weariness, and a stubborn enemy defense. Still, a crack appeared in the solid German defense. It would be a crack that would fracture the Siegfried Line.

Since it would take many hours to follow the same path secured by the 3rd Battalion, another plan to support them was developed. 1st Battalion of the 142nd, as the sun set on the twentieth, was ordered up a deep pass due west of Ober-Otterbach. This new trail ran dangerously close to the enemy lines, but its direct line to the Grassberg area saved valuable hours of marching. This move was completed without drawing German fire with 1st Battalion arriving early on the morning of the twenty-first. This enabled them to move through 3rd Battalion,

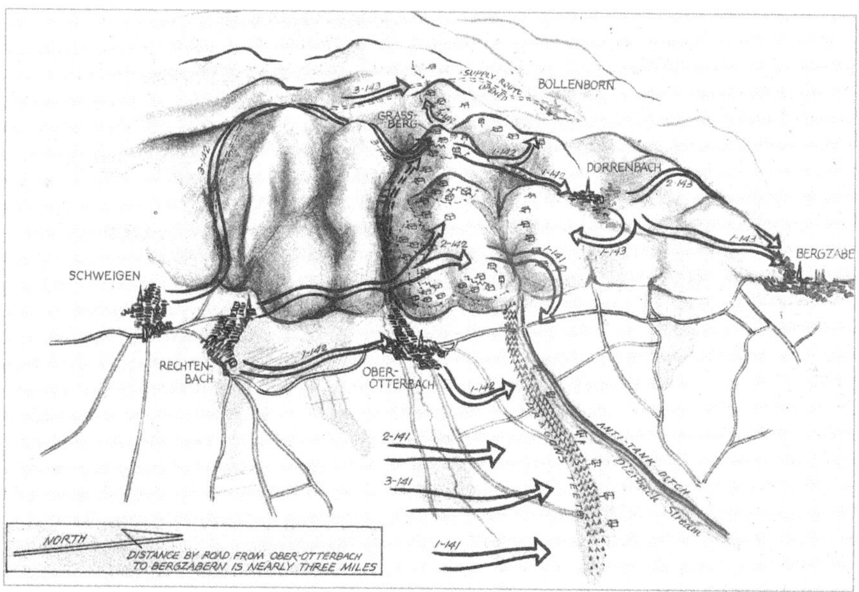

The Siegfried Line would prove to be another tough obstacle for the 36th Division.

and blasting past pillbox by bloody pillbox, work towards Dorrenbach. The well defended German positions took their toll, but the Americans never wavered in taking Dorrenbach, a town behind the Germans' main line.

Pearce, with 1st platoon attached to 1st Battalion of the 143rd, moved into the hills on the morning of March 21. Their mission was to pass through the 142nd and attack east, eliminating the Germans at Bergzabern. Bergzabern was a town located two and a half miles behind the Siegfried Line. Each engineer was equipped with and carried one tetryl pack,[1] which could be used for any required demolitions.

Bobbing and weaving through the deep woods after dark, they found themselves in a precarious position. The battalion had bobbed once too often and was almost a mile off course for Bergzabern. To make matters worse, they had been slashing at the backside of German installations and were trying to penetrate in the wrong direction. In the daylight of the twenty-second, they were able to get back on track and continued towards Bergzabern. 1st Battalion then finished the job of taking the furiously defended German town.

The Siegfried Line now split open so badly no tourniquet could stop the bleeding. The 36th, in a rippling effect of various Battalions volleying past each other, moved deeper into Germany. Resistance west of the Rhine River went kaput as the 36th engaged in their last major battles of the war.[2]

Homer Figler.

With the war near an end, men still risked their lives to save friends. As Company A started on a mission to destroy over thirty German pillboxes near Ober-Otterbach, enemy artillery and mortar blasts drove the members of the company back. Homer R. Figler, after reaching protective cover, "noticed his squad leader lying wounded and exposed to hostile shellfire". Blacking out any thoughts of his own safety, he raced across the open ground and immediately "while shells crashed around him, calmly administered first aid". With the aid of another engineer, Figler carried his squad leader to an aid station 500 yards behind the front. Then he rejoined his squad and helped with their task of demolishing the enemy pillboxes. Kenneth Weiss of Kent, Ohio, Charles Hickey Jr. of Harvey, Illinois, and Roy Martin from Vesuvius, West Virginia, were three men from Company A injured completing this mission.

The end of the long list of injuries to the engineers occurred in this final push into Germany. On March 23, 1st platoon of Company C continued moving eastward from Bergzabern with the 143rd. After receiving constant small arms, mortar, and artillery fire during the entire advance, Frank Cathcart Jr. and Luther Matlock were wounded. At 9:00 PM, an artillery shell's explosion drove fragments into Cathcart's right leg. The same shell sent flying metal which struck Matlock in both legs and his right foot. Cathcart and Matlock would be the last of Pearce's Company C to receive a purple heart.

German prisoners, captured from pillboxes during the 36th offensive, are led to the rear.

On May 5, a message from Seventh Army Headquarters signaled an end of hostilities and all units ground to a halt with orders not to fire unless fired upon. The 141st plus Company A and the 142nd supported by Company B, in the last engagements of the war for a veteran 36th, captured Bad Tolz, Germany and ended it all in a victorious halt across the Austrian border near Kufstein.

The Nazi government officially capitulated, and all the sounds of fighting fell silent at 11:00 PM on May 8. VE Day (Victory in Europe) had arrived. While the silence was treasured the most by the battle worn GIs, back in the United States, President Harry S. Truman broadcast "This is a solemn but glorious hour. General Eisenhower informs me that the forces of Germany have surrendered to the United Nations. The flags of freedom fly over all Europe."

Sensational news of the Texas Division's success continued to make headlines with their capture of famous German generals and war criminals. Easily the most prestigious celebrity prisoner was Reichmarshal Hermann Goering. Until a falling out with Hitler several days earlier, Goering was the number two man in Nazi Germany. In 1939, he had received the Reichmarshal title and was named Hitler's successor. Commander of the German Luftwaffe, he was a prize catch indeed.

Add in Von Rundstedt, captured on May 1 by the 141st near Bad Tolz, twenty plus lower ranked Generals, and the 36th ended this war in glorious fashion.

The first American unit to set foot on the continent of Europe was fame enough for most Divisions. Simply ordinary people back in the States, two years of fighting in Europe had cast the T-Patchers as blue steel tempered men

Welcome to Austria.

EXTRA - Gœring Surrenders To ADC
SEE PAGE 3
In Austria
T-PATCH
36TH DIVISION NEWS
Vol. 4. No. 1 SPECIAL EDITION 8 MAY 1945
VICTORY

T-Patch 36th Division News.

who accomplished victory after victory. Goering, Von Rundstedt, and twelve Presidential Unit Citations added to its legacy as one of the superior combat units in WW II. Individually, members of the Division were awarded fourteen Congressional Medals of Honor, eighty Distinguished Service Crosses, 2,354 Silver Star Medals, 5,407 Bronze Stars, and 88 Air Medals.

The 36th Division, in almost two furious years of combat, paid a large price in their part to eliminate Nazi tyranny. In this monumental effort, they suffered the third most casualties (27,343) of any US Army Division in the European Theater. The casualties included a total of 5,974 killed in action.

All three lettered companies were honored with their share of medals and, regretfully, more than their part in the casualties' department. During the action in the European Theater, Companies A, B, and C experienced the unofficial loss of fifty-five men killed. The totals came from Company A with fifteen, Company B with fourteen and Company C with twenty-six. Headquarters and Service Company added three and the 111th Medical Battalion another seventeen.

Tuesday 20 March '45

Rode out with Division trucks as they were moving up. Company was at Wissembourg. Quite a lot of artillery going pounding parts of Siegfried line. Helped Popeye drink schnapps & got tite.

Wednesday 21 March '45

"Entered Germany on this day-1945" Got up early and rolled light bed roll & took off with the Infantry on advance. Climbed mountain all day and crawled thru trenches & was shelled & shot at all day. Got lost after dark and we ended up behind German lines dug in by a pill box & six Jerries came out and surrendered. Lieutenant Cathcart & Sergeant Matlock were wounded by shrapnel. We really caught hell from mortars, shells and those terrifying screaming meenies. The mountains were full of pill boxes & trenches & how they were ever taken beats me except they were short of men. We lost more men than Germans.

Thursday 22 March '45

About noon we started out of position and walked for miles thru trenches etc. dodging shells & occasional rifle fire and worked our way back to small town [Dorrenbach] which our Infantry had taken. Found water in hole & filled up. About dark we took off again & advanced thru mountains to take town of Bergzabern which we did about 12:30 AM. Ran into Jerry tanks & quite a battle. As soon as we hit town us Engineers holed up in a hotel & got some rest while Infantry advanced into center of town to hold it. Boy I am dead tired!

Friday 23 March '45

Moved on up town & are staying in a house with good beds. Germans coming out this AM & surrendering. Civilians also coming out. All men are arrested who are young enough to be soldiers. All quiet.

Saturday 24 March '45

Moved on into Germany about twelve miles. Got shelled once. Ended up in town of Rulzheim. Lots of civilians here and white flags hanging out. Made people move out of house & we move in. They give us hard hateful looks.

Sunday 25 March '45

On guard last night as these people are not to be trusted so had heavy guard. We make them stay in house day & night. How they hate us! They sneaked out last night & guards shot at one. Some hear us and others are insolent. Still on guard today.

(March 26 letter to Mother)

Since I wrote you from Paris, I have been quite busy. All my spare moments I have spent trying to catch a little rest. I really have nothing I can write about except that I am now on German soil. It was not so easy for us but here we are. Our squad has a house to ourselves as we can't allow the people to be around us so we make them move out. I wish I could tell you about all the things around here but can't. Some of the people try to be friendly but we ignore them, and some make no pretense of how they feel. This is days which they never expected to see but as usual Hitler was wrong about that. Remember how I wrote about the French hanging out flags everywhere as we came in? Well it's the same here only they are white flags hanging out of windows, table clothes, napkins etc. How glad I'll be when all of Germany hangs out the white flags!

My trip to England seems as if it didn't happen. I was glad when I finally got back as traveling here is very tiring. Everything is going fine with me so don't worry. Each day brings things closer to a finish and I'm counting them till its over.

(March 26 letter to Marvin)

Well I have another country on my list now. At last I am in Germany and I really had quite a time getting in. I walked for two days and nights over mountains, thru trenches and around pill boxes and boy did we have hell. Those bastards really gave us the works, but we kicked hell out of them. We were carrying explosive packs and they really got heavy. Only weigh about 20 pounds but after 2 day & nights it seemed like 200. Am taking it easy now as we have a house to lay our weary bones. Make the people move out as we don't trust or intend to trust them. The white flags are flying as each house has one hanging out the window. Even with all the progress we've made it still is not over but it's getting closer to being.

Wednesday 28 March '45

Am going to mine school. Fine time to teach that now! Practically all the Seventh Army across Rhine but where we are we can't make it as the Jerries has pill boxes all along bank. So far the Germans haven't shelled their own towns much.

Friday 30 March '45

Moved back a few towns today. Have a nice house with good beds. People had to move out. I hate to see old people having to get out. Was quite a lot of sniping here a few days ago. Town of Insheim.

Sunday 1 April '45[3]

Moved out this PM. Moved about 75 miles. Are in town of Wiesbach close to Kaiserslautern. Have a swell home with lights water & radio. A beautiful place inside. Sergeant Duncan & Bruce left for home today! Thousands of vehicles & equipment scattered for miles around here.

(April 1 letter to Iona)

I know you and mother would be all excited over my getting to visit Marvin. You keep asking about how he is. Well really he hasn't changed at all. Still the same old way. His biggest worry is Mary. [Mary Evelyn Hurst of Sulphur Springs] He wants to get home and get married. I didn't say much for or against except that both of them were too stubborn and peculiar to ever get along, but I didn't try to change his mind as it was useless. [Marvin never married] As for the work he is doing it is more like our old line of business and at times I felt like I was back keeping shop for Papa.

Marvin did hate to see me leave but to me it all soon seemed like just another trip. It is different with me because I travel around so much and he doesn't. Really didn't seem so much out of the ordinary for me to be there. I would have liked to stayed longer. Marvin is living in the past too much. I advised him when I left to go places, get drunk, and date a girl and raise hell in general at least once a month. Sounds terrible I know but that is the only remedy for his ailment. I know for I had the same trouble my first year. Things I use to do back in the States are hazy memories now and if it weren't for you and the folks I wouldn't care how long it would be before I got back. I don't mean that I am having the time of my life, quite the contrary, but I am reconciled to this now.

There is one thing. You put too much stress on my condition. Darn it I am as good as ever and am not half of what you seem to think. Don't think it'll be long now.

Monday 2 April '45

Kaiserslautern was a total wreck from bombing & was quite large. Heated hot water tank up & took good tub bath. Have done nothing today but relax and listen to radio. Quite a life. Like home. Won $67 at poker tonight.

Wednesday 4 April '45

Still very little to do. Mostly guard & check points. All civilians with no papers are picked up. So many soldiers in civilian clothes. Also picking up German ammunition. Rumors have it we are getting ready to go to states.

(April 4 letter to Iona)

I wish you could see me at this moment. Here I sit in a nice room listening to the radio and even have house slippers on. Rugs on the floor, good beds, electricity, running water, toilets and a bath with heater. Just like home and very little to do. This squad has a two story house complete with kitchen with an electric stove. Looks like I have this war made unless some changes are made. I have high hopes of being home before too long.

Saturday 7 April '45

Reveille at 7:30 AM. All I did today was to make a trip over a few roads to check all people traveling for passes etc. Was only out about an hour. Squad was issued five bottles of drinking material, cognac etc. Confiscated stuff.

(April 7 letter to Iona)

I received you letter of the twenty eighth of March and was glad to know the package arrived safely. I really hope you are satisfied with the perfume and not just saying that to make me feel good. I wrote another letter while in Paris and hope it got to you as it explained about the deal.

Don't worry about my financial standing as I am not bothered with that anymore as we can't spend money anyhow here in Germany. All we use money for is to play a little poker along. Had a little game the other night and I won back exactly what I spent on my England trip, perfume included. I only spent sixty-five dollars on the whole trip as Marvin and friend wouldn't let me spend much.

As you know I am in Germany and frankly I don't care so much for it. It is not on a friendly basis and we intend to let the people know we are conquerors and not liberators so we can't have anything to do with them except pertaining to business. That is why I have such a nice house to live in. We select the houses we want and tell the people to move out as we are moving in. Of course it kinds of hurts to put old people out of their homes especially when they have lived there so long but that is their first lessons as to the cost of their "total war". They generally take all valuables and keep sakes, but we have all the furniture etc. I figure they are lucky to have a house! They really have lots of conveniences such as electric stoves, radios, in fact about like our homes. Also a basement here with a nice arrangement for washing clothes and plenty of wood or coal stacked in. Oh yes, I am enjoying it immensely.

I don't believe I can tell you just what we are doing but it is not hard. It is quite a job to check all people and see that all is in order but time will fix that up. You should see your boy put his foot down and roar like the devil when some person tries to argue about some point. Me speaking a few words of German? It's the tone of voice and the facial expression which counts. A few laughable incidents happen. I started in on a girl in my meager German and after a moment she began to talk to me in English. I turned her loose!

I hope you all are getting along O.K. As for me I am doing all the good so don't worry about me. Keep hoping on that end and I'll handle this side of it.

Monday 9 April '45

Drove truck today as Lyons [Walter Lyons of Groves, Texas] has malaria again. Out nearly all day picking up gas cans, ammo etc. Went back around Kusel. Lots of young men around and several ammo dumps. Too much for us to pick up.

Tuesday 10 April '45

Have done very little today. Cleaned up tools & guns. Are getting down to routine. Revile & retreat. Went over to see film at B Company on our job in Germany. Also regular film. Developed some pictures tonight in basement.

Developed picture of Pearce in Germany.

Wednesday 11 April '45

Today our schedule started. Reveille, calisthenics, close order drill, lectures. I got three shots today. Typhus, Tetanus & typhoid. My arms are really sore.

Friday 13 April '45

Was out till 8 tonight on recon. Went to Homburg and on south into France around Bitche. Checking all German ammo dumps as to what was there. Sure hard country to follow map in.

Monday 16 April '45

Went down autobahn to within a few miles of Rhine and checked some ammo dumps there. Went up to small town of Battenberg and fraternized a bit. Got lots of wine to drink. Played poker till 1 AM. Lost $54. Two of our men in bad trouble. Shot up a German home and charged with attempted rape. Drunk.

(April 20 letter to Iona)

It was really nice of Arnold to come in to see you. I'm glad he is back in the States as he deserves to be there. He won't tell you much but the reason for that is because these things cannot be put into words. Find out his address and let me know.

It was quite a shock to most of us when we heard of Roosevelt's death. I am wondering what effect it is going to have on us. I hope things work out just the same.

Now Ernie Pyle[4] being killed was another thing that will affect lots of boys. He really did do us guys some good. I'm sorry it had to happen. But no one can keep at this business indefinitely without something happening.

Now don't worry about what these people are doing. So far as I can see no difference in these people from any other except they seem to be a little more educated and have a higher standard of living.

Did I ever tell you that I hear quite a lot from Kathleen Horton? [girl from Sulphur Springs, Texas] I know how you all feel about that, but you could be wrong. Received a package of cookies from her the other day. Darn good too. But don't let it worry you yet. Plenty of time for that when I get back. It is hard for me to explain anything about this.

Saturday 21 April '45

Had inspection today by Colonel Petree. Also had to lay out all clothes. Of course it was not checked. Just same old routine.

Sunday 22 April '45

This PM. I took Sergeant Downing to Battenberg where we got a lot of wine. Cold ride but we were all feeling good when we got back. Jack Cleek came back today. Really got tite tonight.

Tuesday 24 April '45

Company went to A Company where General Stack [Robert Stack of Detroit, Michigan] presented men with medals. Popeye received Silver Star & cluster or Bronze Star. "C" Company had about 25 decorations.

Thursday 26 April '45

Cleaned house and pulled out at 9:15. Crossed Rhine close to Frankenthal. Traveled all day till 9 PM. Am in town of Dunbach. People all along seemed friendly.

Friday 27 April '45

Found out today we are going back into combat. Relieve 63rd Division. This is really a stop over while trucks bringing Infantry. Towns all in good shape except a few.

Saturday 28 April '45[5]

Nothing doing today. So just taking it easy. Peace rumors flying! Captain has gone on up to arrange for quarters. Will move up if trucks get back. We believe war may be over before we get there. Hear that Mussolini was hung in Switzerland and Hitler has 48 hours to live so doctor says. I wonder!

Monday 30 April '45[6]

Up at 5 AM & pulled out at 6. Cold this AM. Traveled all day. Snowed a little along. Roads are jammed with traffic. Came 150 miles. Can see Alps Mountains. Snow covered. Our advance troops have not contacted Germans. Road full of liberated French & Russians.

Tuesday 1 May '45

Spent night in a dairy farm. Only came ten miles today. In town of Weilheim. Not far from Munich and Italy. Snowing tonight. Fried up steak we got at slaughter house. We hear war is practically over. So far have hit no resistance. People say SS troops in mountains.

Wednesday 2 May '45

Went up about twenty miles and repaired bridge this evening. Mountains towering above. Snowed all last night. We heard tonight that the Germans in Italy, Austria & Southern Germany have surrendered. Infantry captured Von Rundstedt.[7] Hope it is true.

Thursday 3 May '45

Moved on into edge of mountains to town of Bad Tolz. A resort town. Carried two kegs of beer but found plenty of wine. We also fixed up a fair auto in a garage. Brand new (38). Got new tires for it. Have to figure out a way to keep it.

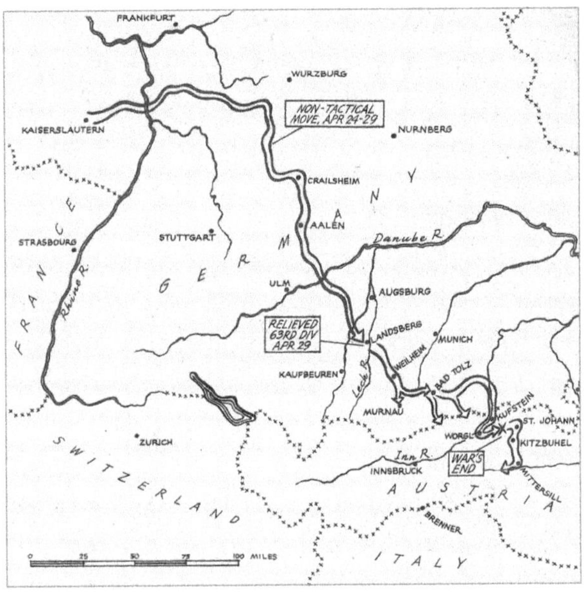

As German defenses collapsed, the 36th Division shifted its advance southeast toward the Bavarian Alps and Austria.

Friday 4 May '45

I came on up with quartering party at 12:20. Company moved to Tegernsee. Am in hotel overlooking a lake with Alps in background. Roads full of German soldiers of all ranks waiting to give up. Most everyone drunk in Company. What a mess!

Saturday 5 May '45

Out all last night until 5 this AM. Had to drive truck as driver and nearly all the squad were drunk or missing. Went up close to Austrian border. Today we move up to same place. Building a bridge and we work tonight. Word came down war over.

Sunday 6 May '45

Worked till 5 AM. Thousands of German troops in trucks etc coming by all night. Our part of the war is over! Such a mess. Freed prisoners trying to travel and Germans coming in. Some pitiful sights. Went into Austria today.

Left: Steve Sinchak and Allen Brewer are excited the end is here. *Right*: Brewer and Pearce celebrate.

Monday 7 May '45

Have done nothing today. Nice warm day. Beautiful country. Still lines of Germans going by. Hear 141 Infantry had quite a battle with Germans today. Didn't know of surrender. Really we don't know whether or not war is over!

Tuesday 8 May '45

We moved today about 25 miles. Am now in Austria at town of Rottenburg. Have nice place to stay. Set in the Alps. Played poker till 2 AM. Won $83. We now know *War* is officially over.

15 104 POINTS EQUALS HOME

"Get on your glad rags for your little boy is coming home! The first Sergeant woke me early this morning and asked me where I wanted to go in the States and I said HOME."

A point system, titled the Plan for Readjustment of the Personnel of the Army was the plan to bring home the most deserving soldiers first. The "points" were accumulated in four categories and then totaled. Service Credit awarded the soldiers one point for each month of service, with a starting date of September 16, 1940. Another point, under the category Overseas Service, could be won for each month a man was stationed overseas.

Combat Credit rewarded those who had actually fought. A GI racked up five points for each combat award his unit achieved and five points for awards like the Purple Heart or Bronze Star, he personally won. The big point category was Parenthood Credit. A far away trooper automatically tallied twelve points each for up to three dependent children left back home.

On June 9, as Frank Pearce boarded a captured Italian luxury liner for home, Doris Day and the Les Brown Orchestra, back in the United States, coincidentally released their new song. "Sentimental Journey." With Day doing the vocal, the song immediately roared to the top of the billboards across the country. Make no mistake about the impact the words of the song had on those returning from war. They touched all the right bases for Pearce and the homesick soldiers. Beautiful Doris Day, with a voice inherited from an angel, instantly cut to the quick of the few sensitive spots the combat veterans retained.

Gonna take a Sentimental Journey,
Gonna set my heart at ease.
Gonna make a Sentimental Journey,
to renew old memories.

I've got my bags, got my reservations,
Spent each dime I could afford.
I'm like a child in wild anticipation,
I long to hear that, "All aboard!"

A barefooted Pearce and his mother on the front porch of 114 Texas Avenue in Sulphur Springs—home, June 27, 1945.

Frank Pearce left New York for San Antonio and its reprocessing center, Fort Sam Houston, on June 18. Once there he drew back pay, had a medical examination, received $300 discharge pay and train fare home. The $300 mustering out pay went to any soldier who had served more than sixty days and had been overseas. Pearce deserved $300 and he would get it, over several months' time. Initial payment, to the money desperate GI, was only $100 with a typical government promise of the rest to come later.

Voucher 7507, distributed to him by Captain Carlos Delima, contained back pay of $70.62, travel home expenses of $17.50 and the $100 dollars. At least he was HOME! Pearce was discharged from service on June 26 and was in Sulphur Springs with his family on June 27.

Within days after his arrival, he received a Bronze Star[1] for "meritorious service in sustained frontline combat operations against the enemy." Just as important to him was his Award of Disability Pension. The pension, for service-connected injuries, would pay him $23.00 a month for the twenty percent disability he experienced from the Anould mortar shell.

Wednesday 9 May '45

Nothing doing today. Braddy has found warehouse 45 miles away full of cognac gin etc and brought some back so we all got drunk and shot up the place. Up till 12 PM on curfew patrol. Broke up a meeting of civilians. All fairly quiet.

Friday 11 May '45

We are doing nothing now. The men are more or less doing as they please. Opened up a beer parlor and it was really a rough house. I nearly had three fights and took a pistol away from one guy. Such a mess.

Saturday 12 May '45

Went out this PM. and destroyed a lot of gun powder and equipment. Men are all classified on who goes home. I have 104 points and about 20th on list. Popeye leaves tomorrow. I may go soon. We have fooled around in platoon or most of us would have more points.

Sunday 13 May '45

Just another day. Popeye & Lieutenant McDonald [Eugene V.] left for home today. Also heard Muley did too. I'll go in next bunch I hope. On guard tonight.

Monday 14 May '45

Still no duties except guard etc. This place stays full of girls. They are using us to get what they can to eat without giving anything.[2] One stayed with me till 11 PM. Just a friendly visit.

(May 14 letter to Iona)

Quite a lot has happened the last few days but here I still am. I'm sure you have all the dope about the point system and are expecting me home any day. Well I am sure of one thing, and that is that I am coming home but don't know just when. I have 104 points and expect to be in the next group to leave. I suppose I should have more but that is a long story. J.P. and Muley are on their way home now. Both were smart enough to have a few decorations so were high enough to be in the first group.

I'm not jealous of the guys who are on their way but it is not fair. More than half of the guys on their way home have never actually been in combat but were lucky enough to be up on top. I don't know when the next quota will come up but I believe I'll be on my way within the next two months. It is too late now for me to get any more points so we will have to make the best of it.

Anyhow it won't be too long before I will be home so I'm sure we all can sweat out the deal a while longer. The good thing is I know I am coming and that's more than I used to know.

Tuesday 15 May '45

Fooled around today. Girl came back to see me this PM. Stayed till 1 o'clock tonight. I am on guard tonight so was up all the time anyhow. What a gal![3]

Wednesday 16 May '45

Cleaned up place and loaded trucks. Left Rottenburg about 11:30 and came about 150 miles back into Germany. Am in town of Marktoberdorf. Say we will be here a long time. Fair place.

(May 17 letter to Mother)

I know the thought of me coming home has you excited and impatient. I have not been told just when it will be but I believe it will be in the near future. Now that this part of the war is over there is no need for many being here and I believe we will be sent back as fast as transportation will permit.

I am anxious to get home, but I am enjoying myself very much as this is such a beautiful country. The weather is just right and the scenery is the best. I wish you could see these mountains and lakes.

As you probably noticed I am back in Germany again. Just to look around one would never know these people have been at war six years. It seems to me they are more like us in customs than any other people. The lakes are well inhabited by them taking sun bathes and do our eyes stick out: The girls are some lookers and well dressed. This non-fraternization policy just keeps us looking—well darn near anyhow. It really feels good to be able to have electric lights and radios and to be able to enjoy ourselves without expecting the worse at a moment. I didn't get up till nine this morning.

Just giving you a little warning what to expect when I get there. We are in a nice town by the name of Marktoberdorf in the vicinity of Munich. Have a pretty nice place to stay. Really I believe that I will be home within the next month. So just start getting stuff together as I probably eat all your ration tickets up.

(May 18 letter to Marvin)

I wonder if you have gotten over your blues yet. I know darn well that you are down in the dumps about the whole thing. But heck the Pacific can't be so bad after all. You should appreciate being in the ground crew for there is things a lot worse. If I don't get to go home until this whole thing is over I will consider myself lucky that I am alive and able to go home. You should look on the other side of this thing and you will see what I mean.

As you probably notice I am back in Germany again. I was in Austria up in the Alps and it was the most beautiful country I have ever seen. The snow-capped mountains and lakes and rivers are something to see. I lived in some of the resorts and in places that people pay a lot to stay in. And since it is very warm now the girls are taking sunbaths and brother there are some good looking ones here too. This non-fraternization is pretty hard to obey as most of the girls are willing and able.

As I told you I have 104 points. Guess that will be all I am allowed as I understand it is frozen now. I figure you must have about sixty. Maybe if you do go to the CBI[4] you will come by the way of the states and get a furlough.

Saturday 19 May '45

Loaded up and moved about six miles to Unterthingau, a small town. This PM went about thirty miles and loaded up enemy equipment. Six A Company men badly burned by powder. We wrecked one truck. Made Sergeant today.

Sunday 20 May '45

Had day off. Took a good bath. I am all excited as I hear I am going home on the 22nd. Am not sure as they say transportation is scarce.

(May 20 letter to Mother)

Here is the letter you have been waiting for! If nothing is changed I will be on my way within two days! I don't know how long it will take to be processed but I have lots of traveling to do before I reach the port. It shouldn't be at the most over three weeks and maybe not that long before I set foot on the soil I have found out means more to me than anything outside of you all. The other good news is that I am now a Sergeant. So you see a few breaks are coming my way. I know how happy you will be and believe you me I am too.

If things move along fairly fast this will be my last letter to you from Europe and I hope it is! Now don't start dusting the house, mowing the lawn, clipping the hedge etc but you might put the evil eye on those pullets you were intending to save. The 22nd is the day and I am just like a boy going to the fair. No bawling now for I have tears.

(May 22 Letter to Mother)

It seems I was wrong about not writing from here again. It seems a transportation situation has arisen which is going to keep me here a while longer. Now it has been raised till the first before I leave. The only thing I am sure of is that I am coming in the next group. And I am sure that as soon as transportation is available I will be on my way. I am not in a hurry as maybe things will be in better shape in the rear to handle us and then I won't have to fool around a week or so before leaving port. So keep your chin up for I'll be there in June.

Wednesday 23 May '45

Went to Munich today in order to locate points of interest and act as guide for Company. Saw all of Hitler's beer halls etc. Munich is a "total" wreck. A large city all rubble & gutted buildings.

(May 24 letter to Iona)

Since the war is over I am having quite a lot of time to do things I enjoy. The military duties are not too severe now and the army is attempting to give us a chance to see some points of interest. Yesterday I was sent to Munich to look up points of interest so as to be able to act as a guide for the company.

The city of Munich is comparable in size to a city similar to Dallas but the building are more crowded. This accounts for all buildings being destroyed. During the bombing Munich underwent 50,000 civilians were killed. The whole city is either a pile of stone or gutted buildings. I can well understand why so many were killed and the reason it was bombed so much was because there was quite a few war industries there. Believe you me the people there have had enough of war for a long time.

The oddest thing about Germany as a whole is the impression one gets in regard to their religious beliefs. In the country along the roads, one sees the crucifixion of Christ portrayed on stone crosses any number of times between towns and in all villages there is generally a large cross with Christ transfixed, in the main square. I have no doubt that many are very religious and to a person who has never come in contact with their brutality it would be hard for him to believe any other way. Too, large groups of people can be seen on Sundays walking several miles from one village to another to attend the church. I sometimes wonder just how their minds work.

There is one thing I can say and be positive about it. The birthplace of Nazism and the breeding place of this war has been totally destroyed and if it ever rises again it will be the fault of the people who put an end to it. Let's hope it never happens and now have some "Peace in our Time."

Friday 25 May '45

First Sergeant woke me early and told me to turn in stuff as I am going home in four days! A seven year old kid picked up grenade just outside building and pulled pin. Killed him. Where he found it, I don't know. I feel sorry for his mother.

(May 25 letter to Mother)

Get on your glad rags for your little boy is coming home! The first Sergeant woke me early this morning and asked me where I wanted to go in the States and I said "HOME". So, I told him where I call home.

I will be leaving the Company Sunday the 27th and how long it will take I do not know as one has to go thru a lot of junk before getting to a port. I have hopes of going thru fairly fast but may be a couple of weeks or so getting there. I will end up at Fort Sam Houston, San Antonio and then I'll be on my own and on my way. After a few days all the past will seem like a dream.

Sunday 27 May '45

Left Company at 11:30 Really hard to leave some of the boys as we have been together so long.[5] Went to Kaufbeuren (Division Headquarters). General Dahlquist made a talk. Left there by truck at 4 PM. At 2 AM we arrived at 2nd depot at Worms on Rhine.

Wednesday 30 May '45

Same old routine except we drew stuff we were short and got an Eisenhower Jacket.[6] Rains a lot and gets cold at night.

Friday 1 June '45

Did nothing yesterday. Turned in barracks bags today. Ate at 3:30 & started getting ready to load at 5 PM. Roll called five times before we mounted train. Finally started boarding around at 7 PM & at 8 pulled out.

Saturday 2 June '45

Train jerks along slowly. Have two meals a day-9 & 5 and takes two hours so we don't make many miles in the day. I have never been thru this part of France we are moving thru.

Sunday 3 June '45

Darn train sure going no where fast. Finally came around Paris today. Stalled on hill & had to split train & waited 3 hours. We manage to curl up & sleep but it is not too comfortable.

Wednesday 6 June '45

Arrived at Le Havre on the 4th about 10 PM. Walked out to 15th Replacement depot. Still fooling around on 5th. Don't know the score! Told today we would load tomorrow! Who knows?

Thursday 7 June '45

After getting ready today we didn't go. Told us we leave day after tomorrow on a liner. No one seems to know a thing. Walked around woods today. Lots of big bomb craters here or there as there was a German ammo dump here.

Headed home.

Friday 8 June '45

Another day of laying around. We are leaving tomorrow. Went to stage show tonight. Pretty good. Doesn't get dark till after 11 here.

Saturday 9 June '45

Had an early dinner and formed at 12:30 to load on ship. Came aboard at 2 PM. Pretty good size liner. Name is Hermitage. Pulled out of Le Havre at 9 PM.

Sunday 10 June '45

Have 2 meals a day. 7000 men aboard. Get kind of hungry. Sure does ride smooth and fast. Cool & foggy out. I am on E deck. Should make crossing in 6 days as we are on straight course.

Monday 11 June '45

Today this compartment was put on guard on boat. I went on at 12 to 4 today. Nothing to do & no need of it. Standing by stairs on B deck. Sea is smooth.

Thursday 14 June '45

Didn't get up for guard last night 12 AM to 4. The Major in charge is sure a hell cat. Throws guys in brig for least things. So, I figured to hell with him. Fifth day out.

Sunday 17 June '45

Came up on deck at 6:30 and we anchored in Hudson River. At noon we pulled into dock. Quite a lot of whistle blowing but not much reception altho I didn't expect one. Caught a train to camp Shanks, N.Y.

Monday 18 June '45

Drew khaki suit last night. It is so hot we are melting. Did nothing today. Suppose to leave at 5 PM.

16 THE RUPTURED DUCK

"I was sick and disillusioned and wanted the privacy of my home to shield me from unappreciative and greedy people. I took my discharge button off my lapel as I was no longer proud to wear it."

There were few parades welcoming a soldier back to America. No town, unless it spawned the most decorated soldier in the war like Farmersville, Texas, did with Audie Murphy, lined the streets to get a glance at their boys as the train or bus pulled into town. Located in Collin County, the tiny community of 2206 honored their hero by declaring a local holiday, shutting down all the business establishments, and weathering 98-degree heat to listen to Murphy's coming home speech. The reality of returning home for the rest was simple. It was time to move forward and forget the past. Even the hugs of family soon wore thin. Many more vets than one would like to mention, began to feel like they were being treated as if they had only been working at some nine to five job the past war years.

This became true of the last military decoration a discharged soldier received, the Honorable Discharge Lapel Pin. It was a small metal pin which could be placed on civilian clothes to indicate the wearer was a veteran who served with honor. The design was a proud eagle with outstretched wings inside a gold wreath. As only soldiers will do, someone noticed the eagles head was turned sideways, legs apart. Every discharged veteran, with all the medical exams given in the army, at one point had a doctor order him to turn his head and cough, when checking for a hernia. Still many more felt the eagle resembled a duck. This brought on the unflattering name "Ruptured Duck." Worn with the euphoria of freedom from the military when first coming home, the

The end of the war did not necessarily mean the end of hardships and troubles.

ruptured duck quickly lost its distinction to the general populous as well as the veteran. Soon many, turned off by the lack of respect for their service, simply removed them, forever putting the past behind.

Finally, the Servicemen's Readjustment Act of 1944, called the GI Bill of Rights, offered hope to many returning veterans. It included unemployment compensation, loans for purchase of a home or business, and educational aid. Wrapped within all the good of the bill were numerous stipulations making it appear to be more of a Bill of Rules. Working through all its red tape just added to the despair the vets felt.

As a sign of the times, the December 31, 1945, Life Magazine, with its "Speaking of Pictures", ran a cartoon of Sad Sack finally being discharged from the army. The frames of the cartoon started with Sad Sack jumping and dancing with joy after being released. What he saw next was housing shortages, inflation, international diplomatic crisis, unemployment, and threat of an atomic rocket wiping out the USA. The final picture shows Sad Sack, after three and a half years fighting for his country, sitting on a street curb totally disillusioned. Many soldiers rode the same roller coaster of emotions once home.

Frank Pearce's last notes penned in November 1945 reflect on his difficult and often painful adjustment to life in the "real world".

Over the horizon appeared the coast of America. To me it was one of the happiest moments of my life. America, the land of opportunity. How I had longed just for this moment. A peculiar feeling swept over me and all the past seemed so far away. I could vision things I could get that had been just a dream for so long. Things that were common place and taken for granted by so many of us a few years before.

No, I was not an immigrant seeing this great country for the first time. I had seen it for twenty-five years without knowing the things it meant. I was merely another soldier, tired of hardships and blood shed returning to my native country, a country that I thought could not fail to understand me and millions of others like me. I knew these people could not understand war in all its horror and suffering, of men fighting and dying in a world gone mad. That, I thought, was why I suffered so much to keep America from all that, but yet I expected them to understand us.

My mind was filled with thoughts of things to come, freedom from the over bearing attitudes of men who were selected to lead, freedom from the social barrier that existed between conceited men of rank and the lowly ignorant men who paid for their mistakes with flesh and blood, freedom from an army that had no principles of democracy for the masses. Yes, I know our armies were the greatest in the world or so I was told but there was none of the freedoms in it that we were fighting to give it to the rest of the world.

Yes, we had been told of all the good things our government was going to do for us, a great bill for the fighting men, the manna from an appreciative people to give us all a chance to go back into a world of civilization and prosper. Yes, I was happy and full of enthusiasm. Until this moment, I had been in doubt as to why I was fighting in this war of wars. I had been told by various forms of print and speech, but it was hard to believe what with the news of strikes in essential war plants and black market activities that hindered our progress both physically and mentally. I had convinced myself that I like others, was fighting merely in order to keep alive.

But seeing the skyline of a great American city slip into view, undamaged and humming with activity I seemed to feel that this is what I fought for and my sacrifices were worth all I had endured. Please, before I go further, the term "I" which I am using does not come from conceit or egotism. No, I do not feel I won the war. I am merely trying to put into words, of which I have very little command, the feelings of one man and I know all I feel and felt has been and is being felt by millions just like me. My beautiful dream suddenly burst into atoms like a bubble. The first contact with civilians left me slightly disappointed, but I contributed this to the fact that it was I who had changed. But slowly and surely the realization was forced on me that I was entirely wrong in my expectations. The war to America had meant very little. People griped about being rationed and the inconvenience they had suffered. Others bragged about the huge salaries they had received and some even lamented the end of the war because the wage scale was dropping. Some even seemed to hate us for ending the war. I was sick and disillusioned and wanted the privacy of my home to shield me from a unappreciative and greedy people. Even that afforded no real protection. Even my family became hard to understand. Friends shook my hand and immediately launched into their tales of woe until I began to doubt my sanity. In an effort to protect myself and my thoughts I attempted to explain to people my problems and received answers and solutions that came from narrow mind ness and not from anyone who understood my problems. "What have you to worry about? The government is going to take care of you. You're lucky and we poor civilians are having to pay for it." One person who managed to stay out of the army told me that I was unlucky and he was lucky. Another told me that I had no right to gripe as I was drafted anyhow. This remark hurt me deeply for actually I volunteered.

I wish it were possible for me to put in words my mental feelings but words cannot express the uncertainty, the hurt, the humiliation and distress that I began to feel. I knew without a doubt I was a misfit and lost all confidence in myself and my fellow man. I dreaded to meet a friend on the street. I took my discharge button off my lapel as I was no longer proud to wear it. I found that prices increased when I attempted to buy if I was recognized as an ex-soldier. People appeared to me as being money crazed.

Yes, I like countless others turned to the false impression that alcohol would ease the mind. This made matters worse as I know of no place one can really hear people say what is on their minds than in a bar or beer garden. SO, you see now I was at a loss as to why I fought.

Then the thing that can lift a man from the bottom of despair happened to me. Yes, a girl. I met her quite by accident. To me she was everything I could vision in a woman. Friendly, innocent and an understanding that sets a worried mind at peace. I was swept off my feet with the return of a feeling that at last I was beginning to feel like a citizen of the United States. At last I had found the reason why I had fought. I had fought in order that there could be girls like her, untainted by war and want and the loss of decency that is forced on girls of other countries ravaged by war. At last I was happy and my mind was at ease.

I set out to make myself into a man she would be proud to marry. I realized that the first step in that direction was to be financially able to give her what she had a right to expect. This was a more difficult task than it appeared on the surface. As a result of wounds received I could not go back to any of the work I had done before the war. So, I was faced with the realization that I would have to work at some job which afforded lower pay. I accepted this as fate and acquired a job at a reasonable livable wage. I informed my employer in regard to my physical abilities, but to my dismay I found that people who feel no pain or discomfort have no regard or respect for those that do. As a result, I was discharged because I was unable to do work which my employer demanded although I was capable of doing the job I started on.

My world had again fallen about my feet and physically I was unable to work. So I decided to ask for aid from the source I had attempted to avoid all these months. I went to my unemployed board and applied for the unemployment benefits open to all veterans. I was received with indifference and was informed that I was not eligible for this benefit unless I was able to take any job suitable to my training at any time offered.

My argument was to no avail so again I felt that my country had let me down again. In my despair I wished with all my heart that I had not lived thru the two years of hell and come back to be trampled beneath the feet of the people I believed were the most generous and understanding on the earth. But there was still one hope left.

The G. I. Bill of Rights, that beacon in the dark for returning men. That was also a failure and not being a man of law and understanding documents of this sort I realized it was not for the men who needed it most. I gave up any hopes of assistance from these quarters. My only source of income being a pension for disabled veterans by which I am receiving twenty-three dollars a month, I could see no future filled with opportunity and happiness, a home, a dream way of life for me.

Why must this be? Is our country only capable of making empty promises? Have we again fought in vain? Why must we, having just completed a war, be talking of another when we can't recuperate from this one within the next generation? Why are we financing other countries with billions of dollars when we haven't homes or materials enough for ourselves? No doubt all this will be answered by our politicians when we go to the polls. I am tired of all this flag waving on their part. I do not regret doing my part in this war but now it is time to face all the problems growing out of it and take action instead of idle words and promises.

I am a normal human with few desires outside of the ones every man has. A right to have a home and children, the chance to live decently and respectfully in harmony with my neighbors. So far, I have found this impossible in a country that the world looks to for help in doing the same for themselves.

In spite of my disappointments and experiences with Mr. & Mrs. America I have found one human who could give me advise and advise that was sincere and from the heart. A simple little remedy that the majority of people are overlooking.

The reward of a job well done.

This advice came from an old dorky friend of mine who seemed to sense my frustration. "I am old" he said "and have seen lots of things. People get scared of all the noise and confusion about them. Me, I ain't scared no more. The only thing you can do when you reach the end of your wits is to put your trust in Jesus and he will take care of you when all others fail you."

Oddly enough I had never looked at it from this point of view. I suddenly seemed to see that I had the same faults of other people, yearning for material things only and overlooking the thing that can solve my problem. If I can live up to HIS simple beliefs I believe that I can eventually find the answer to the questions that have so far eluded me and regain confidence in my fellow countryman.

The brave men, by the grace of God, who survived the day to day struggle of the ultimate conflict would see the end of the war in Europe and read the news concerning the ultimate weapon exploded over Hiroshima and Nagasaki. Erupting mushroom clouds, in August, smothered the ideologies of the Axis and replaced them with the awe and fear of the Atomic era. On September 2, the war officially ended with the signing of Japan's surrender document aboard the USS Missouri.

In February of 1946, Frank Pearce married his dream girl, Mary Jean Thornton, bought a home in Sulphur Springs at 113 Kyle Street with help from the GI Bill of Rights, and fathered two sons and a daughter. He would remain in Sulphur Springs at the Kyle Street address for the rest of his life.

He also returned to his prewar job of selling automobile parts city to city by establishing Pearce Auto Supply, and eventually retired in the mid-1970s. After the war, he never kept a single letter or diary of his post war life. One diary and letters home, containing the scars of combat, was enough. Forty years to the month of Salerno, Pearce was buried, with full military honors, in his hometown.

Appendix: Casualties

CAUSALTIES OF THE 111th ENGINEER COMBAT BATTALION

NAME	DATE	PLACE	CAUSE	INJURY
North Africa				
Thomas McTeer	25 June 43	North Africa	training accident	killed
Italy				
George MacLaine	9 Sept 43	USS Lyons	fell during debarkation	broken bones
Jess W. Hudnall	9 Sept 43	beach below Paestum	hand to hand combat	KIA
Truman A. Rice	9 Sept 43	beach near Paestum	German or friendly shell fire	KIA
Joseph Abbott	9 Sept 43	beach near Paestum	unknown	neck wound
Albert Phelps	11 Sept 43	near Altavilla	artillery	forearm
Robert Jobes	13 Sept 43	near Albanella	booby trap	abdominal/legs
Clyde W. Couch	14 Sept 43	near Sele-Calero Rivers	artillery or friendly shell fire	KIA
Robert Preston	16 Nov 43	near Mignano	artillery	chest
Clifford Mitchell	18 Nov 43	near Mignano	artillery	index finger
Stanley S. Dardginski	22 Nov 43	near Mignano	booby trap	KIA
Edward Brungardt	24 Nov 43	Conca	artillery	shrapnel/broken leg
John A. Bettis	4 Dec 43	Monte la Difensa	artillery	KIA
Willie Smith	4 Dec 43	Monte la Difensa	artillery	arms/legs/abdomen
Andy Bochusz	5 Dec 43	near Venafro	artillery	shoulder
Walter Wosik	5 Dec 43	near Venafro	artillery	slightly
Charles George	5 Dec 43	near Venafro	artillery	KIA
Milary King	5 Dec 43	near Venafro	artillery	seriously
Eugene Keegen	5 Dec 43	near Monte la Difensa/ Monte Maggiore	artillery	back/hand
John Marquart	5 Dec 43	near Monte la Difensa/ Monte Maggiore	artillery	slightly
Miles Hill	5 Dec 43	near Monte la Difensa/ Monte Maggiore	artillery	bruised leg
Eugene E. McDonald	11 Dec 43	near Venafro	aerial bombing	leg

Robert Hughes	15 Dec 43	near Venafro	falling tree	not listed
James Evans	19 Dec 43	San Pietro	aerial bombing/strafing	KIA
Felix Gus	19 Dec 43	San Pietro	aerial bombing/strafing	KIA
Joseph Jaegar	19 Dec 43	San Pietro	aerial bombing/strafing	not listed
Glenn Rabb	19 Dec 43	San Pietro	aerial bombing/strafing	not listed
Willie Cope	19 Dec 43	San Pietro	aerial bombing/strafing	not listed
Charles Anderson	19 Dec 43	San Pietro	aerial bombing/strafing	not listed
Kenneth Hand	19 Dec 43	San Pietro	aerial bombing/strafing	not listed
Richard "Terry" Nims	19 Dec 43	San Pietro	aerial bombing/strafing	not listed
Anicet Fournier	19 Dec 43	San Pietro	aerial bombing/strafing	not listed
Leroy Gloor	19 Dec 43	San Pietro	aerial bombing/strafing	not listed
Kenneth Wagner	26 Dec 43	near Ceppagna	accidental	internal injuries
Walter B. Scott	26 Dec 43	near Ceppagna	accidental	killed
Frank Calabrexe	17 Jan 44	Rapido River	mortar	lightly
Harry Rutzisay	27 Jan 44	near Sant' Angelo Theodiche	anti-personnel mine	KIA
Raymond Nichols	27 Jan 44	near Sant' Angelo Theodiche	anti-personnel mine	face
John Rogers	27 Jan 44	near Sant' Angelo Theodiche	anti-personnel mine	face/arm/leg
Albert Lubin	27 Jan 44	near Sant' Angelo Theodiche	anti-personnel mine	bruised leg
Okey Edge	27 Jan 44	near Sant' Angelo Theodiche	anti-personnel mine	face/hand
John Tekus	27 Jan 44	near Sant' Angelo Theodiche	anti-personnel mine	hand/foot
Raymond Feazell	30 Jan 44	Monte Belevedere	artillery	leg
John Owenby	30 Jan 44	Monte Belevedere	artillery	leg
Altus Griffin	31 Jan 44	Monte Belevedere	artillery	stomach
Frank Plechmid	31 Jan 44	Monte Belevedere	artillery	leg
Charles Hinson	1 Feb 44	Monte Belevedere	artillery	leg
George MacLaine	1 Feb 44	Monte Belevedere	artillery	ankle
Attilio Affuso	1 Feb 44	Monte Belevedere	artillery	cuts/bruises
William Rohde	1 Feb 44	Monte Belevedere	artillery	perforated ear drums
Louis Mitschke	1 Feb 44	Monte Belevedere	artillery	cuts/bruise
Clifford Martin	1 Feb 44	Monte Belevedere	artillery	cuts/bruise
Glendon Bowers	2 Feb 44	near Sant' Angelo Theodiche	machine gun	buttock
Joseph Pohl	4 Feb 44	Monte Castellone	artillery	neck
Charles Teramano	4 Feb 44	Monte Castellone	artillery	leg
John Malauskas	5 Feb 44	near San Pietro	own falling anti-aircraft shells	lightly
Roy Staton	5 Feb 44	near San Pietro	own falling anti-aircraft shells	lightly
Clyfton N. Jones	5 Feb 44	near San Pietro	own falling anti-aircraft shells	lightly
Melvin Bunkers	8 Feb 44	near Cassino	Schu mine	seriously
D. B. Mainord	8 Feb 44	near Cassino	Schu mine	lightly
Winston Roberts	8 Feb 44	near Cassino	seeking shelter	broken limb
Thomas Cooney	8 Feb 44	near Cairo	own falling anti-aircraft shells	lightly
Larry Westbrook	12 Feb 44	Cairo	artillery	lightly
Joseph Ronany	13 Feb 44	Monte Castellone	artillery	heel
Willis Bell	14 Feb 44	Monte Castellone	artillery	KIA
Omer Fortier	22 Feb 44	near Cairo	artillery	arms/chest/face
Vernon Bright	22 Feb 44	near Cairo	artillery	hand
Melvin Hamby	22 Feb 44	Cervaro	artillery	lightly

Welton Blagden	26 May 44	near Velletri	mine	lightly
Julio DeVincentis	30 May 44	near Velletri	small arms	lightly
William Jones	30 May 44	near Velletri	small arms	lightly
Earl Powers	1 June 44	near Velletri	machine gun	face
Ernest Speicher	1 June 44	near Velletri	mortar	lightly
Ralph Raymond	1 June 44	near Velletri	mortar	lightly
Albert Lubin	1 June 44	near Velletri	artillery	hand
Henry Capozzi	3 June 44	near Velletri	artillery	seriously
Andrew Mitro	3 June 44	near Velletri	artillery	lightly
Vincent Sinicropi	3 June 44	near Velletri	artillery	lightly
Danna Thomas	3 June 44	near Velletri	artillery	lightly
Richard Bieri	3 June 44	near Lago di Nemi	artillery	lightly
Robert Swehla	3 June 44	near Lago di Nemi	artillery	lightly
Archie Diesel	3 June 44	near Lago di Nemi	artillery	lightly
Reginal Ferguson	3 June 44	near Lago di Nemi	artillery	lightly
Carl McCluggage	3 June 44	near Lago diNemi	artillery	lightly
Arthur Kerr	3 June 44	near Lago di Nemi	artillery	eye
Henry Geer	5 June 44	Rome	artillery	lacerations
Ralph Poole	5 June 44	Rome	artillery	lacerations
Frank Newbold	5 June 44	Rome	artillery	lacerations
Byron Woodward	5 June 44	Rome	artillery	lacerations
Straughn Parker	6 June 44	near Mt. Clvero	incendiary grenade	burns
Ernest Owings	6 June 44	near Mt. Clvero	incendiary grenade	burns
Albert Chambliss	6 June 44	near Mt. Clvero	incendiary grenade	burns
Warren Ausland	6 June 44	near Mt. Clvero	incendiary grenade	burns
Zygment Backus	11 June 44	near Capalbio	artillery	KIA
John Lindsay	11 June 44	near Capalbio	artillery	lightly
Marvin Luckett	11 June 44	near Capalbio	artillery	lightly
Denzol Corn	11 June 44	near Capalbio	artillery	lightly
Raymond Woznicki	14 June 44	near Orbetello	artillery	lightly
Clyfton N. Jones	14 June 44	near Orbetello	artillery	lightly
Raymond Schick	17 June 44	Grosseto	not listed	lightly
France				
Charles Simpson	15 Aug 44	Invasion of Southern France	artillery	hands
David Wray	15 Aug 44	Invasion of Southern France	artillery	hand
Murray Mattleman	15 Aug 44	Invasion of Southern France	artillery	hip
Erwin Knuth	15 Aug 44	Invasion of Southern France	barbed wire entanglement	arm
Stephen Sinchak	15 Aug 44	Invasion of Southern France	air raid	foot
James Cave	15 Aug 44	Invasion of Southern France	artillery	head
Richard W. Conrad	16 Aug 44	near Boulouris	machine gun	KIA
Aubrey Jeter	16 Aug 44	near Boulouris	machine gun	seriously
Charles P. Kemeny	25 Aug 44	Bonlieu	not listed	KIA
Volney B. Simpson Jr.	25 Aug 44	Bonlieu	not listed	KIA
Ephraim F. Watson	25 Aug 44	Bonlieu	not listed	KIA
Louis F. Rullo	25 Aug 44	Bonlieu	not listed	KIA

George B. Butt	25 Aug 44	Bonlieu	not listed	KIA
Norval E. Sparks	25 Aug 44	Bonlieu	not listed	KIA
Terry Rimes	25 Aug 44	Bonlieu	wounded	wounded
Frank Szczesny	25 Aug 44	Bonlieu	wounded	wounded
Malcom Cox	25 Aug 44	Bonlieu	wounded	wounded
Philip Maior	25 Aug 44	Bonlieu	not listed	MIA
Rosario Cyr	25 Aug 44	Bonlieu	not listed	MIA
Otis Watson	25 Aug 44	Bonlieu	not listed	MIA
George Achora	25 Aug 44	Bonlieu	not listed	MIA
Robert Jones	25 Aug 44	Bonlieu	not listed	MIA
John Beaty	25 Aug 44	Bonlieu	not listed	MIA
Rocco Rich	25 Aug 44	Bonlieu	not listed	MIA
Rex Badder	25 Aug 44	Bonlieu	not listed	MIA
John Dodd	25 Aug 44	Bonlieu	not listed	MIA
Leon Leura	25 Aug 44	Bonlieu	not listed	MIA
James Nichols	25 Aug 44	Bonlieu	not listed	MIA
John Yantis	25 Aug 44	Bonlieu	not listed	MIA
Gene Engledow	25 Aug 44	Bonlieu	not listed	MIA
Grady Fordham	25 Aug 44	Bonlieu	not listed	MIA
Michael Gallagher	25 Aug 44	Bonlieu	not listed	MIA
Clovis Helm	25 Aug 44	Bonlieu	not listed	MIA
Samuel Middleton	25 Aug 44	Bonlieu	not listed	MIA
John D. Pierce	25 Aug 44	Bonlieu	not listed	MIA
Chester Rukas	25 Aug 44	Bonlieu	not listed	MIA
Fred Shepherd	25 Aug 44	Bonlieu	not listed	MIA
Talmadege Walker	25 Aug 44	Bonlieu	not listed	MIA
Arthur Henderson	25 Aug 44	Bonlieu	not listed	MIA
David Wray	25 Aug 44	Bonlieu	not listed	MIA
William Jones	25 Aug 44	Bonlieu	not listed	MIA
Murray Mattleman	25 Aug 44	Bonlieu	not listed	MIA
Paul Lupia	22 Sept 44	near Remiremont	machine pistols	shoulder
Alex Kuntz	22 Sept 44	near Remiremont	machine pistols	ear
Thomas Nichols	22 Sept 44	near Luxeuil	air raid	lightly
Lee Lassiter	23 Sept 44	near Remiremont	mine	wounded
Dee Winn	23 Sept 44	near Remiremont	mine	wounded
Arthur Rose Jr.	23 Sept 44	near Remiremont	mine	wounded
Domenic Caldereone	23 Sept 44	near Remiremont	mine	wounded
Carl McCluggage	23 Sept 44	near Remiremont	mine	jammed neck
Benjamin Fennell	1 Oct 44	near Tendon	self-propelled guns	lightly
Richard Halley	1 Oct 44	near Tendon	self-propelled guns	lightly
Edwin Arnold	2 Oct 44	near Tendon	artillery	lightly
Anthony Amari	9 Oct 44	near Herpelmont	artillery	seriously
Samuel Howard Jr.	11 Oct 44	near Tendon	artillery	lightly
George Altschul	11 Oct 44	near Tendon	artillery	seriously
Paul Tuck	12 Oct 44	near Fimenil	artillery	lightly
Joseph Friday	13 Oct 44	near Le Panges	artillery	finger

Joseph Corazza	16 Oct 44	near Bruyeres	artillery	thigh
Eugene V. McDonald	17 Oct 44	near Belmont	mortar	lightly
James E. Dyer	19 Oct 44	near Bruyeres	R-M-43 mine	KIA
George M. MacLaine	19 Oct 44	near Bruyeres	R-M-43 mine	KIA
James P. Maher	19 Oct 44	near Bruyeres	R-M-43 mine	KIA
Thomas Cooney	19 Oct 44	near Bruyeres	R-M-43 mine	KIA
Milton Fondberg	19 Oct 44	near Bruyeres	R-M-43 mine	lightly
Leonard Halpern	19 Oct 44	near Bruyeres	R-M-43 mine	lightly
Martin Nunberg	19 Oct 44	near Bruyeres	R-M-43 mine	lightly
Oliver Bowland	19 Oct 44	near Bruyeres	R-M-43 mine	lightly
Gerald Bullis	19 Oct 44	near Bruyeres	R-M-43 mine	lightly
Michael Thomas	20 Oct 44	near Champ le Duc	artillery	hand
Millard Earman	24 Oct 44	near Biffontaine	tank fire	head
David Johnston	24 Oct 44	near Biffontaine	tank fire	head
Lester Shaw	24 Oct 44	near Biffontaine	tank fire	head
Albert Chambliss	24 Oct 44	near Biffontaine	tank fire	concussion
Fritz Johanson	25 Oct 44	near Devant	small arms fire	not listed
Thomas Baker	25 Oct 44	near Belmont	artillery	head/limbs
Thomas Corwin	26 Oct 44	near Devant	artillery	shoulder
Frank Santacroce	26 Oct 44	near Devant	artillery	hip
Clinton Hall	28 Oct 44	near Belmont/Bruyeres	S mine	hip
Harry U. Oesterien	30 Oct 44	near Laval	S mine	KIA
Arthur Truman	30 Oct 44	near Laval	S mine	KIA
Joseph Dlugos	30 Oct 44	near Laval	S mine	lightly
Robert Findley	30 Oct 44	near Laval	S mine	lightly
Anthony Cardillo	4 Nov 44	near Rouges Eaux	artillery	lightly
John Sparks	5 Nov 44	near Rouges Eaux	S mine	lightly
Joseph Nines	6 Nov 44	Biffontaine	S mine	seriously
Bryson Hayden	6 Nov 44	Biffontaine	S mine	lightly
Lind Salmela	6 Nov 44	Biffontaine	S mine	lightly
Andrew Cromarty	6 Nov 44	Biffontaine	S mine	lightly
Eugene E. McDonald	6 Nov 44	Biffontaine	S mine	lightly
Gilmer Ellis	6 Nov 44	Biffontaine	S mine	lightly
Marvin Braune	6 Nov 44	Biffontaine	S mine	lightly
Raymond Lauchlen	15 Nov 44	Neume	Artillery	lightly
Wilber Gasper	15 Nov 44	Neume	Artillery	lightly
John Lusick	17 Nov 44	near Liezey	S mine	seriously
Floyd Duren	17 Nov 44	near Liezey	S mine	lightly
James Ramsey	17 Nov 44	near Ivoux	mine	lightly
John Borovsky	18 Nov 44	near Liezey	mine	lightly
Robert Hinson	18 Nov 44	near Liezey	mine	lightly
David Johnston	18 Nov 44	near Pinefaing	Schu mine	seriously
D.B. Mainord	19 Nov 44	Sarupt area	S mine	leg
Joe Warren	19 Nov 44	Sarupt area	S mine	chest, head, legs
Kenneth Brodbeck	20 Nov 44	Anould	R-M-43 mine	KIA
Stephen Sinchak	20 Nov 44	Anould	R-M-43 mine	lightly

Kenneth Hand	20 Nov 44	near Le Souche	Schu mine	leg/foot
Frank Pearce	21 Nov 44	Anould	mortar	back/leg/arm
Anthony Vesce	21 Nov 44	Anould	mortar	lightly
Robert "Bobby" Sleator	21 Nov 44	Anould	mortar	lightly
Walter Baker	22 Nov 44	Anould	Schu mine	leg
Lawrence Turner	22 Nov 44	Anould	Schu mine	lightly
George W. Smith	23 Nov 44	Anould	Schu mine	foot
Oran Stovall	25 Nov 44	near Ban de Laveline	artillery	lightly
Rolland Allen	25 Nov 44	near Ban de Laveline	artillery	lightly
Clarence Smith Jr.	27 Nov 44	Sainte Marie Aux Mines area	artillery	lightly
Luther Matlock	27 Nov 44	Sainte Marie Aux Mines area	Schu mine	lightly
Jack Scott	30 Nov 44	near Haut Koenigsbourg Chau	Nebelwerfer rockets	lightly
Leonard Hooker	30 Nov 44	near Haut Koenigsbourg Chau	Nebelwerfer rockets	lightly
Michael Baritelli	30 Nov 44	near Haut Koenigsbourg Chau	Nebelwerfer rockets	lightly
Calvin Comstock	30 Nov 44	near Haut Koenigsbourg Chau	Nebelwerfer rockets	lightly
Jamie Holmes	30 Nov 44	near Haut Koenigsbourg Chau	Nebelwerfer rockets	lightly
Andrew Stefanick	30 Nov 44	near Haut Koenigsbourg Chau	Nebelwerfer rockets	lightly
Ernest Vanier	1 Dec 44	Kintzheim	artillery	KIA
Edwin Newmann	1 Dec 44	Kintzheim	artillery	lightly
Thomas Frost	1 Dec 44	Kintzheim	artillery	lightly
Kenneth Engelhardt	1 Dec 44	Kintzheim	artillery	lightly
Joseph Friday	1 Dec 44	Kintzheim	artillery	lightly
Leroy Gloor	1 Dec 44	near Aubure	artillery	lightly
John Waroblak	2 Dec 44	near Ribeauville	artillery	abdomen
Edward Ludwig	5 Dec 44	Guemar area	sniper fire	lightly
Michael Thomas	6 Dec 44	Ostheim	booby trap	lightly
John Sudatz	6 Dec 44	Ostheim	booby trap	lightly
Earnest W. Wickham	6 Dec 44	Ostheim	friendly fire	KIA
Ralph Thompson	6 Dec 44	Ostheim	booby trap	KIA
Thomas B. Gautier Jr.	7 Dec 44	near Chatenois	S mine	KIA
Wilbur Gasper	9 Dec 44	near Selestat	S mine	lightly
Fred Molsbarger	13 Dec 44	near Riquewihr	artillery	lightly
Victor Roney	13 Dec 44	near Riquewihr	artillery	lightly
Bruno Pistoni	13 Dec 44	near Riquewihr	artillery	lightly
Clarence Hunter	13 Dec 44	near Riquewihr	artillery	lightly
Arthur Hertel	14 Dec 44	near Riquewihr	hand to hand	KIA
Ernest Boddye	14 Dec 44	near Riquewihr	not listed	KIA
David LaLicata	14 Dec 44	near Riquewihr	not listed	KIA
Francis Berchem	14 Dec 44	near Riquewihr	not listed	KIA
Nis Nielsen	14 Dec 44	near Riquewihr	not listed	KIA
Floyd Lewis	14 Dec 44	near Riquewihr	not listed	KIA
Franklin M. Philpott	14 Dec 44	near Riquewihr	not listed	KIA
Clarence Aldrich	14 Dec 44	near Riquewihr	not listed	lightly
George Taylor	14 Dec 44	near Riquewihr	not listed	lightly
Eugene Whitlock	14 Dec 44	near Riquewihr	not listed	lightly
David Watson	14 Dec 44	near Riquewihr	not listed	lightly

John Samonds Jr.	14 Dec 44	near Riquewihr	not listed	MIA
Arthur Bauch	14 Dec 44	near Riquewihr	unknown	MIA
Donald Barnett	14 Dec 44	near Riquewihr	unknown	MIA
John Benedetto	14 Dec 44	near Riquewihr	unknown	MIA
Don Shoemaker	14 Dec 44	near Riquewihr	unknown	MIA
Robert McFarland	14 Dec 44	near Riquewihr	unknown	MIA
James Gordon	14 Dec 44	near Riquewihr	unknown	MIA
Leo Kraus	14 Dec 44	near Riquewihr	unknown	MIA
Virgil Leishman	14 Dec 44	near Riquewihr	unknown	MIA
Lawrence Rieve	14 Dec 44	near Riquewihr	unknown	MIA
Daniel Ryan	14 Dec 44	near Riquewihr	unknown	MIA
Patrick Barry	14 Dec 44	near Riquewihr	unknown	MIA
Basil Caldwell Jr.	14 Dec 44	near Riquewihr	unknown	MIA
Crescencio Flores	14 Dec 44	near Riquewihr	unknown	MIA
William Llewellyn	14 Dec 44	near Riquewihr	unknown	MIA
Harvey Moore	14 Dec 44	near Riquewihr	unknown	MIA
Robert Moore	14 Dec 44	near Riquewihr	unknown	MIA
John Peabody	14 Dec 44	near Riquewihr	unknown	MIA
John Ruane Jr.	14 Dec 44	near Riquewihr	unknown	MIA
Wilbur Skallion	14 Dec 44	near Riquewihr	unknown	MIA
Biagio Tramontano	14 Dec 44	near Riquewihr	unknown	MIA
Ervin Knuth	14 Dec 44	near Riquewihr	unknown	MIA
Clinton Hall	14 Dec 44	near Riquewihr	unknown	MIA
Luca Dimicelli	14 Dec 44	near Riquewihr	unknown	MIA
Willard Mellin	14 Dec 44	near Riquewihr	unknown	MIA
Claude Weber	14 Dec 44	near Riquewihr	unknown	MIA
Oliver Bashore	14 Dec 44	near Riquewihr	unknown	MIA
George Brown	14 Dec 44	near Riquewihr	unknown	MIA
Gerald Bullis	14 Dec 44	near Riquewihr	artillery	KIA
Joseph D. Brown	14 Dec 44	near Riquewihr	artillery	seriously
George Pengressi	14 Dec 44	near Riquewihr	artillery	lightly
Elmore Scafidel	16 Dec 44	near Riquewihr	artillery	hand
Earl E. Watson	18 Dec 44	Ribeauville	artillery	KIA
Philip DiCarlo	18 Dec 44	Ribeauville	artillery	KIA
Albert Coker	18 Dec 44	Ribeauville	artillery	lightly
Arnold Glenn	18 Dec 44	Ribeauville	artillery	lightly
Oral Shelton	19 Dec 44	near Riquewihr	work related	lightly
Domenic Calderone	19 Dec 44	near Riquewihr	work related	lightly
Doy Marks	20 Dec 44	Strasbourgh area	artillery	foot
John R. Simons	21 Jan 45	near Bischwiller	accident-mines	KIA
Chester A. Huebner	21 Jan 45	near Bischwiller	accident-mines	KIA
Albin A. MacHeese	21 Jan 45	near Bischwiller	accident-mines	KIA
Roy A. Pfleger	21 Jan 45	near Bischwiller	accident-mines	KIA
Frederick V. Hibbard	21 Jan 45	near Bischwiller	accident-mines	KIA
Joseph J. Bliss	21 Jan 45	near Bischwiller	accident-mines	KIA
Joseph A. Ford	21 Jan 45	near Bischwiller	accident-mines	KIA

Isadore Keller	21 Jan 45	near Bischwiller	accident-mines	KIA
Louie V'Dovick	21 Jan 45	near Bischwiller	accident-mines	seriously
Stephen Somal	21 Jan 45	near Bischwiller	accident-mines	seriously
Jack F. Cleek	21 Jan 45	near Bischwiller	accident-mines	lightly
John Giordano	21 Jan 45	near Bischwiller	accident-mines	lightly
Robert Hall	21 Jan 45	near Bischwiller	accident-mines	lightly
Boguslavis Kayota	21 Jan 45	near Bischwiller	accident-mines	lightly
Carlton Cowan	21 Jan 45	near Bischwiller	accident-mines	lightly
Thomas W. Walker	21 Jan 45	near Bischwiller	accident-mines	lightly
Earl Green	25 Jan 45	near Bischwiller	work related	ear drums
Wellington Gilbert	31 Jan 45	near Bilwisheim	accident-mines	KIA
Lawrence D. Fye	31 Jan 45	near Bilwisheim	accident-mines	KIA
Lawrence E. Saline	31 Jan 45	near Bilwisheim	accident-mines	KIA
Winfred Weems	31 Jan 45	near Bilwisheim	accident-mines	KIA
Herbert Loree	31 Jan 45	near Bilwisheim	accident-mines	KIA
John Meese	31 Jan 45	near Bilwisheim	accident-mines	KIA
Richard "Terry" Nims	31 Jan 45	near Bilwisheim	accident-mines	KIA
Robert "Bobbie" Sleator	31 Jan 45	near Bilwisheim	accident-mines	KIA
William Brady	1 Feb 45	near Bischwiller	artillery	lightly
Russell T. Young	6 Feb 45	near Rohrwiller	anti-tank mine	KIA
Joseph H. Pohl	8 Feb 45	near Oberhoffen	mortar	KIA
Leo Howell	15 March 45	near Mietesheim	artillery	lightly
George Pengressi	15 March 45	near Mertzwiller	Schu mines	eyes/arm
Carl McCluggage	15 March 45	near Mertzwiller	Schu mine	foot/eye
Kenneth Wilt	15 March 45	near Mertzwiller	Schu mine	lightly
Charles York	16 March 45	near Haguenau	artillery	lightly
Raymond Goodman	19 March 45	near Wissembourg	artillery	torso/arm
Troyce Reich	20 March 45	near Wissembourg	unknown	face
Leon Jones	20 March 45	Riedseltz	artillery	eye/arm
Marvin Luckett	20 March 45	Riedseltz	artillery	cheek
Anthony Cardillo	20 March 45	Riedseltz	artillery	shoulder
Germany				
Salvatore Colietti	22 March 45	near Ober-Otterbach	accident	lightly
Kenneth Weiss	23 March 45	near Ober-Otterbach	artillery	lightly
Charles Hickey Jr.	23 March 45	near Ober-Otterbach	artillery	lightly
Roy Martin	23 March 45	near Ober-Otterbach	artillery	lightly
Frank Cathcart Jr.	23 March 45	near Bergzabern	artillery	leg
Luther Matlock	23 March 45	near Bergzabern	artillery	both legs

Endnotes

Chapter 1

1 The construction of Camp Bowie began on September 27, 1940. The original size of the camp was approximately 61,000 acres. This acreage was divided into 2,000 acres for a campsite, 8,000 for infantry training, 28,000 for maneuvers, and 23,000 for artillery ranges. Pearce was among a group of six engineers from the Division temperately sent by train from Camp Bowie to Ft. Belvoir, Virginia on May 5, 1941. The Engineer Replacement Training Center at Ft. Belvoir, opened in March of 1941, furnished the inexperienced men with a twelve-week course covering an enormous spectrum of subjects. The Electrical, Motors, and Mechanical Equipment Course for Enlisted Men consisted of sixteen student hours in electrical, 88 hours in motor and motor vehicles, 8 hours for field phones, and 416 hours for engineer mechanical equipment. Physical conditioning added to the training. The world's first known obstacle course, soon the popular army training device at all military bases, opened a few days before Pearce's arrival.

2 The Louisiana Maneuvers, nicknamed the "Big One", involved nineteen Divisions and support groups numbering half a million men. It was the largest military exercise ever held in the United States. The activities of the maneuvers covered over 3,400 square miles of the state of Louisiana.

3 September 13, 1941, became the date the former guardsmen were introduced to leadership. By the direction of President Roosevelt, Brigadier General Fred L. Walker was ordered to take command of the Division. Walker, replacing General Claude V. Birkhead, instantly zapped his new unit with the electrical energy of his regular army background.

4 A furlough, granted by a company officer, was a reward for work well done. It could number no more than fifteen days at a time or a maximum of thirty days in a single year. Pearce, on January 23, returned to Sulphur Springs to see his parents. A week later, January 30, he traveled by train back to Massachusetts. He would not see Texas again for two and a half years.

5 Marvin was drafted on January 19, 1943, and reported for active duty with the Army Air Force in February. His new assignment was in Huntsville, Texas.

Chapter 2

1 Henry Gibbons was launched in November of 1942 and commissioned USAT Henry Gibbons on February 27, 1943. It had a troop capacity of 1976

2 On a filthy, nameless street, in some soon forgotten town, an off-duty soldier from the 143rd, wheeling a gun, shot two Military Policemen who were trying to disarm him. A third MP's shot killed the out-of-control soldier. From this time on, the MP's orders from General Walker were to shoot to kill any person, American or other, endangering them with a weapon.

3 The Division moved west from Algeria to French Morocco to spend most of the summer in or around the cork oak forests near Rabat and Casablanca.

4 Perkins Brothers, where sister Iona was employed, was a clothing store located on the south side of the red brick town square in Sulphur Springs. Sam B. Perkins founded his first store in Kaufman, Texas, in 1898, and established a second store in Sulphur Springs in 1900. One of the employees' war time goals was to send letters and cards to Sulphur Springs boys stationed overseas. They called themselves the "store force" and were determined to do more than sell jeans, dresses and shoes. The following was a letter written by Pearce to the Perkins Brothers "store force".

5 Thomas McTeer, of South Carolina, joined the 36th Division in June of 1942. He was killed on June 25, 1943, in a tragic training accident in North Africa. While crawling through a minefield, under barbwire and with 50-caliber machine fire only three feet above his head, a stray bullet fell short hitting McTeer. He died in the hospital that night.

6 V Mail was used by the military from June 1942 until November 1945. Realizing mail was as important to the soldiers as ammunition, the government devised a scheme to photograph numerous letters onto compact 16-mm reels of black and white camera film. Once the film arrived at its destination, a copy of the original letter was printed onto a piece of 5" by 4" black and white photographic paper. This system left more room for vital supplies, along with the mail, to be shipped to the fighting men.

7 A Bangalore torpedo, first designed in 1912 by the British Army in India, was an explosive charge placed at the end of several segments of long reaching tubes. Without having to advance into dangerous fire, the soldiers could extend it forward allowing them to explode bunkers, machine gun nest, and barbed wire entanglements from a safer distance.

8 The Samuel Chase, named for a signer of the Declaration of Independence, was a Coast Guard assault transport used in the invasion. It also was used to land troops on D-Day, 1944, at Normandy's Omaha Beach.

9 The 36th Division carried out a practice landing operation titled "Cowpuncher", about thirty miles east of Oran, between Porte aux Poules and Arzew. This area was selected to duplicate as much as possible the beaches they would come ashore on at Salerno (Paestum).

10 The L. C. T. was the military term for Landing Craft, Tank. These ships were 117 feet six inches long and traveled at eight knots. They were used to ferry trucks, artillery, tanks or as much as one hundred fifty tons of cargo to the invasion shore.

11 The M7 was a self-propelled artillery vehicle, manned by a crew of seven, allowing for quick movement and adequate firepower to support infantry advancements.

12 A steel bridge, invented by British engineer Sir Donald Bailey, designed to be moved in several parts and assembled quickly where needed to cross a river.

13 Although green concerning combat experience, the engineers were definitely ripe and rotten from training. Spats between the young soldiers, usually verbal eruptions, now turned physical. Except for a few disasters like the Magenta incident in May, most fights between Americans were fists flying left and right hoping for a quick KO. Some might think it was pride in state put on the line during this hot Thursday night, at a movie ironically about professional boxers. It wasn't pride in Texas or Kansas, as Pearce later noted, that sparked the slug fest, but the frustration of continual training for war inflaming the cutting edge of the soldier's nerves.

14 General Dwight D. Eisenhower, the future 34th President of the United States, was the Supreme Allied Commander of the Mediterranean Theater. General Walker noted in his book *From Texas to Rome* Eisenhower visited the Division in the afternoon. "Each unit formed in line on the highway near bivouac. Since he had to drive many miles to see all the troops, he reviewed them while standing in a moving jeep. He was in a jovial mood and complimentary of many units, critical of none."

15 Mark W. Clark was the Commanding General of the newly formed Fifth Army which included the 36th. At 46, he was one of the youngest Lieutenant General in the history of the United States.

16 C Rations were utilized for troops on the move, with no access to a field kitchen. C Rations, stored in cumbersome cans, could be served hot or cold. The rations contained meat, bread, and accessory items. Included were potatoes, pork and beans, lima beans, and various vegetables. Their taste created no problems with the hungry soldiers. There was also coffee, sugar, chewing gum, and cigarettes in each daily supply of the ration. The stumbling block centered on the meat. The GI's uproar over this was the lack of variety it presented. They continually were fed repetitious meat and hash combinations over and over again.

Chapter 3

1 The Silver Star Medal is the United States' third highest award given for valor in combat while battling the enemy.

2 While final plans were being made for the invasion, on September 3, Eisenhower suddenly removed the entire 82nd Airborne Division from the Fifth Army strike force. Now, in the heat of battle, another battalion vital to a successful breakout of the Paestum front was removed.

3 The hills and mountains, in the path of attack, were identified by the number of meters they were above seas level.

4 Approximately 75 paratroopers were injured in the drop and eliminated from combat.

5 The 82nd had again been reassigned to the Fifth Army out of necessity on September 11. Designated as an Airborne Division in August of 1942, this was their second combat jump. Their only previous experience parachuting into a combat zone was two months earlier in Sicily.

6 The 489 foot long Samuel Chase also carried General Walker, 96 officers and 1163 enlisted men of the 36th and 45th divisions.

7 Each company had three half-tracks, one for each platoon. The seven-man half-track crew for 1st platoon of Company C consisted of John Beavers of Grand Haven, Michigan, Stephen Sinchak of Lakewood, Ohio, Allen Brewer of Niles, Michigan, Albert Forbear of Shelby, Michigan, Junell, Benedict, and Pearce.

8 There were four major convoy departure points for the invasion force. They sailed from Oran, Tripoli, Bizerte and Sicily on staggered schedules before combining in the Gulf of Salerno.

9 The fleet was protected by cruisers U.S.S. Philadelphia, U.S.S. Savannah, and U.S.S. Boise plus numerous destroyers.

10 Due to threat of an Allied invasion, the 16th Panzer Division was moved in late August to the Eboli-Battipaglia area southeast of Salerno.

11 Barrage balloons were large balloons attached to long, thick cables, hopefully eliminating bombing raids by German planes attacking at low altitudes. The cables were designed to build a fence in the air over the ships destroying any aircraft contacting them.

12 On the night before the invasion, a convoy of 450 vessels of all shapes and sizes stood ready to place the first American invasion troops on Hitler's Europe.

13 There were two air attacks on the Bizerte convoy resulting in the sinking of one L. C. T. The first attack consisted of three planes and the second with ten aircraft. None were shot down.

14 The German 88 mm dual-purpose gun, designed in the 1930s as antiaircraft-antitank weapon, delivered telling blows on the troops dashing ashore.

15 The feared German Messerschmitt Bf 109E-4, with speeds near 360 mph, was a heavily armed plane with the ability to dive faster than any British or American aircraft.

16 The Supermarine Spitfire was the classic British single-seat fighter in WWII. Introduced in 1938, its maneuverability over rival German planes made it a legend in the air war of 1940-41, known as the Battle of Britain.

17 The Division, on the night of the fourteenth, was reinforced by the parachuting in of 2100 men of the 505th Parachute Infantry Regiment (82nd Airborne Division).

18 1st platoon of Company C, working under the cover of darkness, placed 320 yards of concertina wire between the Germans and the defending 141st. Concertina wire was a barbed wire, with razor sharp points, extended in a twisted spiral shape across a defensive front. It was an effective deterrent to advancing soldiers and vehicles.

19 The P-38 Lightning twin engine fighter was used in limited numbers in Europe, due to a sub-par performance at high altitudes. The engines, mounted on twin booms, were located too far from the pilot to efficiently heat the cockpit. The P-38 was famous for its part in the Pacific Theater and the only American fighter, with modifications, produced from the beginning of the war until the end.

20 Engineers under James Mueller, at 3 PM on September 15, contacted the British Eighth Army near Loureena.

21 The Mark IV, with a crew of five, was a highly effective German twenty-ton Panzer tank. It sported a protective 1 ¼ inch steel covering and was armed with a 75 mm gun and two 7.92 mm machine guns.

22 Atabrine, a bitter yellow pill, was a synthetic drug developed before WWII to fight malaria. It took the place of quinine, which came into short supply when the Japanese took control of key South Pacific countries.

23 Stars and Stripes was the official newspaper of the United States Armed Forces overseas. It was printed by soldiers and distributed to soldiers keeping them informed of the latest developments and news.

Chapter 4

1 Time, The Weekly Newsmagazine, Monday featured on its cover the picture of Fifth Army Commander Mark Clark. He would be one of a select group of fifty-two people from around the world in 1943 featured on the cover of the nationally read magazine. The cover story detailed his life, military leadership, action at Salerno, and concluded with, "Now, in Italy, backed by the men of the Fifth, Mark Clark is getting his first full trial as a field general. He is still a man to watch."

2 The engineers built a water line with twenty-five faucets, so the thirsty people could fill their various buckets and containers. The frantic crowd, seeking water, created so many problems that the engineers had to put guards near the faucets to maintain order.

3 The Italian government, Germany's partner in crime only a month earlier, declared war on them. With two-thirds of the country in German control, the declaration had little effect on the 36th Division's situation.

4 Schrapnellmine, known as the S Mine, was a deadly anti-personnel mine. Nicknamed the "Bouncing Betty" by the Americans, when stepped on, it would spring into the air, explode waist high, and spit hundreds of ball bearings over a two-hundred-yard radius.

5 Geoffrey Keyes took command of the II Corps which included the 3rd and the 36th Divisions. A three-year football letterman at West Point, he was a close friend of Eisenhower when they both lettered on the Army squad in 1912. He also served as head football coach at West Point in 1917 where he won 7 of 8 games.

6 The 141st, without the normal companionship of the engineer's company A, loaded on ships for an apparent invasion near Gaeta, on the Italian coast. The proposed site, by plan, was leaked to the Germans. It was hoped that they would remove troops from key positions facing the Allies and transport them to defend the upcoming landing site. The hour of departure, timed for after sundown, never came. The troops, after dark, unloaded and returned to a camp built in and around an apple orchard.

7 A pontoon bridge, used to cross streams and rivers where no normal bridge exists, is a temporary bridge using various floats (in this case rubber boats) as support.

8 Finally, a break in the combat gave the men time to be boys. Spinning a little down-home humor, this letter appeared in the Hopkins County Echo, a small weekly paper, covering the Texas County where their homes were located.

9 Ernest Smith, a member of the 168th Infantry Regiment of the 34th Division, was killed on October 13. Known as "Snuffie" to his friends, he was 26 years old. He was killed storming a hill filled with a German machine gun nest. He was later buried in the Sicily-Rome American Cemetery in Nettuno, Italy.

10 Lee E. Beahler Jr. served with distinction in World War II. Yet, his greatest honor came during the Korean War in 1950. With the 2nd Engineer Combat Battalion, 2nd Infantry Division, he was given a "stand or die mission" where he singlehandedly rallied a "battered and shaken unit" thus eliminating a superior North Korean force. "By his superb leadership and aggressive action through out the entire day, the town (Yongsan) was saved and the threat to the whole position eliminated." He was awarded the Distinguished Service Cross for the September third heroics. The Distinguished Service Cross is the nation's second highest award given for bravery in combat against the enemy.

11 Marvin was assigned to the Army Air Forces 706 Bombardment Squadron, 446 Bomb Group. He departed October 27, on the Queen Mary, for duty in England. He would be stationed there for the duration of the war.

Chapter 5

1 Tellermines were anti-vehicle mines. The fuses would be set as not to trigger when a person walked across it. An explosion would come when the weight of a tank or truck rolled on top of the pressure point. The Germans designed them to allow a trip wire to be attached so they could be used in booby traps situations. Tellermines weighed

seventeen to nineteen pounds and were made of steel which at least allowed the engineers to use mine detectors to expose them.

2 Area between Monte Sammucro, the town of San Pietro, and Monte Lungo earned the name "Death Valley."

3 The engineers relocated about a half-mile southwest of Presenzano. The camp site was protected from the northwest German artillery barrages by Monte Cesima and surrounding lower heights.

4 Working three miles south of Mignano on a supply road for the 142nd, all three platoons of Company C were subjected to artillery fire from German positions in the Camino Hill Mass. With Company B furnishing the corduroy material, the road was completed at 11:00 PM on Thursday.

5 Faced almost daily with the stress of life and death situations, many soldiers felt they needed their own self called time out to get away from it all. AWOL was the official term for this maneuver and although not socially accepted by the army brass, it was a far more common occurrence than some would admit. In the States, as happened to Pearce, this impulse could and would cost a man his stripes and/or guardhouse time, but in combat areas usually resulted only in a down grading lecture from an officer.

6 Although rain canceled part of its sorties, the XII Air Support Command flew 274 sorties on this day.

7 The single seat P-51 Mustang, capable of extended periods in the air, was a fighter plane valuable in escorting American bombers during long missions. Introduced in 1942, it became one of the most respected planes in the U. S. Army Air Force.

8 On the II Corps front alone, in a single hour, some 346 pieces poured 22,500 rounds of explosives and white phosphorus shells on Germans in the Camino Hill Mass.

9 There were 612 sorties on targets in front of Fifth Army.

10 Canteen was a military store that sold cigarettes, candy, etc. to the soldiers.

11 The Italian 1st Motorized Brigade, commanded by Vincenzo Dapino, consisted of 5,486 Italian soldiers. They reported to the II Corps front lines on December 7. They were part of the Italian Co-Belligerent Army, former Axis soldiers now working as allies.

12 Goumiers were Berber tribesmen from Morocco. Trained by the French as soldiers, they showed little mercy to their enemy. Their skill with knives and brutal ways sparked fear in everyone. Not only did the Germans feel their wrath, but even the Italian citizens were robbed, raped, and killed. Eventually the French brought Berber women, as a form of camp followers, to calm the marauding men.

13 Active first in 1942, the single seat A-36A, unofficially named Invader or Apache, was a ground attack dive bomber version of the P-51B. It was equipped with dive breaks in the wings allowing for greater stability in a dive. By 1944 it was out of action, being replaced by the more effective P-51 and P-47.

14 The Focke-Wulf FW 190 ranked with the best fighter planes of the war. Designed as a successor, in 1939, to the Messerschmitt Bf 109, it had a maximum speed of 408 miles per hour and a range of 560 miles. The attack on the men was probably by a modified

version, a FW 190 F or G fighter-bomber, which carried less 20mm cannons and more bomb racks.

15 Company A of the 753rd Tank Battalion suffered a catastrophic defeat as only four of sixteen medium U.S. tanks and one British Valentine tank could return. Seven were destroyed and five disabled. Because of the shell fire, mines, and terrain the tank incursion was crippled and forced to retreat.

16 On this day, Eisenhower relinquished command of the Mediterranean and was appointed Supreme Commander of Allied Expeditionary Forces to plan and direct the invasion of Europe. British General Sir Henry Maitland Wilson became Supreme Allied Commander of the Mediterranean Theater.

17 On December 30, the 34th Division moved up and occupied positions held by the 36th Division. The division, except for the 142nd, again moved into a reserve status. The 142nd was attached to the 34th Division and occupied Monte Sammucro.

18 Concerned with the families continuing financial woes, Pearce decided to send two thirds of his monthly check home. A private's pay was low, half as much as a sergeant's, but every dollar helped. The Army encouraged these "allotments" and even added extra incentive money to it. In Pearce's case, the Army almost doubled the monthly deduction he was sending home. For the next two years, the check was always a monthly blessing to those left behind.

Chapter 6

1 The Garigliano River flows from the juncture of the Liri and Rapido (also known as the Gari) rivers to the coastline of the Tyrrhenian Sea. Although the rivers along the battlefront slither for many miles, the distance, as the crow flies, from the Benedictine Abbey to the mouth of the Garigliano, near the city of Minturno, is only nineteen miles.

2 The VI Corp suffered less than three hundred casualties while securing the beachhead at Anzio.

3 Drift pins were steel rods twelve to fourteen inches long. They were used to nail down bridge and road timbers to make them secure for transportation over.

4 On December 29, 1943, Dwight Eisenhower issued the order "We are fighting in a country . . . rich in monuments which illustrate the growth of the civilization which is ours. We are bound to respect those monuments so far as war allows. If we have to choose between destroying a famous building and sacrificing our own men, then our men's lives count infinitely more, and the building must go."

5 Rest camps, serving as places to get away from the war, were critical to morale. Men got new uniforms, felt the warmth of hot showers, ate food out of something other than a mess kit, laughed through movies, enjoyed band concerts, and were even given individual freedom to come and go if discipline was maintained. All this sounded great, but in any situation, there is reality. Rest camps had theirs. Men traded their worn thin, battle scarred clothes in and often got faded repeat issue uniforms in return. Seems some rear echelon troops, as the new uniforms were moved to the dispersal areas, did a little

early trading themselves. Showers were in dilapidated facilities where the sputtering showerheads did or did not provide lukewarm water. The projectors for the movies instantly flashed to a halt in mid scene far too many times to count, and five day passes to Naples met a disease filled end.

6 Piedimonte, ten miles from the rest camp, was one of two places movie theaters set up to entertain the troops. Alife, approximately three miles from camp, was the other.

7 San Vittore, a village a couple of miles north of San Pietro, fell after bitter fighting to the 135th infantry of the "Red Bull" 34th Division.

8 The invasion from sea at Anzio put over fifty thousand American and British soldiers ashore about thirty-five miles southwest of Rome against a sprinkle of enemy resistance. The troops, failing to take advantage of the early success during landing, were hemmed in and trapped. With thousands of Germans in front of them and the waves of the sea splashing ashore behind them, German radio broadcaster "Axis Sally" (also known as "Midge at the mike") went so far as to broadcast that Anzio was the largest self-supporting prisoner of war camp in the world.

9 Two men from Company C accompanied a 143rd Infantry patrol and mined many of the still useable reconnaissance boats left by the river.

10 The term Screaming Meemies was the feared name given lethal rockets fired by the six-barrel Nebelwerfer rocket launcher. The noise created by the 15 cm rockets, when unleashed, was scary enough to have the Americans coin a name for the nightmarish sound.

11 A truce, on January 25, was arranged between the two sides so they could remove the dead and wounded from the horrific battlefield. The three hour arrangement proved time only to remove a fraction of the losses suffered.

12 First platoon of Company C filled shell holes and poured gravel to repair a road three miles southeast of Sant' Angelo Theodiche.

13 German air force executed four bombing attacks in a two day period.

14 North of Cassino, the Germans dammed part of the river and it overflowed into the flat lands nearby. With Italian rain added to the mix, the situation became a constant headache for the engineers.

15 Pope Pius XII reigned as Pope from March of 1939 to October of 1958. The Italian Pope (born in Rome in 1876) has been criticized for his soft public stance against Hitler and the Nazi regime.

16 Monte Castellone, Hill 593, Hill 468 and surrounding terrain were directly behind the Abbey and under attack from American forces.

17 The Germans, beginning in the early hours on the morning of the 12th, unleashed a two-hour-long artillery and Nebelwerfer bombardment on the 36th. It was the heaviest the Division had faced in Italy.

18 The B-17 Flying Fortress was a four-engine heavy duty bomber. It carried a crew of ten and depending on the bomb load, had a range of 1700 miles. When the war ended, the B-17's were credited with dropping more bombs on the enemy than any other American aircraft.

19 The twin-engine B-25 Mitchell, named in honor of famous pilot Billy Mitchell, carried a crew of six. With a range of 1350 miles, 16 B-25B bombers were used by Jimmy Doolittle in the famous bombing raid on Japan in April of 1942.

Chapter 7

1 Iona received a much-deserved reward in 1974 when she was honored as the Sulphur Springs "Business and Professional Women's Club Woman of the Year" for her life works.

2 Caserta became the top rest camp, if only for five days, for the tired Division. Located seventeen miles from "off limits" Naples, the recuperating soldiers slept when wanted, ate when desired, and were "off limits' when they felt like it. This was one great rest stop for men totally wanting to get away from the rigors of combat.

3 Sulphur Springs buddy Billy W. Young was with the Navy stationed in Naples.

4 The T-Patchers were officially taken off the river and mountain battlefronts, giving their positions to French units and elements of the American 88th Division, which was seeing its first action in the front lines.

5 The pneumatic drill, also known as a jackhammer, was a heavy portable drill powered by compressed air. Controlled by one man, it was designed to break up concrete, asphalt, or other hard flat surfaces. TNT (Trinitrotoluene) is a chemical compound renowned for its explosive force yet with easy handling and transportation qualities free from threat of accidental detonation.

6 The Allies attempted another attack on Cassino. This attack lasted until March 23 with an unbelievably high causality rate inflicted on the overly ambitious New Zealand and Indian soldiers. The scoreboard of success still registered a zero for the accomplishments of the Allies.

7 514 medium and heavy bombers supported by 300 fighter bombers and 280 fighters dropped high explosives on Cassino.

8 While division was recouping in Maddaloni area, Mt. Vesuvius had its most active eruption of the century. The 1227-meter-high mountain near Naples was famed for its AD 79 eruption that buried Pompeii, Herculaneum and Stabiae claiming over two thousand lives. In the interim, it had erupted thirty times but never with the devastation of AD 79. The 1944 eruption of March 18 was the third (1905 and 1929) and last of the twentieth century.

9 Brother R.A. owned and operated an automotive parts store and lived in San Augustine, Texas. He never served in the military.

10 The pup tent is a small A-shaped canvas structure designed for easy construction. It normally housed one or two men and was considered so rustic they were good only for a dog (or puppy).

11 Peninsular Base Section was a noncombatant rear echelon personnel group considered by regular fighting men as scavengers. They occupied the cities the fighting men paid the price in blood to take. Then they would declare an area off limits thus saving and

enjoying the excitement there themselves. Their self-centered actions, in the thoughts of the men who had laid it on the line at the front, may have made them more hated than the Germans themselves.

12 Lieutenant Beahler's fine fortune, a pass to Naples, resulted in Pearce's gain. A person had to be on call to provide transportation while in Naples. Officers didn't hitchhike like enlisted men. Officers rode in the front right seat of their jeep. Average Joe was forced to catch a lift in the back of a truck or bum a ride from anything that moved to get from point to point. The value of being a jeep driver for an officer gained him the joy of Naples.

13 In early April, Walker secured the Pensione Mueller, Piazza Mergellina 43, in Naples as an officers' club for the Division. Each week Walker approved twenty-one officers to go for an escape from the war. Enlisted men weren't as lucky in quality of housing, but excited just the same to be in Naples.

Chapter 8

1 The towns of Anzio and Nettuno, stretching for approximately three miles along the Italian coastline, wedge together practically forming a single city.

2 The defensive positions were known as the Caesar Line. It was a loosely fortified line running east from Anzio to a position two miles south of Valmontone.

3 Two German 280 mm railway guns, nicknamed "Anzio Annie" or "Anzio Express" brought agonizing destruction down on the men at Anzio. The 130-foot long guns had a range of 38 miles. This enormous weapon of destruction fired a 563-pound shell, creating many moments of fear for those at the target area.

4 Official records for Company C recorded, "The 143rd Infantry Regiment with Company C moved to an area five miles northeast of Cisterna, Italy. The site they witnessed there was ghastly. Enemy dead cluttered up the entire countryside given off a stench which only the combat soldiers can bear."

Chapter 9

1 Any military photographer, who accompanied Clark, was permitted to take pictures only from the General's left side (as featured on the cover of the October 4, 1943 Time Magazine and front page of the Dallas Morning News on June 5, 1944).

2 Incendiary grenades, using the chemical agent thermite, were designed to produce extreme heat capable of burning through metal objects.

3 In July 1944, McNair became the highest-ranking American soldier killed in World War II. He lost his life while in France when American planes accidentally bombed his position. When Walker reported to work, it was for the new Commanding General, Army Ground Forces, Benjamin Lear.

4 111th Engineers completed two pontoon bridges over the Albegna River. This allowed vehicles to cross the waterway and replenish the 143rd. In the picture, troops move over one of two pontoon bridges built by the engineers across the Albegna River.

5 An estimated seventy percent of those captured in action around June 14 were non-Germans. These "volunteer" fighters came from eastern countries like Russia (Mongolians) and Poland.

6 Before dawn, 143rd crossed the Ombrone River and occupied the city of Grosseto.

7 The After Action Report for the 111th Engineers recognized "probably the most spectacular event during the month. First Lieutenant Robert Findley and Private Jorge A. Diaz of Muskogee, Oklahoma, were conducting a reconnaissance when they came in contact with a strong partisan group which was massing for a raid on a German stronghold in the vicinity. After taking charge of the situation these two with the partisans proceeded on the strongpoint and forced the surrender of two hundred and fourteen Germans." Each received the Silver Star Medal.

8 The Messerschmitt Me 210 was a heavy fighter/attack aircraft developed by the Germans. It entered combat in 1943 but was not popular with the pilots. It was quickly replaced by the Me 410 which was a much-improved version of the Me 210. The Me 210 carried two pilots and a speed capability of 385 miles per hour.

9 Ecstatic due to the end of combat, the Division would get a short well earned, stay in Rome before returning to Salerno to prepare for a third amphibious landing. The soldier's soldier, General Walker, made sure his men were paid before the first of the month, so they would have the finances to enjoy the pleasures of Rome. Just another example of what each fighting man, from buck private to officer, meant to this man personally.

10 James "Ace" Mueller was one of the most active and respected officers in the 111th. His combat readiness, from Salerno to present, was an inspiration to all. A Mechanical Engineering graduate of Auburn University, he was famous for action at Rapido River in January, where he, Edwin B. Haynes of Victoria, Texas, James D. White of Detroit, Michigan, and William Dold Jr. acted as sheepherders. They herded numerous sheep, under the very nose of the Germans, over mined and booby-trapped areas to clear a potential path for Allied soldiers.

11 The DUKW was a 2 1/2 ton, thirty-one foot amphibious truck equipped with six wheel drive plus a water propeller. This allowed it to move at speeds of 50-55 miles per hour on land and up to six miles per hour in water. DUKW were initials standing for D (first year of production code-1942), U (utility truck), K (front wheel drive), and W (tandem axle).

Chapter 10

1 It was originally named Operation Anvil, but in July 1944 the code name changed because it was believed the Germans had uncovered its secret meaning.

2 Montelimar was known worldwide for its famous chewy almond nougat. The first commercial nougat factory in Montelimar opened in 1770.

3 The Invasion Training Center, near Salerno, was the location for tuning up the 36th and 45th Divisions for the pending invasion. The 3rd Division used Pozzuoli, on the northwest rim of the Gulf of Naples, as its site for training.

4 Composition C-2 was a molded plastic demolition explosive consisting of RDX, other explosives, and plasticizer. It could be shaped by hand into the size to fit the job needed.

5 The L.S.T. was an abbreviation for Landing Ship, Tank. These ships, approximately 328 feet in length, were seaworthy and capable of self-transportation. They could carry up to sixty tanks and vehicles.

6 The American public needed bravo pictures glamorizing the great Allied victories overseas. The showing of "Guadalcanal Diary" in Italy turned out to be more of a slapstick comedy to vets participating in combat there. A year later, Burgess Meredith would star as Ernie Pyle in "The Story of G. I. Joe". To the fighting man, who had experienced Italy, this was as movie close to real as it gets. No glamour or fluff, just the reality of the rain, mud, grappa, and heartbreak like they experienced it.

7 Accommodations for the enlisted men didn't quite match that of the commander of the VI Corps. While they scrambled for a bunk and attempted to fan away the stifling heat and bodily smells of men tightly packed together, Truscott and his immediate staff enjoyed an air-conditioned war room. Punctuating the rewards of rank, he always insisted on having fresh flowers daily and all meals prepared by his personnel Chinese-American cooks.

8 Eventually the task force would have over 885 self-propelled ships and landing vessels plus more than one hundred fifty thousand soldiers. Companies A and C, with the 141st and 143rd, left Naples on August 12. Company B, supporting the 142nd didn't depart till August 13. The troop carriers linked up at sea.

9 Early in the AM of the fifteenth, under the code name Rugby, Allied paratroops, bailing out ten miles behind the beaches around Le Muy, secured as much ground as possible before glider troops arrived to strengthen them. The American's goal was the small town of Le Muy. Through it ran two major highways the Allies needed to leapfrog deeper into France. Route Napoleon eased northward to Grenoble, while National Highway 7 branched west and then north to the Rhone Valley.

10 Operation Dove was a glider-borne assault of more than three hundred gliders carrying three thousand soldiers and equipment. They were reinforcements for the paratroopers already on the ground the day before. Only one hundred twenty-five soldiers had been injured landing on the broken terrain, despite more than fifty gliders being destroyed by manmade obstacles.

11 The 142nd, breaking through the last German resistance in the Argens Valley, hooked up with the paratroopers and triumphantly entered the city of Draguignan.

12 The only serious setback to invasion was the sinking of a L.S.T., carrying ammunition, by single German airplane. It was hit, near Green Beach, at dusk on the first day of the invasion.

13 The Partisans waited since 1940 for this time. Called the French Forces of the Interior, they dealt the enemy telling blows. Hatred flourished, and revenge was handed out. Several villages in the south, with few prisoners taken, were liberated by these men and then handed over to the advancing Allies.

14 The bridge was over the Durance River south of Sisteron. Helped by French Indo-Chinese troops and French civilians, the engineers build a bypass over an existing railroad bridge. Over six hundred feet of single railroad track was removed to allow construction of a bridge that would allow ground traffic to cross the river.

15 1st platoon of Company C moved from near Crest to an assembly area a mile east of Marsanne.

16 Robert Sleator of Ossining, New York, and John Benedict manned the machine gun until heavy sniper fire forced a retreat. In a letter after the war to Sleator's family, Benedict described how as they reluctantly fell back, Sleator pitched the weaponless Benedict his own forty-four pistol yelling "Here Benny, use this!" Both men were able to fight their way to safety.

17 Jarrel Julian of Commerce, Texas, an earlier winner of the Bronze Star, remembered "1st platoon was split between defending part the town and to its left where I was. After shelling, German's came down the mountains to this town with infantry and tanks. We had no support. I did not know I could run so far, but I ran and retreated about ten miles . . . we could not fight tanks, so we retreated".

18 They repaired an eighty-foot gap in a railroad bridge by removing the train tracks and placing timber decking down for road use.

19 Company B, working with 142nd Infantry, constructed a 140 foot, Class 40, double bent trestle bridge over the Doubs River near Byans. After twenty-two hours of nonstop work, the bridge was open to traffic.

20 In a historical moment in the war, French armored units of the Seventh Army, on September 11, physically linked up with elements of Patton's Third Army. Four days later, after the hookup of the two armies, central control of the Seventh Army moved from the Mediterranean Theater command to the Supreme Headquarters Allied Expeditionary Force (SHAEF) under Eisenhower.

21 They stopped to build a twenty-eight foot wooden trestle bent bridge over a small stream less than a half mile southwest of St. Maria.

22 When the engineers swept a road for mines, they earlier only cleared the existing road plus a four foot buffer to each side of it. As the Americans neared Germany, the number of anti-personnel mines set by the enemy multiplied. The importance of unrestricted troop movement to the front, over narrow mountain paths and roads also increased in number. To allow for more freedom of movement, the engineers established a new guideline of clearing the road plus fifteen feet on each side of it.

Chapter 11

1 Self-propelled artillery were vehicles mounted with various types of weapons (anti-tank guns, infantry field gun) for quick mobility.

2 The abatis is a field fortification using branches of trees laid in a row with the tops aimed towards the opponent. In this case, it was an obstacle created by interlocking entire trees, interlaced with mines, to form over a quarter mile of blockage.

3 The tank dozer was a medium tank equipped with a bulldozer blade on the front.

4 Riegel mine 43, also known as a bar mine, was a long, narrow rectangle filled with over eight pounds of explosives. It became the most effective German anti-tank mine of the war but could be rigged as a booby trap against foot soldiers.

5 The advancing evolution of mine warfare continued to maim and kill the advancing soldiers. The Topf mine, first encountered in December, defied the search pattern of the metal sensitive mine detectors used by the Americans. This mine was constructed of plastic and glass and hard to locate except with time consuming probing.

6 Frank Pearce in 1982 remembered Gautier, a 1942 graduate of The Citadel, as an easy-going personality plus man who constantly talked about his girlfriend back home. Pearce termed him "a nice guy, a damn good man". James Mueller, in 2005, recalled going to Boston several times with "Tommy" to see their girlfriends. Sadly, one wonderful girl never got to greet a TRUE HERO on his return home.

7 Frank Cathcart of Champaign, Illinois, joined Company C as an officer in April of 1944.

8 Near Jussarupt, the engineers of Company A were committed to the mountainous front as infantry. They were placed in a defensive sector between the 141st and 143rd. Fortunately, several days of consistent artillery and small arms fire produced zero killed or wounded.

9 One soldier out of the entire 111th, for some forgotten reason, was rotated to the United States. His replacement had neither engineer or infantry training nor the prescribed course for firing a rifle. The replacement could not be utilized and was returned to the replacement depot.

10 Germans held encircling hills to east and shelled the town when targets became available. From high in the hills, forward observers could direct a deadly spray of artillery on the ant-like American figures swarming through the streets.

11 The 442nd eventually took the heights over Bruyeres and the small village of Biffontaine to help eliminate the artillery threat to forces in Bruyeres.

12 The radiogram was a format to transmit messages from place to place. The message was transmitted by voice or Morse code. It was usually a brief statement received and written on a standardized form.

13 Lucian Truscott, Jr. was promoted and assigned command of the Fifteenth Army. Major General Edward H. Brooks assumed leadership of the VI Corps.

14 The P-47 Thunderbolt was the largest single engine fighter/bomber produced by the Americans. Introduced to combat in 1943, it combined both high speed and long range

ability. Known for its durability, the P-47 became legendary for its low level bombing and strafing in support of Allied ground troops.

15 A Presidential citation was awarded to the Engineer Battalion for its achievements in building the road used to save the Lost Battalion. General Dahlquist boasted "This action by the 111th Engineer Battalion was the most outstanding feat of combat engineering I have seen since the Division came to France."

16 After an unsuccessful sweeping for mines on a road one half mile east of Biffontaine to La Houssiere, Griffitt's squad stumbled upon an enemy patrol. In the face off, all the American soldiers escaped unharmed.

17 The Field Ration, Type K was introduced in 1942. They were noted for their compactness and packed in wax coated cartons. The cartons were placed in a second container labeled and colored to indicate in large letters breakfast, dinner, or supper. They included, according to the meal, a canned meat product (canned pork with carrot and apple or beef and pork loaf), biscuits, gum, cigarettes (in a 4 pack), salt tablets, a canned cheese product, and coffee. It also included a warning on both the boxes stating "for security, do not discard the empty can, paper, or refuse where it can be seen from the air. If possible, cover with dirt, foliage, sand, etc."

18 The new campsite was three fourths of a mile southeast of Mormomosse. The pyramidal tent, probably the M-1942, Olive Drab, housed twelve men. This tent was sixteen feet wide, over thirty-two feet long, and twelve feet high. It replaced the M-1934, Olive Drab tent which could house only eight men.

19 The 36th Division reached the Meurthe River at St. Leonard.

20 Schu mines, containing a detonator and explosives, were placed in a small six-inch by six-inch wooden box. With no metal parts, the Schu mine was undetectable to mine detectors.

Chapter 12

1 Oran Stovall, on January 1, was transferred to the 343rd Engineer Regiment. He was replaced by Pearce's nemesis Ernest L. Petree.

2 Travel back to the front included a dismal ride in the infamous French "40 and 8" box cars. These numbers didn't mean they were forty feet long and eight feet wide. They stood for the loading capacity of each box car. In these, forty men or eight horses could uncomfortably fit.

3 1st platoon of Company C placed one hundred-sixty anti-tank mines and twenty anti-personnel mines from one quarter mile northeast to one quarter mile north of Bischwiller. 3rd platoon of Company C laid ten anti-personnel mines one mile south of Bischwiller.

4 There are criminal elements in every society who sponge off the hardship of others, and Paris held the monopoly on such slime. The French black market, aided by over two thousand wayward U.S. Army deserters, was efficient in making money off stolen Army items. Supply theft was as common as a glance up at the Eiffel Tower. It not

only included gas, food, cigarettes and identification theft, but even the vehicles that carried them.

5 Pearce replaced Winfred "Hunky" Weems as corporal of first squad.

6 A total of 2,193 yards of road was repaired by the three companies of engineers with timber planking and three hundred truckloads of gravel. Company C repaired 520 yards of road with planking plus another seventy truckloads of gravel hauled and spread over the road.

7 French civilians, numbering between one hundred to four hundred, were utilized by the engineers during February to improve drainage ditches and load trucks carrying lumber or gravel.

8 Company C placed 2910 mines in defensive positions near Bischwiller.

9 Pearce wasn't exaggerating. The official After Action Report s of the 111th stated "Sixteen enlisted reinforcements were received by the battalion during February, and as a whole were not satisfactory. A large number of these had been eliminated from other organizations, due to reorganization, and, although their training might be considered sufficient, most of them have been subjects of continual disciplinary actions."

10 This was his first look at the family's new home they moved into after he sailed for Africa in 1943. Although it was new only in terms of the most recent Pearce homestead, it was the place he now dreamed of returning. Pictures of his mother in front of the house at 114 Texas Avenue in Sulphur Springs completely erased the memories of the creaky, drafty, overcrowded rented 209 Oak Avenue home he left behind.

Chapter 13

1 Glenn Miller's music would become a national treasure to World War II Americans. No band created such lasting music as "Tuxedo Junction", "Pennsylvania 6-5000" and the classic "In the Mood". While in the service, Miller formed the Glenn Miller Army Air Force Band. The band would play in over eight hundred performances, including radio broadcasts, and entertain personally in front of more than six hundred thousand people. Preparing to move the band to Paris, Miller's plane mysteriously disappeared between England and France on December 15, 1944. The loss of Miller has never been explained and he became another soldier missing in action.

2 To go to England, one had to look his military best. The issuing of new clothes wasn't such a surprise, but the campaign ribbons were. These simple looking decorations, colorfully displayed on one's chest, added much pride to the men who had been doing the combat. Service bars on the left forearm of the new issue jacket, each representing six months of service overseas, blended with the ribbons to distinguish real soldiers from the rear echelon variety.

3 Before returning to the combat, Pearce was required to return the impressive new uniform and ribbons he flashed around England, so they could be used by others on leave.

Chapter 14

1 The pack, also known as a satchel charge, normally contained eight blocks of tetryl. Tetryl is a combination mixture of 70% tetryl and 30% TNT. The packs were perfect for individual soldiers to transport and use in destroying bridges, pill boxes, and installations.

2 The entire 142nd and 1st platoon of Company B of the 111th Engineers received a Presidential Unit Citation for their efforts of March 19-22. It was the only time in the war that a complete regiment of the 36th would be honored with such a citation.

3 The entire 111th Engineers were relieved from combat duties and moved from Insheim, Germany to an area near Kaiserslautern on April first. Occupation became a welcomed relief. The Division was presented a rear area assignment as the war screeched to a close. All three letter companies became more like military police than combat engineers. Moving to Kaiserslautern, they set up check points patrolled the surrounding area and searched for ammunition dumps the Germans had abandoned.

4 Ernest Taylor Pyle, killed during the invasion of Okinawa on April 18, was the journalistic voice of the American soldiers.

5 Benito Mussolini was executed by Italian communist partisans in the small village of Giulino di Mezzegra, Italy.

6 On April 30, Hitler and his new wife Eva Braun committed suicide in a bunker in Berlin. The end of the Fuhrer came from a self-inflicted gunshot in his mouth. German wireless broadcast "It is reported from Der Fuehrer's headquarters that our Fuehrer Adolf Hitler, fighting to the last breath against Bolshevism, fell for Germany this afternoon in his operations headquarters in the Reich Chancellery." Grand Admiral Karl Doenitz was named Hitler's successor as the Head of State of Nazi Germany.

7 Field Marshall Gerd von Rundstedt was the Commander and Chief of the western front for Germany

Chapter 15

1 There were two types of Bronze Star awards for the soldiers. When the Medal rewarded bravery in combat, the Bronze Star ribbon and accompanying ribbon bar had a small letter "V" for valor included on them. When the award was for meritorious service, the valor "V" was not included with the award.

2 Food, cigarettes, and candy became the official money of a new Germany. With any combination of these, the American soldier, who had plenty of each, could buy anything he desired.

3 "What a gal" was symbolic of many German women. To survive occupation, they fraternized with the enemy so they could endure in frenzied times. This fraulein was a lonely soldier's wife who hadn't seen her husband, fighting on the Russian front, in over three years.

4 The initials CBI stood for the China-Burma-India Theater of Action.

5 During the month of May, the 111th Engineers redeployed seventy-three men back to the USA. Each man sent home under the point system policy created waves of highs and lows to those left behind. Eventually all would experience the jubilation of seeing the longed for American coastline.

6 This issued jacket was known widely by the names "Ike Jacket", "Eisenhower Jacket", or the "ETO (European Theater of Operations) Jacket". The future President, early in the war, admired the short waist style of the upper half of the official British battlefield dress. Before long, he copied it and had it tailor made as part of his own uniform. Eventually it became regular equipment for the soldiers in Europe and even sparked fashions in the United States for women. There the windbreaker-type jacket, complete with drawstring waist, military shoulders and trim soon became a fashion favorite.

Bibliography

Books

Aldeman, Robert H. and Colonel George Walton. *Rome Fell Today,* Boston, Massachusetts: Little, Brown, 1968.

Allen, William L. *Anzio: Edge of Disaster.* New York: Elsevier-Dutton, 1978.

American Military History. Washington D.C.: U.S. Government Printing Office, 1959.

Atkinson, Rick. *The Day of Battle.* New York: Henry Holt, 2007.

Blair, Clay. *Ridgway's Paratroopers.* Garden City, New York: The Dial Press, 1985.

Blumenson, Martin. *Bloody River.* Boston, Massachusetts: Houghton Mifflin, 1970.

Anzio: The Gamble that Failed, Philadelphia. Pennsylvania: J. B. Lippincott, 1963.

Bonn, Keith E. *When the Odds were Even.* Novato, California: Presidio Press, 1994.

Clark, Mark W. *Calculated Risk.* New York: Harper & Brothers, 1950.

D'Este, Carlo. *Fatal Decision.* New York: Harper Collins, 1991.

Faustina, Leonard A., *Memoirs of an Engineer Lieutenant in World War II.* Pittsburgh, Pennsylvania: RoseDog Publishing, 2005.

Garland, Joseph E. *Unknown Soldiers.* Rockport, Maryland: Protean Press, 2009.

Grant, Neal. *Chronicle of 20th Century Conflict.* New York: Smithmark,1993.

Gawne, Johathan. *Finding Your Father's War.* Drexel Hill, Pennsylvania: Casemate, 2006.

Hapgood, David and David Richardson, *Monte Cassino.* New York: Congdon & Weed, 1984.

Jackson, W.G.F. *The Battle for Rome.* New York: Bonanza Books, 1969.

Katz, Robert. *The Battle for Rome: the Germans, the Allies, the Partisans, and the Pope.* New York: Simon & Schuster, 2003.

Kurzman, Dan. *The Race for Rome.* Garden City, New York: Doubleday & Company 1975.

Lockhart, Vincent M. *T-Patch to Victory.* Canyon, Texas: Staked Plains Press, 1981.

Mauldin, Bill. *Up Front*. New York: Henry Holt, 1945.
Mansoor, Peter R. The GI Offensive in Europe. Lawrence, Kansas: University Press of Kansas, 2002.
Nordyke, Phil, *All American All the Way*. Minneapolis, Minnesota: MBI Publishing, 2005.
A Pictorial History of the 36th Texas Infantry Division. Austin, Texas: The 36th Division Association, 1946.
Pond, Hugh, *Salerno*. Boston, Massachusetts: Little, Brown. 1961.
Pyle, Ernie. *Brave Men*. New York: Henry Holt, 1944.
Reader's Digest Illustrated Story of World War II. Pleasantville, New York: TheReader's Digest Association, Inc.
Sheehan, Fred. *Anzio: Epic of Bravery*. Norman, Oklahoma: University of Oklahoma Press, 1964.
Slayton, Robert A. *Arms of Destruction*. New York: Kensington Publishing, 2004.
Scott, Jack L. *Combat Engineer*. Baltimore, Maryland: American Liberty Press, 1999.
Sommerville, Donald. *World War II Day by Day*. Greenwich, Connecticut: Brompton Books, 1989.
Sparrow, John C. *History of Personnel Demobilization of the U.S. Army*. Washington, D.C.: Department of the Army, 1951.
Starr, Chester G. *From Salerno to the Alps*. Washington, D.C.: Infantry Journal Press, 1948
Sulzberger, C.L. and the Editors of American Heritage. *The American Heritage Picture History of World War II*. The American Heritage Publishing Company, 1966.
Wagner, Robert L. *The Texas Army*. Austin, Texas: S.P., 1972.
Walker, Fred L. *From Texas to Rome*. Dallas, Texas: Taylor Publishing, 1969.
Whiting, Charles. *America's Forgotten Army*. Rockville Centre, New York: Sarpedon Publishers, 1999.
Who was Who in World War II. New York: Crescent Books, 1984.

Websites

Ancestry.com
Army Military History
The Aviation History Online Museum
BBC-World War II People's War
Brownwood.tx.us/history
Custerman.com
Dogtagsdirect.com
eHistory.com
Encyclopedia
Engineer's Diary by Warren Toney
Glen Miller Orchestra

Globalsecurity.org
Hyperdictionary
Hyperwar
Indiana Military.org
The 82nd Airborne
Military.Com
Military History Network
National World War II Memorial
Oud Vossemeer
Skylighters World War II Virtual Encyclopedia
The Texas Military Forces Museum
University of Texas Library
United State Coast Guard
United States Army Center of Military History
United States Army Quartermaster Foundation
Wikipedia

Magazines

Hopkins Country Heritage September 2010: World War I Causalities.
Life Magazine May 3, 1943: Land Mines.
Life Magazine August 28, 1944: The Coming Battle for Germany.
Life Magazine September 25, 1944: When You Come Back.
Life Magazine October 9, 1944: Western Front.
Life Magazine October 20, 1944: Lucian King Truscott Jr.
Life Magazine January 25, 1945: George Lott, Casualty.
Life Magazine March 12, 1945: Eisenhower Jacket Starts New Fad.
Life Magazine March 26, 1945: Paris Black Market Robs U.S. Army.
Life Magazine December 31, 1945: Speaking of Pictures.
Time Magazine September 23, 1940: How it Works.
Time Magazine October 21, 1940: First Conscript.
Time Magazine October 4, 1943: Mark Clark.
Time Magazine February 28, 1944: The Bombing of Monte Cassino.
The T-Patch News Letter 2002-2011

Newspapers

The Bull Dozier (111th Engineers during the war)
The Commerce Journal
Dallas Morning News
Hopkins County Echo

Stars and Stripes
Sulphur Springs Daily News Telegram
The T Patch 36th Division News

After Action Reports

141st Infantry Regiment
111th Engineer Combat Battalion

Pictures from Personal Collections

Cleek, Jack
Coon, Earl
Figler, Rob
Glynn, Imogene
Griffitt, Wayne C.
Julian, Jerrel
McCluggage, Helen
Mueller, James N. "Ace"
Pearce, Frank W.
Pearce, Marvin J.
Rugg, Marsha
Sinchak, Ray
Sleater, Happy
Smith, Mike
Toney, Warren
Vesce, Anthony

Interviews

Bright, Vernon
Cleek, Jack F.
Glynn, Mrs. James A. (Imogene)
Griffitt, Wayne C.
Julian, Jerrel
Janell, Daniel "Muley"
Mueller, James N. "Ace"
Pearce, Frank
Pearce, Marvin J.
Scarbrough, Bill
Sinchak, Stephen J.

Other

Military records of Frank W. Pearce
Diary of Frank W. Pearce
Letters from Frank W. Pearce
Letters from Marvin J. Pearce
Letter and diary entries from John Benedict
36th Division Association Board of Directors

Index

B

C

D

G

H

L

M

N

O

P

T

U

V

W

Y

Z

CPSIA information can be obtained
at www.ICGtesting.com
Printed in the USA
LVHW030601141221
706059LV00001B/1

9 781649 670052